HEALTH AND SOCIAL CARE

INTERMEDIATE

GENERAL EDITOR: NEIL MOONIE

RICHARD CHALONER

MARGARET HILTON

KAREN HUCKER

BERYL STRETCH

Including contributions from:

CREESHA ATHERTON

DOROTHY DICKINSON

HEINEMANN

Heinemann Educational,
a division of Heinemann Educational Books Ltd,
Halley Court, Jordan Hill, Oxford OX2 8EJ

OXFORD   LONDON   EDINBURGH
MADRID   ATHENS   BOLOGNA   PARIS
MELBOURNE   SYDNEY   AUCKLAND   SINGAPORE   TOKYO
IBADAN   NAIROBI   HARARE   GABORONE
PORTSMOUTH NH (USA)

© Beryl Stretch, Margaret Hilton, Karen Hucker, Richard Chaloner,
Neil Moonie

First published 1993
96 95 94 93
10 9 8 7 6 5 4 3

A catalogue record for this book is available from the British Library on
request

ISBN 0 435 45240 1

Typeset by Taurus Graphics, Kidlington, Oxon
Printed by Thomson Litho, East Kilbride

Front cover
Designed by: Tad Kasa
Photograph by: The Image Bank

CONTENTS

CONTENTS

What the book covers

This book is designed to provide a guide to the GNVQ at Intermediate Level in Health and Social Care. GNVQs are entirely new qualifications based on nationally defined standards. The assessment standards are fixed but a learner's pathway to achieving them is not laid down. Indeed, part of the strength of GNVQ awards is that learners are encouraged to monitor their own learning and own personal development.

The book aims to support learners to gain Merit or Distinction grades for the award by offering:

- An introduction to GNVQs.
- An explanation of the structure of standards.
- An overview of assessment and evidence collection.
- Guidance on portfolio design and test preparation.
- The knowledge, skills and values associated with each of the four GNVQ mandatory units:
  1 **Provide emotional support**
  2 **Influences on health and well-being**
  3 **Health emergencies**
  4 **Health and social care services.**
- The knowledge and skill associated with core skills of Information Technology, Communication and Application of Number at Intermediate Level.
- An integrated approach where core skills are integrated into the theory base of the mandatory units.

Special features of the book

- ICONS are used throughout the book to identify sections. They are also used to indicate:

 areas for **reflection** (thought) and

 ideas for **evidence collection** to meet the requirements of national standards.

Icons are also suggested as a way of labelling your evidence collection.
- Self-assessment tasks to test understanding (with suggested answers) are included in each chapter.
- Fast Facts – each chapter contains a quick reference section for key concepts.

How to use this book

The book is designed to be used as a source of knowledge. It *can* be read from the beginning to the end, but it is also designed to be used whenever you need information. Fast Facts are listed alphabetically so that concepts can be checked quickly.

Following an introduction to GNVQs, there are four chapters on the mandatory units. You may not, however, want to use the chapters in this order.

Three further chapters cover the core skills of:

Communication, Application of Number and Information Technology. You may want to study these areas before finishing your work on the mandatory units. Core skills interlink with the mandatory units and evidence for them should be gathered with evidence for the mandatory units. You will probably wish to dip in and out of these chapters as you study the units.

Each reader will have his or her own needs and purposes for using this book. Hence it has been designed with easy reference headings and icons, so that it can be used flexibly – in keeping with the ideas behind the GNVQs.

▪ ACKNOWLEDGEMENTS ▪

The authors and publishers would like to thank the Officers of NCVQ for their help and assistance with this book. They would also like to thank the following individuals and organisations for permission to reproduce photographs:

Barnabys Picture Library; Chris Ridgers; Chubb Fire; Format Partners; Lincolnshire County Council; Network Photographers; Philip Parkhouse Photography; Robert Harding Picture Library; Sally and Richard Greenhill; Science Photo Library.

UNDERSTANDING GNVQS IN CARING

What this section offers:

- The meaning of GNVQ
- Levels and pathways of qualification
- What does a GNVQ caring qualification lead to?
- How GNVQ Health and Social Care at Intermediate Level is made up
- Understanding standards – the technical explanation
- An example: How to interpret one element
- Understanding standards – how they might feel in the end
- GNVQ assessment
- Things that count as evidence

- Collecting evidence
- Reflection
- Action plans
- Grading of GNVQ qualifications
- The portfolio
- What the portfolio might look like
- Using the portfolio design to develop your own learning
- Tests
- Preparing for tests
- Self-assessment of knowledge about GNVQ: questions and possible answers
- Fast Facts

GNVQs are a new system of qualifications designed to fit into a national pattern of 'levels'. GNVQs are also designed so that they can be 'controlled' to some extent by the people taking them. This introduction explains how the national system works and how *you* can control or manage your own learning whilst working on a GNVQ programme. GNVQs are not intended to be simple, but this section will provide the knowledge needed to understand and manage your own study of the GNVQ at Intermediate Level in Caring.

This introduction contains a range of *theory* and *advice*. Before starting it, it may be worth checking what do you need to know. Use the contents list above as a guide to what is on offer. If you know very little about GNVQs then start right at the beginning.

Getting a GNVQ qualification may be a bit like learning to drive a car or learning to ride a bicycle. It takes time and, most importantly, it takes *practice*. This introduction provides ideas for designing action plans and portfolios. What is said here will make most sense when you are actually working to get the GNVQ award. Like learning to drive, there is a limit to how much *theory* you might want to learn in one go. It may be best just to read parts of this section as you need them.

When you have finished the introduction you might like to test your understanding with the questions at the end. Another idea is that you might like to look at the questions to begin with and decide whether you need to know about these things. If yes, then it is worth exploring to get more knowledge. If you just need to understand a technical word, look up Fast Facts.

You are in charge of your own learning, so please see this section as something to explore. Different people will use it in different ways at different stages of the GNVQ programme.

A note on change and development in GNVQs

Learners develop their skills by constantly building on their experience. Good learners are open to change – they drop things that don't work well in practice, and fine-tune behaviours that do seem to work, in order to get the best outcomes.

General NVQs are still very new. While their purpose and philosophy is unlikely to alter, the fine detail of how to achieve a GNVQ will almost certainly continue to build on experience over the next few years. The advice and guidance in this introduction is based on the GNVQ system as it was in the spring and early summer of 1993. Fine detail on issues like grading, revising for test questions and portfolio design will continue to develop.

Anyone reading this book is therefore recommended to check whether new details or new regulations have come about. In particular, the nature of test questions and grading criteria are quite likely to change. It is worth checking the latest information with a tutor or learning manager if you are enrolled on a GNVQ programme.

GNVQs involve exploring ideas and developing skills with information and knowledge. This introduction is designed to help you get started on your programme, but you should use your skills to check that the information has not become dated!

The meaning of GNVQ

GNVQ stands for General National Vocational Qualification:

- **General** means that the qualification is not just for a particular job. General qualifications are broad; they are designed to enable people to move on to higher qualifications or to get jobs in a wide range of employment.
- **National** means that the qualification is valuable nationally. The qualification has the same value everywhere in the 'nation'.

- **Vocational** means that the qualification focuses on areas of employment. A vocational qualification in caring provides the knowledge and understanding a person needs to go on to work in many different caring jobs. The study involved also means that people with Intermediate Level will be ready to take A-levels or an advanced GNVQ if they want to.
- **Qualification** means that an individual has passed at a definite standard. Intermediate Level is equivalent to good GCSE passes at an academic level and is also equivalent to work skills which would enable a person to perform some complex and individually responsible jobs.

Levels and pathways of qualification

There is now a national system of qualifications at five levels, as shown in the diagram. *Level 1* is the starting point for foundational qualifications. *Level 2* (Intermediate) covers jobs that are more complex, and academically it is worth GCSE at good grades. *Level 3* covers jobs that involve high responsibility and complexity, perhaps including supervising others. This level is designed to provide vocational A-levels. *Levels 4* and *5* cover professional and management jobs and are designed to be degree and post-graduate equivalents.

How the ladders work

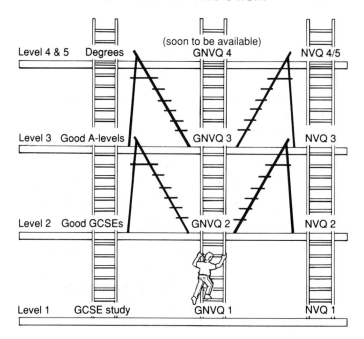

Level 4 & 5 — Degrees — (soon to be available) GNVQ 4 — NVQ 4/5

Level 3 — Good A-levels — GNVQ 3 — NVQ 3

Level 2 — Good GCSEs — GNVQ 2 — NVQ 2

Level 1 — GCSE study — GNVQ 1 — NVQ 1

As well as the five levels, there are three *pathways* to qualifications. The first pathway – the 'academic' one – has been around for many years and has worked well for some people. But in 1986 the government decided to set up the National Council for Vocational Qualifications (NCVQ) so that there would be new ways to get qualifications. To begin with, the NCVQ designed qualifications called National Vocational Qualifications (or NVQs).

NVQs are designed to provide qualifications for particular jobs or professions. Sometimes NVQs can be studied at college, but many of these qualifications are easier for people to get if they already have a job. For many individuals, NVQs opened up the possibility of getting a recognised qualification for the skills and 'know-how' they had already learned at work. NVQs meant that people could become qualified at work without necessarily having to start at the beginning with their studies again.

The third pathway or ladder is a GNVQ. GNVQs first began in 1992 and their purpose was to provide a 'middle way' between academic and work-based qualifications. GNVQs are based on standards in just the same way that NVQs are. However, GNVQs cover a much wider range of knowledge and understanding than NVQs.

What does a GNVQ caring qualification lead to?

From the diagram you can see that a person with GNVQ at Level 2 has at least three options:

1 He/she can decide to stay with the GNVQ ladder and go on and get Level 3.
2 He/she can decide to switch to A-level studies.
3 He/she can decide to look for employment in Health and Care. It may depend on where they work, but after a while they might be offered the chance to collect an NVQ at Level 2. Level 2 should then be easy because they would already have the knowledge at this level. There may be some new skills and 'competencies' which are different from GNVQ though. Most jobs involve some new things to learn. Some people might not wish to get an NVQ at Level 2, but might prefer to work until they had the chance to go to NVQ at Level 3.

Of course some people may not want to spend the next few years climbing ladders, in which case a GNVQ at Level 2 in Caring should help them to get a job in Social Care or in Health Care. Level 2 standards guarantee a level of achievement that many employers will look for in the future. Finally, some individuals might even decide that they don't want to work in Health and Care. Level 2 is still a good qualification which should interest other employers.

How GNVQ Health and Social Care at Level 2 is made up

All GNVQs are made up of **units**. Making a qualification up of units is a useful idea because a unit can be 'passed' and then awarded to the person who has achieved it. GNVQs can be 'passed' bit by bit, unit by unit. If a person leaves a GNVQ course, they still keep the units they passed. This means that they could start again without having to go right back to the beginning. The whole qualification consists of **nine** units. The nine units are made up of four mandatory (no choice), two options and three core skills units.

Mandatory unit

Title: 'Provide emotional support'
Required evidence includes a test

Mandatory unit

Title: 'Influences on health and well-being'
Required evidence includes a test

Mandatory unit

Title: 'Health emergencies'
Required evidence includes a test

Mandatory unit

Title: 'Health and social care services'
Required evidence includes a test

Optional unit

Chosen from a small range provided by your awarding body (BTEC, City & Guilds or RSA)
No test

Optional unit

Chosen from a small range provided by your awarding body
No test

Core skills

Three core skills units in Communication, Application of Number, and Information Technology

Core skills units are different from mandatory units or optional units. This is because they are meant to be studied *with* the other units. The evidence needed to 'pass' core skills is meant to be collected with the evidence to pass the mandatory and optional units.

The idea of core skills is that communication, number and information technology skills are needed in *all* work situations. GNVQs will probably cover 14 areas of work in the future, and Health and Social Care will be just one area. Core skills *standards* will be the same across all the areas, but the *evidence presented* will be different because it will be linked to practical assignment work for each qualification. In Health and Social Care, evidence

opportunities for core skills like information technology will link with assignment work in Caring.

Only core skills units in communication, number and information technology have to be assessed and awarded for the award of a GNVQ qualification. There are three other areas of core skills though: 'Problem Solving', 'Working With Others' and 'Improving Own Learning and Performance'. These core skills are worth including in a portfolio of evidence because (1) they can be recorded in your National Record of Achievement, and (2) they help towards getting evidence for Merit and Distinction grades (see later).

An Intermediate GNVQ in Caring will usually take one year of full-time study to complete all the work and evidence collection.

Understanding standards – the technical explanation

To collect GNVQ units and qualifications, candidates have to demonstrate that they have achieved a defined **standard of work**. GNVQ standards are definitions of what is required in order to 'pass' and be awarded the qualification. Because standards are definitions, they are not always easy to understand. This part explains the technical detail of units, elements, performance criteria, range statements and evidence indicators. Some readers may prefer to go straight to the part on 'how standards might feel in the end'. A glance at that section might help to make sense of the detail here, but some people prefer the facts first!

The whole set of standards for a qualification runs to many pages. Most people who sit down and read standards will say that they are boring. Many people will say they cannot really understand them!

Why are standards so complicated?

Standards are difficult for three reasons:

1 Standards are a system for defining outcomes.

Because standards define things to be understood or done, they become a bit like legal statements. Standards try to give exact details of what is required rather than discuss ideas about what would be useful. Standards end up being technical rather than interesting simply because they are definitions. Definitions are necessary because they have to be applied in the same way across the nation. Standards are a guide to assessment: they explain what has to be done in order to pass the GNVQ. Standards don't really explain what has to be studied; rather, they define what has to be achieved in order to get the qualification. So standards are like goal-posts in football – they define the goal that has to be reached. Standards don't explain how to get there!

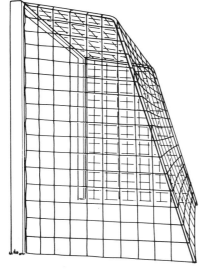

It's boring just standing here looking at the goal –

It's much more fun if you're doing something with it!

2 The value of a qualification will depend on the definition of standards.

There are two kinds of qualifications. One kind is based on what people can do or understand, and the other kind is based on who comes first in a competition. Many qualifications have exams, which are like a competition or a race. The people who run the fastest get to the end first – these people pass. In a running race, the people who come in last are not so good; in the exam, the people with the lowest marks fail. Not all exams are marked in terms of top and bottom, but they all have some degree of competition about them. Standards allow a different way of qualifying – instead of doing better than others in an exam, the candidate has to show that he or she can definitely do or knows the details needed for the qualification.

Exams give people qualifications because they have come in the top group. Standards give people qualifications because those individuals have proved they can do what is needed. The problem with standards qualifications is that the qualification is only as good as the standards. If

standards are not well defined, or if they don't cover much, then the qualification isn't worth a lot. Standards need to define complicated details carefully if the qualification is going to be worthwhile in the end! The standards show how much someone knows and can do when they get their qualification.

Climbing to the top = achieving a standard – do it in your own way at your own pace. Running a race is different – you have to beat the others!

3 Standards are impossible to understand without the knowledge of the area they are about.

Because standards define areas of skill, values and knowledge, they are impossible to understand without the necessary knowledge. At the beginning of a course of study, the standards will be difficult because people will not know all the terms and detail involved. As a person learns about the issues, so the standards should become easier to understand. When a candidate's work is ready for assessment, the standards should be clear.

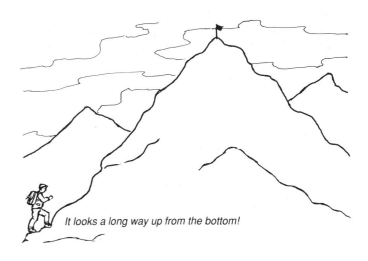

It looks a long way up from the bottom!

The way standards are written

Standards are written for guiding the assessment of GNVQs. They start with units.

- **Units**. GNVQ qualifications are split into units. Units cover particular areas of knowledge, values and skill. For instance, Unit 1 covers the knowledge and skill needed to give emotional support to other people. This is a complicated area which is very important in care work. Units can be awarded and recorded in your National Record of Achievement. A person who is awarded Unit 1 has demonstrated that he or she has the skills and knowledge and can work within the values defined in the standards for that unit. Unit 1 isn't a whole qualification, but it is the first part of an Intermediate GNVQ in Health and Social Care.

- **Elements**. Each GNVQ unit is split into elements. Unit 1: 'Provide emotional support' is split into three elements. Each element defines an area of skill or knowledge. Elements are the smallest areas to be assessed, and *evidence* has to be presented for each element. When there is enough evidence, an element can be 'passed', but a person has to provide evidence for all the elements in a unit before the unit is awarded. Elements are not awarded – they are not recorded in your NRA.

  Elements have a title such as 'Use conversational techniques to maintain social interaction'. This may be a good definition, but it is not easy to see exactly what it means or how it should be assessed. To explain this definition, elements have *performance criteria*.

- **Performance criteria**. Performance criteria define what is required to pass the element. In a sense, they help to explain what the element title is all about. Performance criteria are *not* extra things to assess, they are there to help to explain what is needed to pass the element. When evidence is gathered to 'pass' an element, that evidence has to meet the requirements defined by the performance criteria.

  The element title therefore gives the focus of what has to be done, and the performance criteria help to explain this focus and provide rules for assessment. However, '*range*' is also needed to explain what the evidence has to cover.

- **Range**. This covers what is in range for evidence or out of range for evidence. The word 'range' comes from

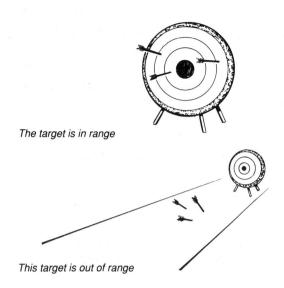

The target is in range

This target is out of range

archery or from shooting ranges. To be in range means something has to be covered by evidence. If something is not in the range, then it does not have to have evidence when achievements are assessed.

So standards are defined by units and elements: elements have titles, performance criteria and range statements which explain what has to be done or known in order to pass. Finally, each element has *evidence indicators*.

- **Evidence indicators**. Evidence indicators give a brief guide as to what type of evidence would be desirable in order to achieve the standards defined in an element. A project would be one way of providing evidence or 'indicating evidence' to meet requirements.

An example: How to interpret one element

In the following example **2HSC1** means Level 2 Health and Social Care Unit 1. The 2 stands for Level 2, (or Intermediate Level), HSC stands for Health and Social Care, 1 stands for Unit 1. The unit is all about the provision of emotional support.

Element 1.1 means Unit 1, Element 1. The title is 'Use conversational techniques to maintain social interaction' – this is what has to be done, or what has to be achieved. How should it be done?

**UNIT 2HSC1: PROVIDE EMOTIONAL SUPPORT
(1993 standards)**

Element 1.1: Use conversational techniques to maintain social interaction

Performance criteria:

1 reflective listening is used to display interest and attention
2 non-verbal messages convey interest and attention
3 questioning techniques are used to develop conversation
4 communication is adapted to, and displays respect and value for, others' individuality

Range:

Conversation: individual and group
Reflective listening: direct repetition of others' content; paraphrasing and interpreting of content
Non-verbal messages: eye-contact; facial expression; posture; gesture; distance; tone of voice
Questioning techniques: open and closed questions; organised question sequences; probes and prompts
Individuality: culture; religion; age; gender; physical appearance; physical ability; mental ability

Evidence indicators:

Demonstration of performance, to include individual and small group discussion. In addition, the candidate should demonstrate an understanding of the implications of the range dimensions and the key principles in respect of them. The unit test will confirm the candidate's coverage of range.

(Example reproduced with permission from NCVQ)

Performance criteria

These explain how the use of conversational techniques should be performed – that's why they are called performance criteria! The right techniques are: (1) reflective listening, (2) non-verbal behaviour, (3) questioning techniques, and (4) adaptation of communication. Each of these techniques has to be used to achieve an outcome – like showing interest and attention, or developing the conversation.

If there were no performance criteria, then any conversation style or methods might do. To get Level 2 Element 1.1, candidates have to provide evidence of particular skills.

Range

Here, range gives a definition of what the words above cover. For example, 'conversation' range explains that both individual and group conversation should be covered. Three kinds of reflective listening are described, so all of them have to be used. What does non-verbal messages cover? Again, the detail is listed. Questioning techniques covers use of probes, prompts, open and closed questions and the organisation of questioning sequences. Individuality is a 'values' area: particular things which must be respected in other people are described.

All this may still not be clear, because range lists the detail but it doesn't explain the knowledge involved in that detail. See Chapter 1 for the knowledge and theory of conversation!

Evidence indicators

It says that candidates have to demonstrate the skills knowledge and values above. Individual and small group discussions have to be demonstrated to the standards for the element. Perhaps the discussion could be videoed or tape-recorded. Some detail might be watched by an assessor, perhaps some detail will be written about.

Anyone who can do all of this must be skilled at keeping a conversation going (maintain social interaction) in a caring way. The standards show just how much is learned and can be done by someone who gets the unit. This is a real qualification!

Understanding standards – how they might feel in the end

You are having lunch with those that you know, and after a while one of them says: 'I keep getting a headache and my eyes go funny – I can't see things for a while – do you think I'm all right. What would you do – should I take something for it?' One of the others says: 'Don't worry, it's the tube

You →

lights – they affect me sometimes, it soon goes.' The third person says: 'Yes, I hate these lights – think they'd do something about them wouldn't you – it's not right!'

You watch the first person with the headache, who looks disappointed. You can tell from his eyes and face that he doesn't feel that he has been taken seriously. So you say something like: 'Tell me about the headache – when do you get it.' He looks more interested and answers you. Perhaps you repeat a few words that he said in an understanding way. The person with the headache tells you more. You ask about his eyes, nodding and showing interest as he keeps talking. The other two become interested and start to join in, but the first person centres his attention on you. You realise that you are the person who is keeping the conversation going, and that you have gained the first person's trust.

This is 1.1 in real life! If you have the skills, knowledge and values involved in each element, you can use them in your work and relationships with other people. The skills in Unit 1 not only cover ways in which you influence others, they can also influence the way others see you. In the above example, 'you' have become the temporary leader of the group.

There is something even more valuable though. A person who really understands all of Unit 1 can probably understand why the people who talked about tube lights weren't very helpful. These two people were not performing to Unit 1 standards – they were thinking about themselves, and just letting the conversation drift. Perhaps they didn't really know much about conversation skills. Some people go through life without understanding how to make conversations interesting, or how to support

others, or how to enable others to trust and like them. People who get 2HSC Unit 1 don't have to be like this; they will understand what behaviours make a person interesting and caring in a conversation.

Not all of Intermediate GNVQ units can be used directly in social settings, but they all lead to greater understanding of caring and people. GNVQ core skills cover practical day-to-day abilities needed at work.

GNVQ assessment

Each element of each unit has to be assessed before the unit is awarded. Assessment takes place when there is enough evidence to be assessed. In order to know what counts as enough evidence, candidates need to have their own assessment skills. Self-assessment of evidence is necessary in order to achieve good grades on GNVQ.

The individual working for a GNVQ qualification will go through a process of action planning, assignment work, checking and submitting the work for assessment. This is not the whole story though. When work is submitted or 'given in' for assessment, a whole system comes into operation.

The assessment

In the past, work was given to teachers or tutors who marked it. This approach was often much simpler than on GNVQ. Now when work is given in, it is more than just 'work'. Assignments are now designed to provide evidence. Evidence has to be judged to decide if there is enough, and if it is the right quality to show that a standard has been reached. The person who decides whether there is enough quality evidence is called an **assessor**. Often the people who act as assessors will be teachers or tutors, but when they collect the work in, they become assessors.

Assessors have to have qualifications and knowledge in the field that they work in. They also have to understand fully the standards that they are checking evidence against. In time, assessors will also have to have gained an NVQ award which will guarantee that they understand the

GNVQ assessment process. All these checks are required to try to ensure that the quality of GNVQ assessment is fair and works properly. But it is more complicated still. The assessments themselves have to be checked.

Assessments have to be checked by an **internal verifier**. 'Internal' means internal to, or inside the centre (inside the college or school, etc.). 'Verifier' means they check the correctness of assessment. Internal verifiers will look at samples of assessment work and check that evidence is being correctly and fairly measured in relation to standards. If candidates don't think their work is being fairly assessed, then they can appeal to the internal verifier to look at their work and re-check it. All the assessor's decisions can be checked by the internal verifier.

There is also an **external verifier**. 'External' means outside, from outside the centre (a school or college, etc.). External verifiers are appointed by the awarding body. An awarding body is BTEC, City & Guilds, or RSA. The awarding body checks the overall quality of the centre's assessment. The external verifier checks the quality of both the assessor's and the internal verifier's decisions. The idea of all this checking is to ensure that standards *really work* – what is accepted as evidence must not become too simple or too complicated. A qualification gained at one college or school should require the same amount and quality of evidence as elsewhere.

The system means that candidates can appeal to the internal verifier, or after that, to the external verifier, if they feel that their assessment is not fair or reasonable.

Evidence, then, is the main issue in understanding assessment. Because standards are a bit like legal documents, as in law evidence is needed before it is fair to give out an award. Evidence is information that goes together to prove that a person has achieved the outcomes the standards require.

Things that count as evidence

Element 1.1 wanted a demonstration of performance, so activities that are done can count as evidence. Projects and written assignments count as evidence.

The following list provides examples of evidence:

Practical demonstration of skills can be watched by an assessor or they can be videoed or tape-recorded (with everyone's permission).

Assignments can provide evidence of knowledge achievement, records of practical work and projects. Most units will require some assignment work.

Past records of achievement and qualifications can count as evidence towards GNVQ units. For instance, GCSE work might count toward core skills assessment.

References from other people such as placement supervisors or employers can provide evidence of practical caring skills, and core skills.

Notes: not all written work needs to be put together into assignments – notes will often be enough to provide evidence for knowledge, or perhaps evidence of planning skills.

Log books or record books are a way of providing evidence to meet grading criteria standards. Log books may be easier to use than loose notes.

Photographs of placement work, perhaps of events organised by a candidate, can sometimes count as evidence towards achieving standards. Photos can often make assignments more interesting.

Things that are made, such as computer printouts, can provide evidence of skills and knowledge. Computer printouts will sometimes need to be 'certified' by an appropriate person to prove that they were done by the candidate.

Portfolio: usually, many different types of evidence will be put together into a collection. This collection is called a portfolio. When the collection is looked at, there should be enough information and evidence to judge that the candidate has performed to the level set by the standards.

Collecting evidence

Each element suggests a way of getting the necessary evidence in the 'Evidence indicators' section. Usually, tutors will provide more information and ideas on practical ways the evidence can be gathered. There are some practical points to watch:

- **Permission**. It is *always* necessary to have other people's permission before written details about them can be used. For instance, written details of a conversation can give evidence of conversation skills, but things other people have said must not be written down without their permission and knowledge of what is written. Where someone is unable to understand, perhaps because they are too young, then their parents or guardians have to give permission.
- **Videos, photos and tapes**. Records of conversations and events also need the permission of the people who appear in them. This might be easy to get if the photograph or video is of a student group. Permission might be hard to get if the tape or video is about clients in a care setting.
- **Group work**. Working with other people is often the best way to plan to collect evidence. Sometimes a group project can meet the evidence requirement for an element. The only problem is that each individual's own work has to be separately recorded or noted, so that they have individual evidence of planning and achievement for their portfolio. Naturally, the general outcome can be recorded as well.

- **Evidence from others**. Evidence of skills used on placements is really valuable, but it will need to be confirmed by a manager or supervisor in the work setting. Usually the supervisor will also have to explain that he or she has watched practical work, and give reasons for agreeing with claims for evidence. Sometimes a report or reference will be needed.

Quality of evidence

Being assessed involves convincing an assessor that your evidence is good enough. Usually, candidates will get a lot of help and guidance to make sure the evidence is all right.

The process of assessment will probably start something like this:

1 Tutors suggest a project or assignment or demonstration to provide evidence for particular units. Written guidelines are given out.
2 Candidates discuss the guidelines, probably with a tutor, and think of ways of planning practical work.
3 Each individual designs an 'action plan' (see later) for the assignment/project/demonstration.
4 Each individual discusses the action plan with a tutor.
5 Candidates do the practical work and write about it.
6 The written work is checked by an assessor. If it is all right then it counts as evidence. If not, then further work can be done until the evidence is right.
7 When there is enough evidence for an element, it is credited as complete.

At the start of a GNVQ programme, tutors and teachers will probably help with action plans and other practical work. Towards the end of the programme, candidates will have to do this work without help, in order to get Merit and Distinction grades.

Reflection

Planning to collect evidence can be interesting, and it involves a special skill. This skill is called **reflection**. Think of a mirror. When a person sees themselves, their image is being bounced back from the reflective mirror. Reflection is the bouncing back of the original image. In social care, 'reflection' means the same sort of thing, except here we are thinking about thoughts and ideas rather than images. Thoughts and ideas get bounced backwards and forwards between people.

Reflection is often very useful. When a person looks in a mirror, they can see what they look like, they can change their make-up or hair until it looks right. The same idea goes for thoughts. If a person can have their thoughts mirrored or reflected by another person, then they have a chance to change or alter their thoughts. Like changing hair style, reflection allows a person to experiment until their ideas are good.

Providing reflective listening is a special skill that is needed in Unit 1. People who can help others to reflect are giving a care service with this skill. When people get very good at reflecting with other people, they can sometimes reflect in their own mind – alone. This becomes a powerful learning skill as people can adapt their own thoughts using an internal mirror rather than using another person. Reflection is also needed in order to plan the collection of evidence.

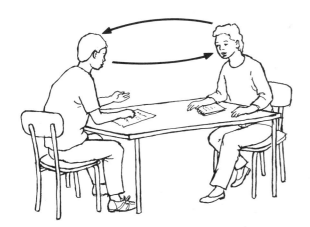

After having some guidance about assignments and evidence gathering, candidates should have ideas about how they will write the assignment or do the practical work. These ideas should be discussed with other people so that they can be developed and improved on. Usually, ideas should be reflected with the tutor, bounced between people until the ideas get more practical and more useful.

Designing an action plan (see below) involves discussion and reflection. For example: getting evidence for Element 1 of Unit 1 involves planning for a discussion with another individual and with a group. The following things might need to be checked out, or organised before going ahead with practical work:

Practical work checklist

1 Are all the performance criteria clear? Are all the range statements clear? If not, then more reading and learning are needed.
2 Have there been opportunities to practise the skills involved before trying to get evidence? If not, then practise the skills with others until they seem easy.
3 Will the discussions be videoed, taped or watched? What permission will be needed? Will people agree?
4 How will people, space, equipment be organised? Who will set it up?
5 What topic is going to be discussed, and what planning is needed?

Action plans

Action plans are records of the ideas that go into getting ready for assignments and evidence collection. They are used to assess the grade of the final GNVQ qualification. Action plans record ideas for the following:

Finding information
● looking up books for information and ideas
● asking people for their opinions
● asking tutors, learning advisors, librarians for advice on how to find information

Reflecting on ideas
● discussing with tutors, with other candidates
● discussing with placement supervisors
● working out what information is needed in order to do assignments, etc.

Preparing to gather evidence
- plans for practical activities
- plans to get evidence during placement
- plans for doing assignments
- plans for what to include in notes and written work

Self-assessment and monitoring
- self-assessment of evidence before it is formally assessed
- self-checking of own progress
- checking of ideas against assignment guidelines
- checking own study patterns and use of time.

Many people like to use a form to help record their ideas. An **action plan form** might look like the one below. People often invent their own forms, so the one shown is just one possible example. People also fill in their own ideas in different ways, but it is a good idea to aim to be consistent in how you go about it and to do it neatly.

Forms are useful because they can focus attention on what needs to be done. They also keep a record of planning activities which can fit neatly into a portfolio. Records of planning are needed in order to get Merit and Distinction grades.

Forms are just one way of organising and recording a 'plan for action'. Some people prefer to write everything down in notes or to use notes to go with their forms. Some people like to make 'pattern notes' to help display things visually.

Suppose a person wants to collect information to help with practical work on 'Providing emotional support'. Collecting information is a theme for grading, so some planning should be recorded before asking other people for ideas. What do you need to know about if you are doing an assignment on emotional support? One possibility is to identify areas of information with **pattern notes**. Pattern notes might be more useful than forms when planning for reflective or self-assessment work.

The diagram shows one person's pattern notes on information she needed for her assignment. She collected the words from the standards. The pattern has five long legs with branches coming out from the legs. The five legs list the main topics that the person wants to find out about. These topics are reflective listening, non-verbal messages, supportive behaviour, individuality and self-esteem. Other smaller areas of knowledge are linked with each of the five legs. Because of all the legs, some people like to call this

GNVQ ACTION PLAN

Candidate's name ....
Planning dates ....
Unit title ....
Time period ....

Elements	Type of evidence	Knowledge needs	Sources of information	Placement activities which provide evidence	Opportunities for reflection	Self-assessment and progress checks	Dates for completion
Element 1	Demonstration, observed group, taped conversation with friend (name)	Check reflective listening, non-verbal, probes, prompts, individuality. (Do first – this week)	Next chapter, lectures, tutor, look up books on interviewing and psychology. Share ideas with group. (Check this week)	Talking to clients, asking carers how they run their conversation, talk to supervisor.	Tutorials, with palcement supervisor, with friends. Dates completed:	Tape record a practice session with a friend – discuss it (next week). Write notes as extra evidence (2 weeks time)	Complete individual conversation work in 4 weeks' time. Group planned for (date)
Complete Element 1 first before going on to Element 2							

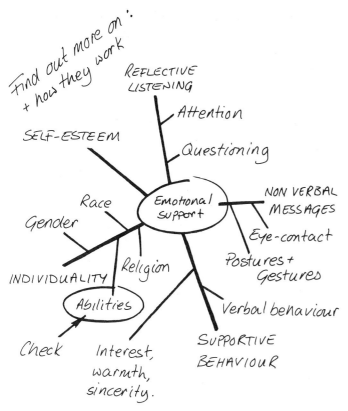

Find out more on ∴ + how they work

REFLECTIVE LISTENING

Attention

Questioning

SELF-ESTEEM

Race

Gender

Emotional support

NON VERBAL MESSAGES

Eye-contact

INDIVIDUALITY

Religion

Postures + Gestures

Abilities

Verbal behaviour

Check

Interest, warmth, sincerity.

SUPPORTIVE BEHAVIOUR

An example of pattern notes

kind of pattern a 'spider-graph'. Whatever it is called, it provides a record of 'identified information needs' and this will help towards a good grade.

It isn't very useful to work out what needs to be known without going on to the next stage! The next stage involves looking for the answers – finding out more about the topics noted.

The best place to find out more is probably the first chapter in this book. There are other sources of information which can be used as well. For instance, a candidate could go to a library and look for useful books. So, to start with, the plan of action might read:

1. Knowledge needs – pattern notes
2. Read next chapter
3. Look in library

Looking in the library may sound all right, but it's not that straightforward. A person could just look along the shelves to see whether he or she could find books with titles like 'Reflective Listening', 'Individuality', etc. This idea probably won't work. One problem is that the books

may be out! So the person could look in the library catalogue. This probably won't work either, because there may not be any single books with these titles! So what next? The person could ask the librarian and show his or her pattern notes. This might get a helpful response, but the librarian won't have read all the books and won't know for sure where all this knowledge could be found. The person could ask a tutor. This again should get a helpful answer – but the candidate can't get a Distinction grade if he or she always has to ask other people for advice.

Finding information and knowledge is always a problem. When something is a problem, it is important to try to use problem-solving skills! People should never give up, there will be a way around the difficulty. There will be some ways to experiment and get a better answer.

The problem with finding the information identified in the pattern notes is that this information is hidden. It is hidden inside chapters of books with quite different titles. In order to find out what the person needs to know, they might have to look at books on helping skills, caring, interviewing, social skills, psychology, sociology. To find out where to start, the person might need to look up the index or the glossary at the back of a book. Another idea is to look at the chapters and contents section at the beginning of a book.

If you start to look through books, you will probably find something useful; but each answer often creates new problems. Suppose what you have found is difficult to understand, you should never give up! The next question to ask is why is it difficult? It may be difficult because the book is really about something different from emotional support. If this is the case, then look for another book. Perhaps another book is too difficult? An idea might be to get an interpretation of the difficult sections using tutorials? Perhaps it is worth taking a few photocopies of pages and discussing them with others?

Usually the hunt for information shouldn't be too difficult. There are often booklists, articles and notes which get people started. Sometimes, information won't be in books anyway. You might sometimes do assignments where the information involves talking to people who work in health or care settings. Sometimes there may be projects which involve searching newspapers for information. The important thing is to plan a strategy for collecting the information and to keep well-written notes which explain how information sources have been identified.

So the full action plan which started with the pattern notes might look like this:

Sheet 2 – Unit 1

Information action plan

1. Information needs for assignment (project) work to be done with pattern notes.
2. Read next chapter.
3. Undertake information search in library by (a) looking up catalogue to identify headings and shelf areas, (b) looking at contents and indexes of books to tell if they might be useful.
4. Talk to staff whilst on placement, or at work. Ask them for advice on how the theory might work in practice.
5. Practise and discuss issues connected with evidence requirements.
6. Get advice where necessary from tutors, supervisors, learning resource staff.

Following this planning stage, the next thing to do will be to **monitor** the planning. (Monitoring is needed to get Merit and Distinction grades.) Monitoring means keeping a record of how the action plan worked. One idea might be to use the action plan form to help monitor how things went. Another idea is just to keep notes. The best idea might be to keep a record or log book where notes are recorded. The notes might look like this:

Sheet 3 – Unit 1

Notes on monitoring
Used chapter in this book, made notes (enclosed). Searched in library: nothing useful in sociology, psychology, but found book on helping skills – photocopied two pages for discussion (enclosed – date). Made notes from book on interviewing (enclosed – date).

Talked to placement supervisor about Emotional Support pattern notes: points recorded in notes (enclosed – date).

Still haven't got information on interest, warmth, sincerity and how they are supposed to link with work. Action plan: ask for advice on such and such a date ....

continued ....

There are three reasons for keeping all these notes and records:

1 They will contribute to meeting the grading criteria for the GNVQ. They will help to provide the evidence needed to get Merits and Distinctions.
2 All this planning and note-taking will create records which can be reflected on. Reflection on your own notes will help to develop skills of problem-solving and management.
3 When people can reflect on and are confident about their own learning skills, they are more likely to feel 'in control' and 'on top of' their work. Work can feel interesting, rather than difficult or boring.

Grading of GNVQ qualifications

Once all the evidence for a unit has been assessed as satisfactory and the test (for mandatory units) has been passed, the unit is awarded. At this stage units are not graded as a Pass, Merit or Distinction. The pass grade is automatic for any candidate who has been awarded all the units – nothing extra is needed. Merit and Distinction grades depend on extra evidence of independent action planning and the management of learning and information.

The extra evidence only needs to be assessed for the later GNVQ units, but it is best to start action plans right from the start to make sure the evidence will be there.

To get a Merit grade, candidates have to:

Independently draw up action plans that 'prioritise' or explain the order of activities.

Identify the need to monitor action plans and revise or change them when necessary. This might, for example, involve the 'reflection' and 'self-assessment' sections of the action plan form provided in this chapter. Some reflection with tutors is expected.

Independently identify information needs for tasks. This might involve the 'knowledge needs' on the action plan form.

Independently find and collect information. This might involve the 'sources of information' column on the action plan. Some reflection with advisors is permitted to identify 'additional sources of information'.

To get a Distinction, candidates have to use the action plans as already explained for Merit standard. In addition, these plans must cover more complex activities. Revision and self-assessment have to become independent – done without help. Information needs are expected to be more complex and candidates can get their information without tutor guidance. Candidates must be able to explain and justify their methods.

In practice, action planning may start with guidance and be focused on each element. At Distinction grade, towards the end of the GNVQ course or programme, candidates will plan for whole units and whole assignments without tutor guidance. To be able to do this, candidates will need to be able to reflect on activities within their own minds. Candidates will be independent in their own planning and use of knowledge skills. Naturally, independence doesn't mean that there won't be discussion and sharing of ideas. This independence would mean that at Distinction level, all the final decisions about planning and working would be made by the candidate and explained by them.

At Distinction level, it may be necessary to draw up plans for assignments, study and placement activities, as well as for evidence gathering. The forms suggested here may not be sufficient. Some candidates might design their own forms as evidence of independent skills, or as evidence of Information Technology core skills.

The portfolio

A portfolio is a portable folio – or a portable collection. A GNVQ portfolio is your collection of evidence for the

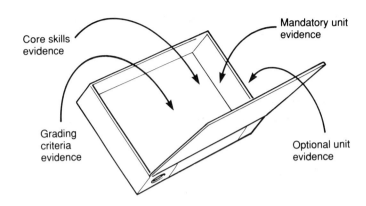

award of the qualification. Evidence for the qualification will probably be contained in:

● assignments
● a record or log book
● extra notes and forms.

Evidence has to cover:
● mandatory and optional units
● core skills units
● grading criteria.

Assignments

Evidence for mandatory and optional units will mostly be found in assignment work. There may be just one assignment per unit so this may be straightforward to present at the end of the course. Assignments will probably contain most of the evidence for core skills units. The evidence for core skills will probably be spread across the six assignments though.

Record or log book

Another way of collecting evidence for core skills and for Merit or Distinction grades is to keep a record. By keeping what might be a diary of study activities, it should be possible to analyse 'personal learning opportunities'. The log book or record can be used to note information needs on placement. There might be questions to ask about placement activities, words or technical terms which need an explanation. Assignments might set tasks to explore on placement. The log book might provide somewhere to record thoughts and opinions gained from others. The log book could take notes and plans for assignment work.

Notes

Sometimes candidates might prefer to use action plan forms for planning. Core skills in Information Technology might be demonstrated by designing action plan forms, or other record sheets. These sheets might be separate from the assignments or from other log books or notes.

By the end of the GNVQ programme, there could be a great deal of evidence to be reviewed for the award of the qualification.

All this evidence could be collected together, dumped in a bag and given to the assessors and verifiers. The problem with dumping it all on the assessors is that they will not understand it all. A disorganised portfolio won't communicate quality, it won't suggest good planning and monitoring. So a portfolio is more than a bag of bits!

Portfolios need to be carefully planned and organised. The planning of the portfolio might even provide evidence for the 'planning and monitoring' grading criteria.

What the portfolio might look like

The portfolio might be a ring binder, an envelope folder or a file of some sort. The portfolio at the end of the programme might need more than one folder. What matters is that there is an explanation of how the evidence in the portfolio meets the standards for GNVQ and the standards for a Merit or Distinction grade if this is claimed.

So, looking inside the folder there will probably be:

1 *A title sheet* stating the candidate's name, the centre's name (school or college) and the name of the qualification (Intermediate GNVQ in Health and Social Care).
2 *An index of assignments and assessments* which have already been made.
3 *A statement or claim* explaining that the assignment work meets the unit standards and has been assessed as meeting the standards (dates of assessment and forms might be included here).

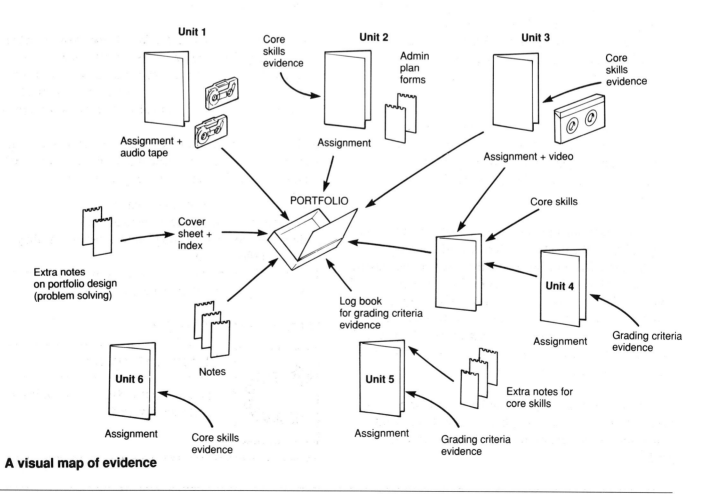

A visual map of evidence

4 Photocopies of the *unit standards* which the work claims to demonstrate (or workbook containing the standards).

5 *An index of core skills evidence*. This index would explain where evidence could be found for Information Technology, Application of Number and Communication skills. Page numbers in assignment work might be quoted. Notes would be placed in order in the portfolio and numbered. Core skills demonstrated by other records (floppy disk, video, etc.) would also be noted, and disks and boxes labelled.

6 *An index of evidence for the grading criteria* of 'action planning', 'monitoring', 'identifying information needs' and 'identifying and using sources to obtain information'. Most of the evidence would probably be on forms, on notes, or in a record or log book. Page numbers should be quoted.

You don't have to supply evidence for the core skills of 'problem solving', 'working with others', and 'improving own learning'. It might still be worth putting in for these units, as they can go in your NRA; and evidence for these core skills might also count towards the grade for the GNVQ. 'Action planning' and 'monitoring' sometimes involve problem-solving. 'Identifying information needs' links with 'improving own learning'. Health and Social Care assignment work will often link with 'working with others'.

The act of designing a really good portfolio involves problem-solving and self-assessment of your own learning. A high-quality portfolio might supply evidence to claim the additional core skills as noted above.

The above indexing might be enough, but remember that the portfolio is the final collection of work for the qualification. The portfolio could therefore contain also an overview of how different types of evidence might link. If you claim Distinction grades or perhaps Merit grades, you might include some writing, explaining the links between additional core skills and the grading criteria. You should explain how some assignment work meets the standards for core skills, and so on.

As well as the indexing, the standards, and the evidence, the portfolio can contain explanations and arguments which support the claim for a Merit or Distinction grade.

Using icons to organise the portfolio

One idea to make indexing easier is to use symbols or 'icons' to label your evidence. A range of icons appears at the back of this book – these can be photocopied for use with GNVQ evidence, free of copyright restrictions. After photocopying, they can be cut out and stuck to notes or pages of assignment or log-book work. When an icon is stuck next to a piece of writing or on a tape box, etc., it means that evidence is being claimed. An icon states: 'Look, this is evidence!'

Using the portfolio design to develop your own learning

Designing a portfolio to achieve a Distinction grade will involve a good deal of self-assessment work. Usually, this work will have to be started early in the programme and developed as the programme goes on. *Good grades may be difficult to achieve if portfolio design is left until the end of the programme.*

One idea is that candidates should be helped to action plan, monitor and gather information towards the first assignment. After the first assignment, candidates should begin to organise their own plans for later work. Portfolio design might begin as soon as self-assessment work begins.

Designing a good portfolio depends upon understanding the subject area and understanding the idea of 'evidence'. Learning and understanding usually depend on:

1 Wanting or needing to learn something.
2 Being prepared to try ideas out in practice.
3 Being able to imagine and picture things so that they can be 'reflected' on.
4 Being able to listen to other people and take advice on how to improve one's own ideas.

Imagine – a reflective task

Think it over

Do you want to design a portfolio for Distinction grade?

If you are still reading on, then you must be interested! It should feel good to do well on your GNVQ. Wanting to do well covers the first area above.

Assignments will provide opportunities to try out ideas in practice. There are many 'evidence opportunities' listed in this book. These opportunities or the assignments that are suggested to you should cover the second issue.

Imagination can become a kind of skill. For some people it develops with learning to 'reflect'. When it comes to collecting evidence, imagination is very important. It is useful to imagine what the standards really mean in practice. It is useful to imagine events which have happened on placement, or between people – and then imagine how skills and knowledge involved in the GNVQ could influence these events. It is useful to picture yourself using skills or information in practical situations. Most of all, it is very useful to imagine yourself in another person's place, and imagine what they would do.

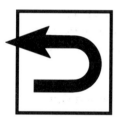

Think it over

Imagine your assessor checking the quality of assignment evidence. What sort of things will he or she be looking for?

Do you know the answer, can you imagine this? If yes, then you have already been doing a lot of work for the GNVQ.

If no, then the fourth area of learning will solve the problem – ask the assessor and learn about how he or she thinks. Learning how other people think is very important in Health and Social Care work.

This last part of learning often needs to be linked with the first three areas. It is very important to get other people's ideas to help develop your own. The best way of developing an understanding of evidence may be to ask tutors and assessors what they think would provide good evidence. Next, try out a practical assignment task. Then use imagination to guess how good your practical work is. Finally, check out your imagination with an assessor – were you right? If not, what can you learn so that you will be better next time?

An example

In 2HSC1 Element 1, you have to demonstrate the use of conversational techniques to maintain social interaction in individual and group settings. Your evidence has to meet the standards. So suppose you recorded the following conversation and suggested it as evidence.

> 'Hello Jasmine, how are you today? How's the puppy, is it well? It's a lovely dog isn't it? How's everyone at home? I'm glad everyone's OK. Got to go now, bye!'

Imagine you were the assessor. Would you accept this as evidence? The answer is no! There's nothing wrong with the conversation, but it's not sufficient evidence for the standards.

The reason such a short conversation isn't sufficient is that it only covers some of the performance criteria for 2HSC1.1. The conversation covers using questions, it might cover reflective listening (if we could hear it or see it on an audio or video tape). However, the conversation doesn't provide evidence of adapting to others' individuality – much more detail would be needed. The conversation doesn't record any non-verbal messages. So the evidence isn't enough here.

Learning by doing

Learning to design a portfolio of evidence will eventually require you to self-assess your own evidence. You will have to be able to show that:

1 The work is your own.
2 There is enough work to cover the performance criteria and range statements in the standards.
3 There is enough detail of planning, monitoring and identifying, and using information sources to meet grading criteria.

Doing all this involves a lot of trying things out, using imagination, and checking with tutors or assessors. *Designing a good portfolio is a major learning task* – perhaps a bigger task than many assignments. This is why Merit and Distinction grades depend on good evidence presentation. It shows that a great deal of learning has been done.

Understanding what is needed for evidence presentation also involves understanding the knowledge content of the various units. Many people say that good evidence presentation will require a deep level of learning. Grades should reflect this deep learning.

Imagine trying to learn to drive a car by reading a book. Very few people could do it. To drive a car you have to *practise* doing it. Collecting evidence and designing a portfolio will be the same kind of learning – try it, imagine how to do it better, listen to advice. Or listen to advice, imagine it and then try it. The order isn't important. What can't be done is to learn the whole idea in one go and then do it.

Evidence collection will look very complicated at first, there is so much that can go into a portfolio. It is important to get some ideas, think about them, try them out in practice and then get advice. If this is done over six months or so, it should become much easier. Like driving a car, it gets easier once you've tried it for real.

Some of the ideas here might make more sense after evidence for the first assignment has been collected. So, if you are reading this before starting your GNVQ, why not plan to read it again in a month's time or in two months' time? Some of the ideas about learning will make more sense when they are tried in practice.

Tests

The four mandatory units are all tested. Tests provide evidence that all the detail involved in the units has been covered. Some people think that test evidence will mean that GNVQ qualifications will be more valued and respected by the public and by future employers.

GNVQ tests should usually be taken after all the other evidence collection work for a unit has been done. Tests

will ask a number of short questions about the unit and will probably last about one hour. Tests have to be passed in order for a unit to be awarded. If a test isn't passed first time, it can be taken again. Indeed, it should be possible to take the test several times if necessary. Fear of failing often worries people when they have to take tests. *GNVQ tests shouldn't cause fear because the tests can be retaken.*

You will already have achieved lots of practical learning for the unit. Before you take the test, you will have planned evidence collection, reviewed your own knowledge, reflected on knowledge with others in discussion, written assignments or notes. All this work will have been assessed. This work should mean that there isn't a lot of extra work and revision to do for the test.

Before doing the test, it might be worth organising discussion sessions so that practical work and information can be shared. *Talking about knowledge can be one of the best ways of learning to remember it for a test.*

The knowledge contained in this book should help cover the needs of the test. Fast Facts won't always cover every question possible for a unit, but they should cover many! Use Fast Facts for revision.

Another idea is to combine group discussion and Fast Facts to make your own quiz game along the lines of 'Trivial Pursuits'. Making revision fun can provide a good way of checking learning. Turning revision into a game may also remove anxiety.

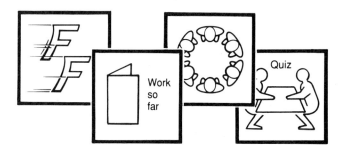

Preparing for tests

You will need a lot of knowledge to pass the test. Sometimes people imagine that getting this knowledge is like filling up a mug with water. The idea is to keep learning until the mug is full. Big mugs hold lots of water, little mugs can't hold so much. Sometimes people try to stretch their memory to hold lots of information – they try to become big mugs!

This idea of stretching memory is usually painful and it makes taking a test a very unpleasant experience. In caring, it shouldn't be necessary to strain your memory.

For example, a candidate just starting a placement may have lots of clients' and colleagues' names to remember. One idea could be to stretch the memory and go around trying to list all the names over and over again until they stick. Usually carers don't do this. An alternative idea is to talk to each person and to get to know them one by one. After a while it becomes easy to remember all sorts of details about the people. Their names become easy and sometimes automatic to remember, because names link to all the other details about the people. This kind of automatic knowledge feels natural – sometimes people feel that it just happens to them. It may be that this kind of learning is 'deeper' than the kind where a memory gets 'full-up'.

GNVQ tests won't be as natural as remembering people on placement, but the ideas about learning may still work. If you have done project work, written assignments, shared ideas with other people, taken notes from other people's explanations and so on – then learning may feel more real and natural. This deeper learning may be interesting. It could even make the tests feel like a fun challenge, rather than an unpleasant pressure.

Whatever the test feels like, it is important to avoid overfilling the memory – cramming things into it for a test. It is usually a better idea to learn from practical experience

and then to use Fast Facts to help revise. Fast Facts probably won't work very well as starting points for learning. They shouldn't be crammed into the memory for the test. One way they might work is that they might help candidates to recognise things that they already know. When a person looks at the Fast Facts list, the words should prompt thoughts. The thoughts should link with the details under each 'fact' heading. Experience of studying Fast Facts may make it easier to recall detail when actually taking a test for a unit.

Think it over

Experiment with this chapter. Use the Fast Facts – do they make sense first time?

An experiment using Fast Facts

There are no tests of knowledge for doing GNVQs, but if there were, questions might look like this:

● 'What is evidence? Why is it necessary to collect evidence in order to be awarded a GNVQ?'

Some people feel mentally 'frozen' by such a question. No matter how long a person stares at it, there is no clue as to where to begin. So, what is evidence?

Fast Facts says these things about 'evidence':

1 It is the key to passing a GNVQ and getting good grades.
2 Evidence is information which confirms that a standard has been reached.
3 Evidence can be gathered in assignments.
4 There are many ways evidence can be presented, such as by video or tape recordings. Demonstrations of skill can be observed and recorded to provide evidence.
5 Tests provide evidence of knowledge.

If a person attempted to memorise all this, it would hurt! Or at least, if a person went through Fast Facts and tried to commit it all to memory, very few memories could take it. So the five points above aren't the answer, they are too difficult to remember just as they are written.

● **Continue the experiment** – try to analyse the five
statements above. What do they mean?

The five points above need to make sense. They need to
feel real; they need to link with a practical know-how of
doing a GNVQ. Do they link with doing?

Point 1 says evidence is the key to passing a GNVQ
and getting good grades. Action planning is one example
of evidence – it is written or recorded information. Point
2 states that evidence is information which confirms
that a standard has been reached. This might remind
someone of the types of information: videos, pictures,
references – they are all types of records of things which
have been done. These records are used to prove that a
standard has been reached. Point 3 says that assignments
are used to gather evidence. Records again, types of
evidence again, examples of assignments might come to
mind. Point 4 talks about examples of evidence. Perhaps
these inspire pictures in the mind? Point 5 says that tests
provide evidence (a difficult point, but then the test is
needed to get the award of mandatory units) – it provides
a record of knowledge. It's another example of
information that confirms that a standard has been
reached.

Is this the kind of thing that came into your mind? If
not, have you done any practical work with evidence
yet?

There is an old Chinese proverb:

I hear and I forget,
I see and I remember,
I do and I learn.

Collecting evidence is something which has to be done
in practice. When it has been done, the Fast Facts will act
as a reminder. The explanations come together after
study.

● An answer to the question: What is evidence?
Answer: Evidence is information, records, details, that
show that standards have been reached.

The above question on evidence is probably harder than
most questions to be set for tests, but even so, it should
become easy if practical work is done which makes the
knowledge real.

Self-assessment of knowledge about GNVQs

1 What are 'standards'? Why are standards used in
assessment?
2 Why are standards sometimes difficult to
understand at the beginning of a GNVQ
programme?
3 Why is it necessary to produce evidence in order to
be awarded GNVQ units?
4 What are action plans? Why is it important to keep
records of action plans?
5 Can a person plan to get a Distinction or Merit grade
and be confident of getting it?
6 What is needed in order to get a Merit or Distinction
grade?
7 What is a portfolio? When should work on a portfolio
start?
8 How should candidates prepare to take a GNVQ
test?
9 Why is it important for GNVQ candidates to assess
their own learning?
10 Why is 'reflection' useful when learning in Health
and Social Care?

Fast Facts

Action planning Evidence has to
be collected in order to pass a
GNVQ. The collection of evidence
needs to be *planned*. What action will
produce enough evidence to demonstrate (pass) the
standard? 'Action plans' equal 'plans to get evidence'.
Evidence of good action planning helps towards merit and
distinction grades.

Assessors These are the people who assess evidence
to decide whether it meets the requirements of National
standards. In other words, they assess work to see if it
should pass. Assessors will also assess the grade of a
GNVQ qualification when the portfolio is presented for
assessment. Assessors will often be tutors or learning
managers. They must be very knowledgeable and
qualified in the area they are assessing. By 1995, most
assessors will hold an NVQ award which demonstrates
that they can operate to the NVQ/GNVQ assessor
standards.

Assignments   Assignments are one way of collecting lots of evidence to demonstrate (pass) an element of GNVQ Caring. Assignments should be planned and negotiated with an assessor, tutor or learning manager.

Awarding body   Either City & Guilds, BTEC or RSA will check the quality of courses and candidates' work. They award the GNVQ qualification (the National Council for Vocational Qualifications does not award qualifications, it just designs and checks the national system).

Candidates   People who collect evidence to get GNVQs are called candidates – they are candidates for assessment. Colleges call all people who study 'students', and 'students' and 'candidates' are the same; but the word 'candidate' emphasises the fact that these people are putting themselves forward for assessment – that they are very active, not just spending time in study.

Core skills   The skills of Communication, Application of Number and Information Technology are needed to get the GNVQ qualification. They are assessed using evidence gathered to pass mandatory and optional units. Core skills of Problem Solving, Improving Own Learning and Working With Others can also be assessed and recorded in a candidate's NRA.

Elements   The smallest parts of standards to be assessed. *Units* are usually made up of between two and four elements. Once an element is 'passed' it has to be collected with other elements to pass a unit.

Evidence   This is the key to passing a GNVQ and getting good grades. Evidence is information which confirms that a standard has been reached. Evidence can be gathered in assignments. There are many ways evidence can be presented, such as by video or tape recordings. Demonstration of skill can be observed and recorded to provide evidence. Tests provide evidence of knowledge.

Evidence indicators   In GNVQ standards, evidence indicators are found at the bottom of element details. They give an outline of the kind of evidence needed to pass a given element.

Grading   GNVQs are graded Pass, Merit or Distinction. GNVQs cannot be failed, but they are not 'passed' until all the necessary units are passed. Here, Merit or Distinction grades depend on extra evidence of skill in action planning and information handling.

Information needs   These are part of action planning and part of the 'criteria' (what is needed) for getting Merit and Distinction grades. Information needs have to be identified in order to do projects and assignments and in order to present evidence for assessment. They might be recorded in a log book or in portfolio notes. At Merit and Distinction grades, candidates will be independent in their ability to find information for assignments.

Knowledge   The word covers information, facts, concepts, theories and also the way people use their ideas to guide their work. GNVQs in Health and Social Care will involve using knowledge in practical situations. Just knowing about things won't be enough for most units.

Levels   Both GNVQ and NVQ qualifications are awarded at five levels. Level 1 is Foundational, Level 2 is Intermediate and equal to good GCSE qualifications, Level 3 is Advanced and equivalent to 'A' level. Levels 4 and 5 are graduate and post-graduate equivalents.

Mandatory unit   Mandatory units are a fixed part of the GNVQ qualification. They have to be achieved or passed to get the GNVQ.

Monitoring   Monitoring means checking what's happening. In GNVQs, action plans have to be monitored or checked and developed, in order to get Merit and Distinction grades. Monitoring links with self assessment where individuals check their evidence before having it assessed. A log book or notes will often be needed to provide evidence of monitoring.

NCVQ   The National Council for Vocational Qualifications. The Council controls the national framework of GNVQ and NVQ qualifications.

NRA   A National Record of Achievement. Candidates should have an NRA in which to keep records of their units as they are awarded. The NRA provides a record of achievement which might be useful to an individual who didn't complete the whole of a GNVQ qualification. The NRA can also record extra units, and extra core skills units for individuals who get more than the standard GNVQ qualification.

NVQ   National Vocational Qualifications are more narrowly focused than GNVQs. They are structured in different units but designed with the same qualification levels as GNVQs.

Optional unit   Intermediate GNVQs at have two 'optional units'. These are not tested at present.

Performance criteria   These define the performance necessary to reach the standard (or criteria) necessary to achieve an element. Performance criteria explain what is to be covered. They are rules to guide the assessors. Performance criteria are not assessed separately. Evidence has to cover all the criteria when it is submitted for assessment.

Portfolio   A portable 'folio' (or collection) of evidence. Action plans lead to the collection of evidence to meet unit requirements. All the evidence should be put together into a folder or perhaps a file box if photos, tapes and videos are included. The portfolio can then be assessed and verified.

Programmes   GNVQs are usually called programmes because units can be taken in any order, and passed in any order. Individuals could – at least in theory – take different pathways to achieving a GNVQ. Many people call GNVQ programmes 'courses'; they can be courses, but this is a more old-fashioned idea which implies a fixed pattern of treatment (like a course of drugs for an illness!).

Qualification   The whole Intermediate GNVQ in Health and Social Care. GNVQ Units are not qualifications.

Reflection   A skill which helps in the process of evidence collection, self assessment and planning. It is a skill also necessary in health and social care work (see Chapter 1).

Skills   Abilities which people can demonstrate and do. GNVQ standards cover instances of knowledge, skills, understanding and values.

Standards   The basis for assessment, national standards are all the unit, element, performance criteria, range and evidence indicator descriptions for GNVQ areas. Standards don't explain what must be studied, but they do explain what must be assessed.

Tests   The mandatory units all have tests. Tests will probably last about one hour, and may involve short questions perhaps involving multiple choice answers.

Tutorials   A term for the discussions with a tutor or learning manager which will guide action planning, evidence gathering and project work.

Understanding   Deep knowledge and skill that can be used in many different circumstances and settings; also, practical knowledge that can be used to solve problems. GNVQ evidence will often show that concepts and theories can be used in practice, or in practical situations.

Units   The building bricks of qualifications. Units are the smallest part of a GNVQ to be awarded. They can be recorded in the NRA. Units are made up of elements.

Values   Viewpoints which are foundational to professional practice. In Health and Social Care, these views include valuing others' individuality (see Chapter 1). Values are part knowledge and part skill. They are partly a skill because they have practical applications. In Health and Social Care, values are emphasised because other caring skills don't work without them.

Verifier   A person who checks assessments. When assessments are made of people's evidence, these assessments themselves have to be checked. The *internal* verifier checks a sample of tutors' assessment work within a GNVQ centre. The *external* verifier checks the operation of systems in GNVQ centres on behalf of the awarding body.

chapter *1* PROVIDING EMOTIONAL SUPPORT

The ability to provide effective emotional support is a skill necessary for working in health and social care. However, the skills discussed in this chapter can be very powerful. People who are good listeners, who can understand other people's feelings, tend to be popular. People who can understand and support others may get a lot more happiness from life than people who can't. Understanding issues like individuality and group behaviour are an important basis for leading and managing other people. Whatever your career ambitions or social goals, this chapter, and this unit of GNVQ, are well worth studying.

So, you want to develop your personal caring skills. How useful this chapter is to you may depend partly on *how you use your own imagination*. Many of the ideas will only begin to work if you can picture them as a real part of your own life. As you read through the theory, ask yourself the question: 'How would I (or do I) use these skills with people?' Use **mental reflection** (described in the previous chapter) to think about your own caring behaviour and how you can adapt it.

Think it over

What makes a person a good carer? Are certain people just naturally born to care for others or is it something people can learn to do?

There are various answers to this puzzle. Sometimes people say that experiences of caring for others early on in life are important. Other people say you have to have a

calm nature or a good sense of humour. One thing is definite – good carers have to be *interested in others,* and good at building a 'sense of liking' between people.

For example, imagine you are talking to a friend on the way to work in the morning. He tells you that he feels sad because his pet cat died last night, and then becomes quiet. How can you help?

In such a situation most people would start with an expression of sympathy: 'Oh, I'm very sorry to hear that – how did it happen?' A skilled carer will do more. The carer will ask about the details, not because of a need to know, but so that the other person has a chance to talk. Skilled carers will show that they are listening and that they understand the feelings of the other person. A skilled carer will try to make the person feel glad that he talked about his sadness. If this is successful, the other person will feel that he matters to the carer.

Listening to someone who is unhappy is a very important caring skill. There is an old Chinese saying: 'a problem shared is a problem halved'. Listening to someone and showing that you care gives that person a chance to think through their worries. Knowing that someone cares might make their situation feel better.

Many people can't listen to others. What happens is that they feel embarrassed – lost for words. So, unskilled people hearing about a lost pet may come out with things like:

[1] 'Oh that's bad, oh well I suppose you can always get another cat – I saw some kittens for sale in the paper.'
[2] 'Oh that's a bit of bad luck . . . still, these things

happen. Oh! about that piece of work, can I talk to you later about it.'

[3] 'Tough! Still, could have been worse; never mind we all lose pets don't we, lots of people have worse trouble than that.'

These statements are not examples of providing emotional support. The reasons for this are as follows:

Statement 1 ignores the feelings of the person who is sad. Saying 'you can get another cat' makes it sound like losing a knife and fork at lunch time – 'oh can't find it, well get another one'. The cat really mattered, it can't just be replaced. The person who said this didn't care enough to listen and to find this out. They just jumped in with some bad advice.

Statement 2 also ignores the feelings of the sad person. This is even worse though, because the person who said it didn't want to listen to the other person at all. Perhaps hearing about sadness upsets them so they switched off and changed the subject.

Whoever said statement 3 not only wanted to avoid listening, he or she wanted to lecture the other person about life. Some people might find this the most uncaring response of all. Hearing that others have even worse trouble than yourself is only comforting if you are in competition with everyone else! This statement is likely to make the sad person angry or perhaps depressed.

Providing emotional support is not just common sense – it requires a range of special skills. Perhaps the most important skill is to be able to listen to others.

· LISTENING ·

In care work, it is useful to separate the idea of listening to what people say from the idea of hearing the noise that people make when they talk!

Here, listening means hearing another person's words, thinking about what they mean and planning what to say back to the other person. Hearing the other person means picking up the sounds they make.

Look at Figure 1.1. The person with the personal stereo can't hear or listen to the others. The person with legs up, looking out the window, is behaving as if he is not listening. The person might hear what the other two are saying, though. In the third picture the people are listening to each other because each person can explain what the last speaker said. They have heard the message, remembered what was said, planned their own comments, before replying.

Listening is a skill, far more than just being around when something is said. Listening involves **hearing** and then **remembering** what has been said. If we are going to remember what someone else has said, we have to **understand** it first.

Some psychologists believe that we usually only remember about one out of every two thousand things that we hear in a day! Most of the sounds that come to our ears are not important enough to bother about remembering.

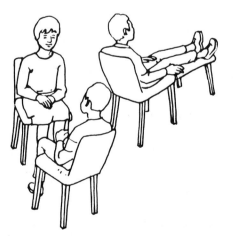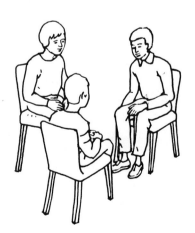

Figure 1.1

Think it over

Last night you may have watched TV or talked to family or friends. Just how much can you recall of what you heard over the hours?

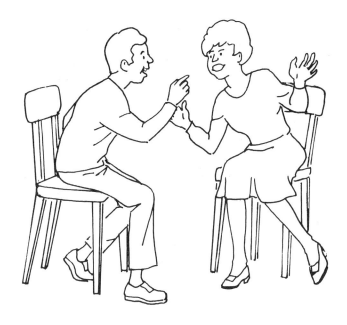

Figure 1.2 *The listening process*

If you can't remember much perhaps it doesn't matter; the important thing may be that you enjoyed it. But it's different when you work with clients. Listening skills are needed here.

To understand a client you will need to know something of their background, lifestyle and personal situation. As well as knowing about these things, you will have to be able to make sense of them to feel that you understand and have some idea of what to expect. This understanding develops from *experience* of listening to people. Perhaps we gradually get better and better at it.

Sometimes, getting ready to listen involves switching into your store of knowledge and understanding. For some people this is a conscious switching-on process. You want to give emotional support to the person who has just lost his pet. You will need to say and do the right things, but what are the right things? Each person is different. Everyone has their own way of thinking. If you know the person who had the pet, you can 'switch on' to your own memories. What used he to say about the cat? What do you know about his feelings: how much did the cat mean to him, and can we guess how he feels?

Listening could feel like really hard mental work. Instead of just living in our own private world planning to say whatever we think, we have to think about the other person. So, if someone is saying that they are sad because they've lost their pet, we have to *first* hear their words and *then* imagine how the other person feels. We have to make sense of what they said, perhaps imagining how we would feel if it happened to us. Having thought through what we've been told, we have to think again before we speak (see Figure 1.2).

Listening *is* hard mental work – it takes time. Because real listening takes thinking time, a lot of people don't bother to listen.

Reasons why people don't listen to others

1 Listening takes up too much mental energy – we might be tired.
2 People say they have too little time and too much work to do. Sometimes this might be true, sometimes it might be an excuse.
3 It feels like we've heard it all before and there is nothing we can do to help someone – it feels easier to switch off.
4 Some clients in care are seen as unimportant and their worries aren't considered worth listening to – so they are not treated with the respect they deserve.
5 Sometimes we don't understand the backgrounds and lifestyles of other people. It becomes easier not to have to learn about people different from ourselves – not listening saves us from having to adjust our views and beliefs.
6 Sometimes clients can make us worry. They might talk about pain, suffering and grief. Some people are afraid to talk about such things, so not listening means that they don't have to.
7 Some people like to control clients. It's quicker and easier to just get on with practical day-to-day tasks – asking the client's opinion gets in the way.
8 Most important of all: some people imagine that they should always be able to offer simple advice to anyone with a worry or a problem. They feel that they have to have an answer for everything. This belief stops them from listening.

Good carers will try to avoid making the mistakes listed in the box, but listening often remains difficult. If you are going to listen, then the other person has to keep talking! Some clients don't find it easy to keep talking, so how can a carer encourage a client to talk? Here are some ideas:

- *Use skilled non-verbal messages.*
- *Use reflective listening skills and silence.*
- *Use questions in an appropriate way.*
- *Always try to show that you respect and value others' individuality.*

These ideas are explained in detail in this chapter.

Task

Working out what these skills mean in practice and how to use these skills can contribute to the core skill 'Improving own learning performance' and to the grading criteria for 'Identifying information needs'. Could you plan to demonstrate skills for encouraging another person to keep talking? Have you an action plan for this skill? If not, start to draw one up now.

· NON-VERBAL COMMUNICATION ·

Verbal means 'using words', so verbal communication occurs when people speak with words. Non-verbal, on the other hand, means 'without words'. Non-verbal communication means that you can send messages to other people, which they can understand, without using words.

The important thing about non-verbal communication is that we are always sending messages to clients by the way we use our face, eyes, voice tone, movement, muscle tension, hand signals, touch and body posture. We can't help but communicate something all the time! And clients send messages to us all the time too!

Observing non-verbal messages

Think it over

In a residential care situation an elderly lady comes to us and mumbles sounds that you can't understand, but non-verbally she looks at the window, points, looks upset, worried and afraid – her eyes send the message: 'Please help me'. How do you make sense of this. Can you help?

The person has communicated that she is anxious; perhaps she has a desire to be outside or back home. Perhaps she is confused as to where she is. Whatever the message, you could help by being calm, trying to explain that all is well – offering to stay with the person, offering to walk outside with her. You could respond to the 'please help' if you listen to the message.

Being able to make sense of non-verbal language from a client grows with thinking about our experience with people, and it grows with knowledge of the background, culture and personality of individual clients.

In many social situations the non-verbal communication is more important than what is actually said.

Think it over

Think of yourself at a social gathering with friends. Perhaps you can think of one in the last week or so. You maybe sat round talking. How much can you remember of what the other people said? The real messages may have been: 'We all like each other – we are all friends'. These messages will have been sent non-verbally. What people actually talk about may not always be important.

Using our senses

All non-verbal messages are associated with what we learn from our senses. We use our senses in the following ways.

The sense of touch

This can send messages for:

- guiding others' movements
- greeting people
- affection
- expressing power and dominating others (aggression).

The sense of sight

A long gaze is used when we feel comfortable, know someone well. Sometimes a long gaze may be used in an attempt to be threatening towards someone.

A short gaze, of a couple of seconds say, is used to:

- catch someone's attention
- check how we are being received
- end/withdraw from conversation
- signal that we wish to bring someone into the conversation
- signal that we wish to exclude someone.

The tone of voice

This is concerned with the tone, the speed, the pitch and the rhythm of speech. Have you ever heard someone speaking in a foreign language and been able to tell they were angry purely by hearing the speed and tone of what they were saying?

The sense of smell

This is probably the sense used least by adult humans for communication. We try to cover up natural smells by using deodorants, perfumes, etc. It is, however, extensively used by animals and by particular groups of human beings. For example, you may know that babies can recognise their mother by her own smell.

Think it over

Can you think which other people might rely on a sense of smell more than others?

People who do not see well rely more than others on the sense of smell. As well as relating smells to people, they use this sense to help them remember their way around new surroundings. For example, a blind child newly arrived at a boarding school will remember the distinct smells of the dining room, classroom, bathroom, to build a 'mind map' of the way around the building.

When we know someone very well we can recognise their non-verbal clues very easily, but with people we know less well, it is necessary to watch carefully to be aware of all the clues given out.

Remember, too, if a client has a disability such as reduced sight or movement, it is necessary to face them to allow maximum view of your non-verbal language. Be aware that conversing is harder for them if they only get the verbal signals. Someone with a hearing impairment will rely heavily on the non-verbal signals you send.

USING THE BODY TO SEND MESSAGES

Understanding people involves understanding their non-verbal communication as well as what they say. The feelings we have about other people are often based on the non-verbal messages they send to us. We use our body to send non-verbal messages, so non-verbal communication is sometimes called **body language**.

Body language is always there and we are not always conscious of the messages we give out. We are usually very careful in what we say and we can usually explain why we have said it. Body language or non-verbal communication is different – most people don't think about it, they just experience it. *Skilled carers need to be able to understand their own and others' body language and be consciously aware of it.*

Some of the most important body areas to use, and to watch others use, are (see Figure 1.3):

- the eyes
- the face
- voice tone
- body movement
- posture (how we sit or stand) and head angles when looking at others
- muscle tension (how tense or relaxed we are)
- gestures (use of arms and hands).

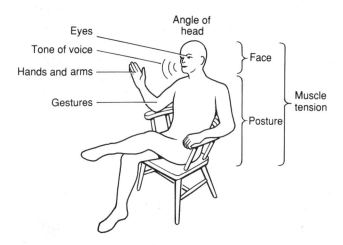

Figure 1.3 *Body language that sends messages*

Important special messages are sometimes sent by:

- touch
- how close people get to each other
- mirroring of body postures and movements.

The eyes

Our eyes can send a vast range of messages and may often be the most important part of our body when it comes to sending non-verbal messages. One poet called the eyes 'the window of the soul', meaning that sometimes we can see the feelings and thoughts of another person by looking at their eyes. Looking at the eyes might be like looking through a window into the other person's feelings!

You may feel that this is too romantic, but your eyes *will* usually send messages as to how you feel emotionally. Skilled actors learn to control their eyes by remembering an emotional feeling and then trying to send that feeling

with their eye movements. Most people don't learn to act to that level of skill, but their eyes still send messages.

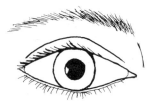 

Our eyes widen when we are excited or interested in someone. If we feel attracted to a person we will probably send them this message just with the look in our eyes! Equally, if we are angry the eyes quickly send this message.

The way our eyes widen and narrow may not be as important as the way we use our eyes to make contact with others. If a person thinks you are interesting or attractive, they will want to look at you. If your eyes meet, there is often a momentary widening (excitement) in the other person's eyes, this followed by quickly looking away, followed by looking back (perhaps to see if you are looking at them). A person who is not interested and just happened to be looking your way may move their eyes more slowly – there will be less jumpiness in the way their eyes move.

Anger and hostility are often communicated by staring. A person who is angry with you might fix their gaze on you. When your eyes meet, they will not look away – eyes can become locked in battle!

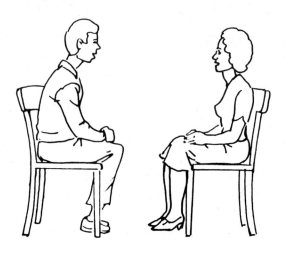

As well as sending messages about emotion, we send all sorts of social messages with our eyes. For instance, many people can say 'It's your turn to talk now' just by using their eyes and the tone of their voice.

This works because when people talk they don't just stare at each other. Usually, the person talking will spend a lot of time looking away, not making **eye-contact** with the listener. This looking away is useful because it helps the speaker to organise what he or she is going to say. The speaker will look back at the other person to see how they are doing: 'How am I affecting your feelings … Are you understanding me?' These looks are often just *glances,* short and quick moments when the eyes meet.

A good listener might choose to keep his or her eyes on the face of the speaker so as to be able to give eye-contact when the speaker looks for it. This says 'Yes, I'm listening, I'm interested, keep going'. As the speaker runs out of things to say, he or she looks back at the eyes of the listener for slightly longer than normal, and drops the voice a little and slows down just a little. This sends the non-verbal message 'I am getting ready to stop – it's your turn next, you get ready to speak'. The next thing the speaker does is to look away – perhaps look down at the floor, stop their sentence and look directly into the eyes of the person listening. This says: 'Go on, I've finished'. The listener sends the message or signal 'OK, here goes' by breaking eye-contact and looking away. Sometimes the listener may emphasise this with an intake of breath and head movements.

Task

People are carrying out this kind of non-verbal communication with their eyes every day when they talk to you. Have you ever analysed it before? Watch a video of people interviewing each other, and use the pause and still buttons to pick up the exact eye-contact between listener and speaker. This may provide evidence for 'Using sources of information' as well as contributing to evidence for Unit 1.

Facial expression

Eye movements are mostly unconscious actions. However, we often *think about* what expression we want our face to have. In other words, facial expressions are often 'acted' or put on *deliberately* to send a message. Most people can smile when they aren't really happy, or can act happy, puzzled or pained just to impress others. Many people can control their faces and can avoid sending out messages from their face about feelings that they don't want other people to know about.

Carers do need to think about the messages they send. It's possible to feel tired and hungry and have a depressed and bored looking face. If you suddenly meet someone and don't change your expression, you send them the message: 'Oh not you – you make me feel bored and depressed'. Sometimes, carers try to overcome this my smiling all the time! But this simply makes them look unreal, because no one is happy all the time. The best thing to do is to smile always when meeting people and *then* vary your expression

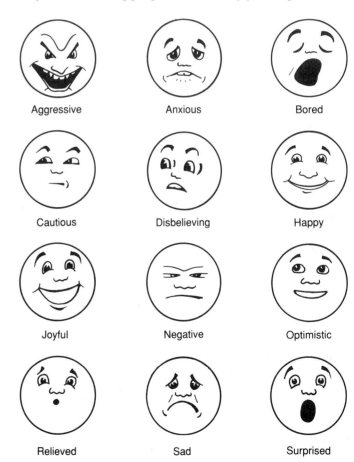

Aggressive	Anxious	Bored
Cautious	Disbelieving	Happy
Joyful	Negative	Optimistic
Relieved	Sad	Surprised

Figure 1.4 *Facial expressions that send messages*

to fit what is happening. Changing your expressions when listening to clients is one way of showing that you are listening and that you *do* care about what is being said to you.

Facial expressions are quite easy to 'read' or interpret. Even simple diagrams can usually be interpreted as having a meaning. How do the sketches in Figure 1.4 work for you?

Voice tone

Words are verbal, but *the way we say them* is classed as non-verbal. The tone of our voice sometimes communicates more than our actual words might. Some researchers say that people often pay attention more to the tone of voice of a speaker than they do to the message.

For example, a person may be told: 'I'm sorry, but your work isn't good enough. Unless it improves you will have to leave'. If the sentence is said in a calm, slow, gentle way with a low but varying tone, the person might get the message: 'Well, things aren't as good as they could be, but there is nothing much to worry about'. If the same sentence is said loudly and quickly in a highly pitched voice, the listener may find it aggressive and become shocked and angry.

It is sometimes difficult to adjust our voices to just the right level to communicate what we want to!

In care work, *voice tone is very important because clients may be unhappy or distressed*. If carers are careful to speak with an appropriate but calm and varied voice, they can sometimes use their voice to relax clients and make them feel safe. Quite often, the real skill is not in what is said to clients but in the way it is said.

Body movements

Very few people keep dead still when they communicate with others. They move their arms, their hands, their feet, their eyes, head, facial expressions and so on. The speed and type of movement can send many messages. People can signal how interested they are by the way they move. They send messages of affection and attraction by the way they tense and relax their body. The way they walk, turn their head, sit down, etc. sends messages about whether they are tired, happy, sad, bored and so on.

Many people use 'head-nods' to signal: 'I am listening to you' and 'I agree', or 'I understand what you are saying'.

Think it over

Spend some time studying the movements of other people. Much of the time you can guess how they feel from the way they move and the other non-verbal messages they send. Try a group exercise: Get everyone to talk without moving a body muscle. This will be very difficult, but if people can do it, it might be a shock to realise how hard it is not to use non-verbal communication.

Posture

The way we sit or stand is often interpreted by others. Standing or sitting stiffly upright may be seen as formal and dominant. Standing or sitting with crossed arms can be seen as being closed to ideas: 'I hear what you say, but I'm not taking any notice.'

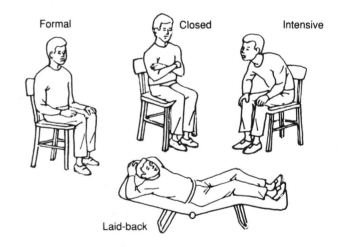

Figure 1.5 *Body postures that send messages*

Leaning at an angle when sitting or standing can send the message: 'I'm tired, bored, or very relaxed.' It can send the message: 'I'm too relaxed to be taking anything in from what you're saying – I'm not listening.'

Leaning forward towards the speaker often communicates: 'Wow! Tell me more, this is astonishing.' Overdoing this posture can send too strong a message of interest.

There is no single *correct* posture to show interest and attention, but most people keep a balance between being too tense and too relaxed. Sometimes, the easiest thing to do is to copy the type of posture of the person you are talking to. This sometimes sends a message of liking the other person: 'Look, I'm like you!' Sometimes it is not a good idea to send this message – especially when you are not like the other person!

Face-to-face encounters

Is it a good idea to face a client 'eye-to-eye'? It has to be realised that this bodily posture can send *many different meanings,* and most of them have strong emotional feelings attached. 'Eye-to-eye' or 'square-on' postures might mean: intimacy, attachment or love, confrontation, hostility or aggression, honesty or openness in commercial dealing.

Sitting face-to-face can indicate formality or a confrontational conversation. However, in *informal* settings it can imply the opposite – closeness, intimacy or love.

Standing at a slight angle can indicate informality and being relaxed. It can send non-verbal messages of: 'I'm calm' or even 'I'm cool!' Sitting at angles can also send messages of: 'This is informal', and 'We can be relaxed' (see Figure 1.6).

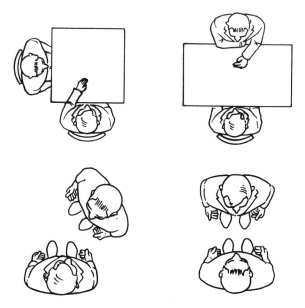

Figure 1.6 *Face-to-face encounters*

As well as keeping a body angle to the other person, if you want to communicate a relaxed, calm message it may be important to adopt a very slight angle to your head (see Figure 1.7). Some people feel that this communicates interest and involvement.

Your Country needs You!

Figure 1.7 *Calm ... or intense?*

On the other hand, face-to-face is *intensive*. The famous First World War poster 'Your country needs you' was intended to influence people to be prepared to fight and die. Is this the kind of intensity you want in your professional work with your clients? A more relaxed (but not over-relaxed) posture may be more appropriate.

Muscle tension (tense or relaxed)

The feet, hands and fingers give away signs of being relaxed or tense. When people are tense they sometimes clench their hands or press their fingers together. Continuous moving of feet or changes of body posture can indicate tension.

When someone gets very tense, their shoulders stiffen, their face muscles tighten and they sit or stand more straightly. When the face becomes tense, the mouth will be closed and the lips and jaw tightened. With a lot of stress, people develop wrinkled lines where the face is always tensed – this may show in the person's forehead.

Tense people always breath more quickly, and you can often observe that their heart is working faster. For you as a carer, *these signs of tension are important to note in others*. If a person becomes tense during a conversation, maybe something is wrong. Perhaps you need to move away from the topic, or be prepared to close the conversation. Perhaps the person is becoming tense because of emotional feelings like grief. The best thing here might be to stay with the person while they cry. There may be nothing to say, but emotional support might be provided through body language.

Gestures

Gestures are hand and arm movements which add meaning to things people say or which carry a particular message on their own. Some common gestures are shown in Figure 1.8.

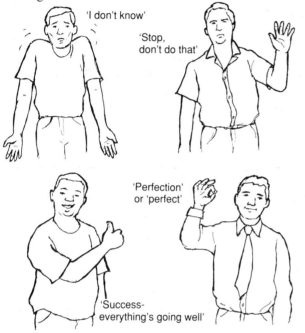

'I don't know'

'Stop, don't do that'

'Perfection' or 'perfect'

'Success – everything's going well'

Figure 1.8 *Some gestures common in Britain*

As well as these signs, people move their arms and hands to indicate emotion whilst they speak, or to place emphasis on what they are saying. Together with other body language, gestures can be important to watch when trying to understand others.

. CULTURE AND INTERPRETING . BODY LANGUAGE

Body language is just that – it's a language. There are many languages in the world and they don't all have the same concepts and sounds. Body language is not the same everywhere.

For example, in Britain the gesture shown in Figure 1.8, with palm up and facing forward, means: 'Stop, don't do that.' In Greece it can mean: 'You are dirt' – a very rude gesture like the English 'V' sign!

Why do the same physical movements come out with different meanings? The explanation lies in culture.

Culture means the history, the customs and ways that people learn as they grow up. One story for the hand-signs says that the British version of the palm-and-fingers gesture means: 'I arrest you, you mustn't do it', whereas the Greek interpretation goes back to medieval times when criminals had dirt rubbed in their faces to show how much people despised them.

Without looking at history and culture, it gets very confusing to understand why gestures mean what they do. No one knows all the history and all the cultural possibilities with body language and non-verbal communication. What is vitally important is that carers should always remember that their clients may have different cultural backgrounds. The carer's system of non-verbal communication may not carry the same meanings to everyone. We can easily misinterpret another person's non-verbal messages.

> **Remember:**
> - *Non-verbal messages do not have fixed meanings.*
> - *They are linked to culture.*
> - *There is no dictionary of non-verbal messages.*

Sometimes cultural differences are very marked. White British people are often seen as 'unusual' or odd when they go outside Europe because they keep a large personal space around them. Other people aren't allowed to come too near when they speak or touch them. In many other cultures, standing close is normal and good manners – touching an arm or shoulder is just usual behaviour. Some British people feel threatened by such non-verbal behaviour because it's not what they have grown up with. For some British people, strangers who come too close or who touch are trying to dominate or have power over them. They become afraid or defensive. However, things often work out because this need for space and distance is understood and allowed for by people from other cultures.

From a caring viewpoint, respect for other people's culture is the right thing to give to people. People learn different ways of behaving, and good carers will try to understand the different ways in which people use non-verbal messages. For instance, research in the USA suggests that white and black Americans may use different non-verbal signals when they listen. According to this research, black Americans tend not to look much at the speaker when they listen. This can be interpreted as a mark of respect – by looking away it demonstrates that you are really thinking hard about the message. Unfortunately, not all white people understand that this is a cultural difference in non-verbal communication. Some individuals misunderstand and assume that this non-verbal behaviour means exactly what it would mean if they did it. That is, it would mean they were not listening.

Learning the cultural differences

There is an almost infinite variety of meanings that can be given to any type of eye-contact, facial expression, posture or gesture. Every different culture develops its own special system of meanings. As a carer, you have to understand and show respect and value for all these different systems of sending messages. But how can you ever learn them all?

In fact, you can't learn every possible system of non-verbal messages – but you can learn about the ones your clients are using! You can do this by first noticing and remembering what your clients do – what non-verbal messages they are sending. The next step is to make an intelligent guess as to what messages the client is trying to give you. Finally, check your understanding (your guesses) with the client: ask polite questions as well as watching the kind of reactions you get.

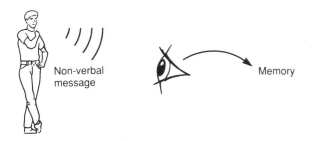

Non-verbal message — Memory

The client gives you more verbal information

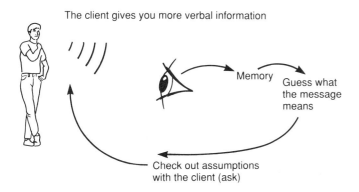

Memory → Guess what the message means → Check out assumptions with the client (ask)

Figure 1.9 *The process of understanding your client's body language*

So, at the heart of skilled caring is the ability to watch other people, remember what they do, guess what actions might mean and then check out the guesses with the client.

> ***Remember:***
>
> ● *Never rely on your own guesses, because often these turn into assumptions.*
> ● *If you don't check out assumptions with the clients you may end up misunderstanding them.*
> ● *Misunderstandings can lead to discrimination.*

Think it over

A simple example: you are working with an older person. Whenever you start to speak to them they always look at the floor and never make eye-contact. Why is this?

Your first thought is that they might be sad or that you make them sad. If you just make this assumption, you might not want to work with this person – they are too depressing and you don't seem to get on. You might even decide you don't like them. But you could ask: 'How do you feel today, would you like me to get you anything?' By checking out what they feel you could test your own understanding. They might say they feel well, are quite happy and suggest something you could do for them – they can't be depressed then!

Why else would someone look at the floor rather than at you?

1 It could be a cultural value. They may feel it is not proper to look at you.
2 They may not be able to see you clearly, so they prefer not to try to look at you.
3 They may just choose not to conform to your expectations. Looking at the floor may be important to some other emotional feeling that they have.

So, how unfair it would be to assume that they were difficult or depressed just because they didn't look at you when you talked to them.

> **Remember:**
>
> *Good caring is the art of getting to understand people – not acting on unchecked assumptions.*

We can never rely on non-verbal messages, we always have to check them. Non-verbal messages can mean different things depending on the circumstances of the people sending them. But all messages are like this. Words can be looked up in a dictionary, and yet, words don't always carry exactly the same meaning.

Think it over

Looking at the whole picture

Think about the statement: 'I really do care about you.' All the words have a dictionary definition, but what does the statement 'really' mean?

It could mean lots of things!

- If there was stress on 'really', i.e. 'I REALLY do care about you', it would mean: 'No, honestly, I really, really care – please believe me!'
- If there was stress on 'do care', i.e. 'I really DO CARE about you', it might mean: 'I am concerned about what happens to you, I am worried, I don't want bad things to happen to you, etc.'
- If there was stress on 'I' and 'you', i.e. 'I really do care about YOU', it might mean: 'I love you, I'm always thinking about you!'

The same words with a slightly different tone of voice can give quite different meanings. If we couldn't quite hear the tone of voice, we could guess the meaning from the circumstances or the surroundings in which things were said.

For instance, suppose the speaker looked anxious and tired, and said 'I wish you could see my point of view, I really do care about you', we could easily guess the words mean I REALLY do care.

If the speaker had an arm round a partner, looked into their eyes and said 'I really do care about you', it would mean:

'I love you'. Messages only make sense when we look at the whole picture. It is important to look at voice tone, body movements, body posture, eye contact and words all together. When we see the whole picture, we are better prepared to check out meanings.

As well as looking at the whole picture of a person's words, their non-verbal messages and where they are, we also need to understand their culture, their individuality and how they see their social situation. This is why caring is such a skilled area of work. People can improve their skills constantly through experience, and through linking new ideas to their experience. The main thing is always to check your assumptions out. It is important to remember that we often misunderstand others. By checking out ideas we can cut down the risks of being uncaring or discriminatory.

• STARTING A CONVERSATION •

As a care worker it is important for you to be good at beginning conversations to gain information. Our non-verbal behaviour may be as important as what we say.

Task

Before reading on, make a list of the non-verbal 'language' someone is likely to use to begin a conversation.

It is likely that they will:

- make eye-contact
- smile
- nod
- have the appropriate facial expression
- change position (e.g. stand up, sit down)
- use a gesture.

All these things are likely to happen before any words are spoken and will give indications of what type of conversation is likely to take place. If the exchange is not a friendly one the facial expression, position and gestures will easily be seen as being threatening.

Opening the conversation

Depending on how well the people know each other, some form of greeting will be used – for example, 'Hi', probably followed by a remark such as 'How are things?' In a friendly and warm encounter, general remarks might continue on such things as the weather etc. In contrast, if the encounter is an interview with the boss who is not pleased with you, it is likely that the subject of the meeting will be introduced straight away!

If a conversation is to be satisfactory to both or all the people taking part in it, it is necessary to take turns to speak and for one person not to dominate the conversation. Have you ever observed a young baby 'talking' with an adult? Think about what happened, how the adult behaved and how the baby responded.

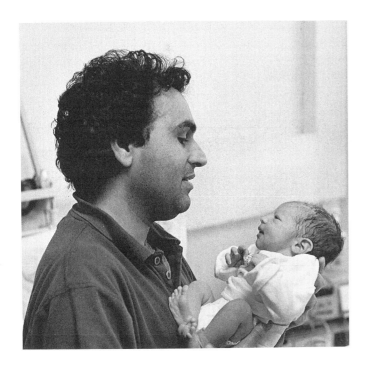

We learn turn-taking rules before we can even speak. The young baby will babble and then stop and wait for the other person to speak. When the person stops, the baby will babble again. The baby will babble for a similar length of time to the person they are 'talking' with. If the person 'talking' were to speak angrily or scowl and look fierce, the baby would become upset and probably cry.

The amazing part about this is that all this takes place without the baby understanding the words used! It tells us a lot about the power of non-verbal communication. Remember, you are giving people messages all the time without saying anything at all.

There are a number of ways by which we judge when it is our turn to speak. You can try this out by closing your eyes during a conversation and trying to judge when it is your turn to come in. Think carefully about what clues you are getting.

Think it over

You should notice:

- *There is a tendency for the last part of the speech to be drawled or slower.*
- *There is a drop in pitch (a change in voice tone).*
- *The statement is completed.*

With your eyes closed you do, however, miss some of the clues that are available – those of non-verbal or body language. When a person has finished their part of the conversation, they may use a hand gesture or relax their body position.

Questioning

Being a skilful questioner is a useful social skill. It means that you are able to keep a conversation going. One thing many people enjoy is talking about themselves, so if you are a skilful questioner you will gain the reputation of being a good conversationalist very easily. Also, as a care worker, you need to get essential information from clients to help you plan the best care for them.

Think it over

Sometimes the answers we get to questions do not tell us what the person really thinks. Can you think of reasons why someone might not say what they really think?

A client may be worried about upsetting staff, being thought of as a trouble causer, if he or she complains. The client may therefore say what he thinks you want to hear rather than what he really wants to say. Can you remember ever doing this? You may have done so when your teacher or parent asked you why you were acting in a certain way. Often when we don't know how to start telling someone how we really feel, we say 'Nothing' when asked what is bothering us.

In other circumstances a person may want to look good, so will agree with the person they are speaking to even when they really disagree. Have you ever tried to impress someone in this way?

At other times a person may make up an answer to a question rather than admit ignorance of the true answer. He or she will do this to avoid looking silly.

Obviously, then, while asking questions can be a useful way of getting a conversation going, it can also seem threatening to the person being questioned. Most of the reasons above for not giving true answers were based on the fact that the person being questioned felt unconfident or needed to protect themselves in some way. Beware, then, of making clients feel they are on trial or being harassed! To repeat the guideline: *It's all about watching carefully to see how the person you are talking with is responding and knowing how far to go and when to stop.*

Closed and open questions

Some questions are known as **closed** questions. This is because it is possible to answer them simply without extending the conversation.

Imagine asking a child if she has been to school today. What might a typical answer be? Many children would simply say 'yes' or 'no', which does not extend the conversation very much. If, however, you used an **open** question – such as 'What did you do at school today?' – you have a better chance of her giving you an answer which you can use to carry on the conversation. Of course, the answer may still be 'nothing', but at least you will have built in the chance of getting more information!

Open questions keep the conversation going, but sometimes you may want to structure it to focus on something specific. For example, you may want to plan some leisure activities for, say, an elderly client group. If you were to ask them what they wanted to do they might all say they don't know. If you were to use a questioning technique called **funnelling** you could get more information.

Funnelling means starting with an open question and then narrowing down to concentrate on something definite. This is an example of a funnelling conversation:

Care worker: What sort of things were you used to doing in the evenings before television came along?
Client: Oh, all sorts really. We used to have some fun though.
Care worker: I suppose you had to make your own entertainment?

Task

Try to write a few more questions and answers following on the above conversation.

It is possible that you could develop the above conversation to see whether the client would appreciate getting in some recordings of old singers or having someone in to play the piano/accordion for a sing-song, or perhaps getting some crafts going such as rug-making, or comparing old photographs. This technique is based on the idea of knowing where you want to steer the conversation, while allowing the clients time to collect their thoughts and develop them in their own way.

Another technique which is useful with all client groups, but particularly with elderly people who may not have a great many exciting events currently happening, is to use **recall** questions such as 'Where did you live when you were a child?' However, you will always have to think carefully about what you are asking, because some areas of their lives may have been painful. Think carefully then about using questions such as: 'Do you feel embarrassed when talking about ... '.

Think it over

Try to remember a time when you were talking with someone about an experience that was painful to them. Make a note of what you needed to do as well as listen.

You would have needed to be very aware of non-verbal signals, such as:

- facial expression
- whether the person leaned forward or pulled back
- how near they positioned themself to you
- how much eye-contact they used
- their tone of voice
- the speed at which they spoke
- the rhythm of their speech (smooth or jerky).

Remember always: the client is 'saying' more than just words.

▪ REFLECTIVE LISTENING ▪

It is very important to understand the people we work with. To understand people, we have to listen to them. But listening is not always easy. Some people will talk easily, some people talk too much! But sometimes, people don't find it easy to talk, and then emotional support is needed.

Think it over

Imagine that you are caring for an elderly man and start talking to him. He is very miserable and perhaps angry about things that haven't gone right. Suddenly he turns to you and says: 'Nobody cares about me. Do you know what my son said to me last time he came to see me? He said: "Well, you won't live much longer, you'll be dead soon and then I won't have to bother visiting you".' He then goes quiet and looks at the floor. You're the carer – what do you do now?

Firstly, you can't just walk away because that would look as if you didn't care either.

You might be able to ask a question – but can you think of a sensible one? You can't say: 'Ah, so do you think your son doesn't like you then?' The man has made the situation clear – you could insult him if you get the question wrong.

You could go silent too. Silence *can* be a good technique (see later) – but not here. Going silent might look like not knowing what to do.

If you feel a bit shocked, if you feel 'that's awful', and if you're lost for words, what's left to say? You could just repeat the words 'he said you'll be dead soon and I won't have to visit you!'

If the client's words are repeated with the right tone of voice – a tone that gives the message 'that's awful' – then you have proved that you were listening to the client, and that you have taken him seriously. The simple act of repeating the statement also invites him to keep on talking: you've proved you were listening, and that you are concerned, so now is there anything he can add to what he has said?

So, simply repeating the client's message can keep the conversation going, but you can't do this too often. If you keep repeating what the client says you will sound like a parrot. The client will think you are making fun of him. However, repeating the client's words once can get you out of a jam. It can keep the conversation going a bit longer. It's now the client's turn to speak again. Perhaps you will be told some details about his life, perhaps you will learn more about his needs and understand more.

Repeating the client's words in this way is the simplest kind of reflection, but a better kind of reflection is to put what the client said into your own words. You might say something like: 'Your son doesn't want to visit you and doesn't care whether you're alive or dead.' When you use your own words, it almost becomes a new question – you are testing your understanding of the client's message.

Putting the client's statement into your own words is usually better than just repeating what he said.

1 It shows that you thought about what he said.
2 Your statement isn't mechanical – you don't sound like a computer program but instead speak in your own usual way.
3 The other person has to do more thinking to check that what you said is what he meant. He is more likely to keep talking, after this extra thinking.
4 Because using your own words often sounds more caring and sociable, you can use this reflective technique more often.

So, repeating what another person has said is a useful way of keeping a conversation going. However, it can be more than that. If you use the right non-verbal messages and your words do make sense to the other person, then repeating the other person's statement is like holding a mirror for them. They can see their thoughts and feelings in the mirror that your words have created (see Figure 1.10).

A person may say 'No one likes me, nobody talks to me here', and you can hold a mirror up to this: 'No one cares at all?' The person will probably want to say more: 'Well, you do, you listen – but nobody else does.'

By the holding up of a mirror, the person has now thought things through a little further. It's not that 'no

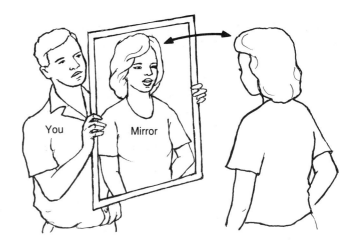

Figure 1.10 *Helping a client to 'see' her thoughts and feelings*

one cares': they think you provide emotional support, so 'you care'. This can be very important; *by learning the technique of reflective listening you can help people to sort out their thoughts.* If you are seen as caring, that is so much better than having no-one who cares!

Reflecting back what someone has just said is a very powerful caring technique. To make it work properly, you shouldn't do it too often in a conversation and you need to be careful not to twist and change what other people might mean when they speak.

If a person said 'No one likes me, nobody talks to me here', and their carer said 'Perhaps no one likes you because you are always sitting here'. Would this be a reflection? It can only be reflection if it does act as a mirror – if it does bounce back just what the person says.

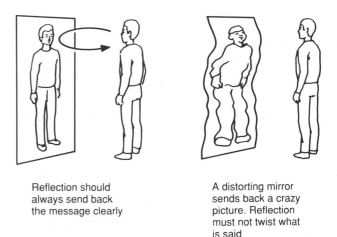

Reflection should always send back the message clearly

A distorting mirror sends back a crazy picture. Reflection must not twist what is said

Figure 1.11 *Ensure accurate reflection!*

This example twists things. The carer goes on about where the client sits, and that's not reflection!

Reflective listening can lead to **reflective learning.** Reflective listening is when the carer bounces the client's message back like a mirror. The client can hear their own message and think about it – is it exactly what they were thinking, can they improve on it, make the meaning clearer, add more detail? The idea behind reflective listening is that it makes both the speaker and the listener think more. This thinking sometimes becomes a kind of reflecting inside our head. Thinking things through in our head is an important kind of learning – reflective learning.

Task

Try it out in practice. Find someone who is studying this unit and get a tape recorder. Sit down with them and explain everything you know about reflective listening to them. Tell them what it is, how you do it, when it could be useful, what would help make it work, what would stop it from working. Ask your colleague to listen to you, and to use some reflective listening if possible, with just an odd question, probe or prompt. Tape-record what you say.

There is a Chinese saying: 'I know what I think when I hear what I say'. Listen to what you said!

Now change over. You use reflective listening, the other person explains it to you.

Keep the tapes (or some notes about it). It may provide evidence for 'Monitoring own learning'. This can contribute to the grading criteria for monitoring and the core skill of 'Improving own learning'.

By trying reflective listening in practice and by thinking the idea through, you can probably learn more than if you read this chapter many times! You will be doing thinking work. If your colleague reflects what you say effectively, you will be able to sort your ideas out by talking them through. Reflective listening may lead to reflective learning.

Remember:
- *Reflective listening may help people to think things out.*
- *Thinking things out helps people to learn.*
- *Thinking things out may help some people to feel better.*

▪ SILENCE ▪

If we are having a conversation with someone and we can't think what to say, it may feel embarrassing. A long silence seems to mean: 'I can't think properly', or 'I don't understand', or 'I wasn't listening'. A bit of a gap puts pressure on our conversation, we feel we have to invent something to say to avoid a silence.

One definition of friends is people who can sit together and feel comfortable in silence. Silence can mean different things depending on the situation. If we have only just met someone and we are trying to get to know them, a silence may look like incompetent questioning. If we do know the person, then silence might be quite OK. Silence might mean 'take your time', 'think about things', 'reflect in your own mind.'

When people need time to collect their thoughts, they might signal non-verbally that they are thinking. We can show respect by just communicating non-verbally, and not speaking.

Imagine, for example, that a doctor or nurse has to tell a patient some bad news. If they say it and immediately continue with details of the next things to do – what hospital the patient will have to go to and so on – the poor patient won't be able to take it all in. The patient may not think of questions he or she would like to ask, being shocked and unable to think clearly.

A more caring way might be to tell the patient the bad news and wait. The doctor or nurse could ask if the person had any questions, they could communicate a caring attitude non-verbally. By them leaving a silence, the patient would have time to think. The silence would be caring.

Sometimes, too, it can be better to stay silent when a person has told you something. You can communicate your feelings non-verbally. You can often communicate 'I'd like you to say more about it' using head-nods, eye-contact and facial expressions. This use of silence can encourage the other person to reflect and to keep talking. Silence is sometimes a good alternative to repeating the verbal message. Silence can be another reflective technique.

Remember:

- Silence can link with reflective listening.
- Silence can give people a space to think.
- Silence can be a skill in caring communication.

'I am me; I am unique'

is influenced by the community, culture, friendships and group situations that we experience. Many adults believe that our sense of individuality is something that we *consciously* choose to develop. Words like 'self-development' and 'personal growth' are used to describe this process.

Three things which many people include in their sense of individuality are:

1 **A need to feel special.** We are different from everyone else. There is no one else exactly like us.
2 **A need to feel that we have 'roots'.** We have a personal history. Whilst we do change, we never stop being the person we were born to be.
3 **A need to like the person we think we are!** This is called self-esteem. There may be things we would like to alter in our life, but we like our own personality.

· INDIVIDUALITY ·

As we grow up, we gradually start to become aware of a sense of who we are: a thinking and feeling of **self**. We need to be 'someone', we need to have a feeling of being something we can call 'I' or 'myself'. This sense of being someone motivates us to do the things we do, choose the clothes we wear, make friends with the people we do, and so on.

Being able to study depends on choosing to be a person who is keen to study. Going to school, college or work depends on our sense of who we are – it's often nicer to stay in bed, but we make ourselves do other things because of this sense of being a special individual, or perhaps we have an idea of what we would wish to be like.

Think it over

What are your earliest memories of choosing things to buy? How did what you bought influence your sense of independence and 'self'? What are your earliest memories of being told you were good at something? How did this influence how you understood yourself? – your sense of individuality?

Think it over

Think about these three things. Do you choose clothes or jewellery that make you feel special? Do you ever think about your past and how your life has changed? Does this give you a sense of having 'roots'? Are you glad to be alive? Do you enjoy life in general? How is your sense or self-esteem?

Our sense of our own 'individuality' or 'self' develops and changes during our lifetime. Our sense of individuality is influenced by our physical body and feelings, and our family or care relationships. As we grow our individuality

If a person has problems with feeling special, or with feeling a sense of life-long development, or with self-esteem, then this may lead to a lot of personal unhappiness. Sometimes people become depressed if they lose their sense of individuality.

Understanding individuality

Each person will have their own special view of themself. For many people this might involve thoughts and feelings which could be listed under headings like 'culture', 'religion', 'gender', 'age', 'physical appearance', 'physical and mental abilities'.

If you care about individuals, you will want to make them feel special. To do this you will need to find out about them and make it clear that you respect and value their individuality. Learning about other people's individuality involves looking at how they present themselves – what clothes they choose, what jewellery they wear, what non-verbal messages they send. A person will often display something of their individual sense of culture, religion, gender and age, just in their clothes and non-verbal behaviour. If you talk to people, you can learn so much more!

Communicating **respect** involves learning about other people, remembering what you have learned and reflecting it back. For instance, first you must learn the names of the people you are working with – the name that the client prefers to be called by. Next you must remember things you have been told, and use them later when you meet the client again: 'Hello Mrs Andrews, how did your son get on at that job interview you told me about?'

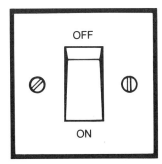

Communicating respect involves getting into conversations with others and showing that you listen to them. You need to show that you value what they have told you enough to remember it. You switch on your memory when you next meet. Naturally, the way you make people feel special will involve sending non-verbal messages of interest and respect as well. So you could greet Mrs Andrews with a smile and make eye-contact (both are messages which say 'I'm interested in talking to you'). If Mrs Andrews wishes, use hand movements to signal interest and then say: 'How did your son get on at that job interview you told me about?' You are sending the message: 'I'm interested in you and I remember what you told me. I respect and value you as an individual.'

Not everyone does this. Sometimes people don't even bother to learn the clients' names: 'There are too many of them so I call all the male old people "pop" and all the women "dear"!' This kind of behaviour sends the message: 'You are not special. I don't care about you as an individual.'

Not only this, but words like 'dear' can send a message: 'I am more important than you' or 'I have power over you'. These messages can be dangerous. They can mean that the client will dislike the carer, and the carer may come to dislike the client!

Another very important issue is to make sure you don't label people together. Because each person is an individual, you have to be careful not to make **wrong assumptions.**

Imagine two people are having a conversation. One is a Muslim and the other person is not, but the second person has tried to learn about the Islamic faith. Perhaps the non-Muslim has heard of Ramadan, a time of fasting during daytime. The non-Muslim might say: 'Oh, it's Ramadan so I didn't get you a drink'. What this person has done shows that he or she was trying to learn about religion – but forgot about individuality! Each individual will keep their own religious observances, so the speaker should have checked what the other person thought, before jumping to conclusions. Many Muslims do not drink during the days of Ramadan, but is that the code this individual actually follows? You need to understand culture and religion on an individual level when you work with individuals. Failure to do this may cause you to stereotype others. This is discussed in the next chapter.

When trying to be supportive to others it is also very important that you show respect for **individual self-esteem needs.** You should always be careful to offer people choices so that they can express their individuality. You should always ask their opinion, rather than guessing what is needed. The idea is this: if a person makes their own choices and is asked for their views and opinions, then they are *in control*. People express their sense of individuality by making choices and having opinions. You can be sensitive to this and thus increase a sense of self-worth in others.

> **Remember:**
>
> *Being sensitive to others involves listening and memory. You build up an understanding which helps you to say the right things, and to send the right non-verbal messages.*

You also need to express **warmth**. Warmth involves not being critical about other people, but being accepting of differences between yourself and others.

Think it over

Think of a person you have met who is totally different from you – someone with different interests, habits, lifestyle, culture, etc. Do you think first about what is wrong with the other person – for example, what you don't hold with, what you would argue against? Or do you think first about what is exciting and interesting in this other person?

'Warmth' describes the feelings of excitement and interest when we meet different people. The judgemental critical view of others is uncaring and unsupportive.

When we begin to think about another person and their life situation, we are bound to be struck by the difference between their way of thinking and ours. Where differences exist, one response is to argue about them, to challenge the other view as 'wrong'. In other words, when people lead different lives or have different problems from our own, there can be a tendency to assume that we have a better way of thinking, a better lifestyle etc., and that we don't really need to know about theirs!

> *To show 'warmth' is to have the ability not to be judgemental – not to compare yourself with others. It is the ability to listen, understand and not evaluate the other person's individuality. You accept that they have the right to be the way they are: you are secure enough in your understanding of your own individuality that you are not threatened when thinking about alternative lifestyles.*

Finding the right behaviours to communicate 'warmth' will also help you to avoid working in a **discriminatory** way with clients (see the next chapter, page 77).

Finally, practical work on supporting individuality in others does require you to be **sincere**. When learning anything new there is a tendency to model yourself on other people. Sometimes we act out what we think are

skills in the hope of achieving a better performance. *The problem is that supportiveness needs to be real or genuine. It needs to be an expression of your own individuality.*

In trying to listen, understand, and be warm, you still have to 'be yourself'. Attempts to use stock phrases, or to copy a performance you have seen others do, destroys the safety and trust that *can* develop if a person believes they are understood and accepted. They must also understand a little about you in order to trust you. So there must be an **openness** in the way you communicate understanding and acceptance for it to mean anything.

Task

Work with a colleague. Take it in turns to talk about the last five years of your life – what has happened, what has been good and what has been difficult. (Negotiate the topic and check confidentiality agreements before you start.) Try to keep your colleague talking for at least ten minutes. Tape-record the conversation. After you finish, analyse the tape-recording for evidence of supportive behaviour. This will include reflective listening, interest, warmth and sincerity.

When you feel confident in your own skills, arrange to video-tape a conversation with your colleague. This time, you might talk about a different topic – plans for the future, perhaps. A good video conversation could provide much of the evidence needed for this unit.

· SELF-ESTEEM ·

As a carer it is important that you become skilful in helping your clients to feel emotionally secure, which comes from having a high level of self-esteem. As we have seen, you need to be able to observe people carefully to see what messages they are sending out, and to be able to respond to these messages. Since the messages will often be unspoken, the skill is in understanding non-verbal signs as well as verbal or spoken ones.

The best way to get an understanding of what another person is feeling is to attempt to see things from their point of view, to 'step into their shoes'. Before this is possible, however, it is a good idea to try to get a picture of how you feel you communicate at present, so you can begin to work on the areas that need improving.

Think it over

On the right is a list of skills which people use every day in order to get along with people and feel good about themselves; in short, to have a good level of self-esteem. Read each skill carefully and give yourself a score.

- *Score 1 if you are NEVER good at it.*
- *Score 2 if you are SELDOM good at it.*
- *Score 3 if you are SOMETIMES good at it.*
- *Score 4 if if you are OFTEN good at it.*
- *Score 5 if you are ALWAYS good at it.*

There are no right or wrong answers. It is only important that you identify your present level of skill and see where you can improve.

Scoring

If you have a high score in points 1 to 3 you are well on the way to being able to demonstrate observational and conversational techniques to identify others' self-esteem needs.

Points 4 to 6 are skills which you will need when listening and using questioning to make information clearer.

Points 7 to 9 examine how you respect and value other people's individuality. It is important to realise that people may have different views and have a right to think differently. You may dislike their views, but you should still value them as people.

Your scores for points 10 to 13 will tell you how good you are at adapting conversations to meet others' self-esteem needs.

Now that you have a good idea of how you relate to people at present, you can work on any areas that are not perfect!

Techniques for identifying others' self-esteem needs

When you are trying to 'step into another person's shoes' it helps to ask yourself how you would feel in certain situations.

1 **Starting a conversation:** Talking to someone you don't know well about general matters (e.g. the weather), and then moving on to more serious points.

2 **Carrying on a conversation:** Starting a conversation, carrying it on and responding to the reactions of the other person.

3 **Responding to contradictory messages:** Recognising and dealing with confusion when a person tells you one thing but says or does something which indicates they mean something else (e.g. if a child is jumping around obviously needing to go to the toilet, but says he doesn't need to).

4 **Listening:** Paying attention to what someone is saying, trying to understand them and letting them know you are trying.

5 **Asking for help:** Requesting help from someone who is qualified to help you handle a difficult situation you cannot handle yourself.

6 **Being open to others' views:** Carefully considering others' opinions and views with your own, and reaching a course of action you feel is the right one.

7 **Expressing appreciation:** Letting another person know you are grateful for something they have done for you.

8 **Responding to anger:** Trying to understand why another person is angry and letting them know you are trying to see their point of view.

9 **Negotiation:** Being able to reach an agreement with someone who has taken a different position to your own.

10 **Finishing a conversation:** Letting the other person know you have listened to what they have said and then skilfully and appropriately ending the conversation.

11 **Expressing a compliment:** Letting someone know you like something about them.

12 **Expressing affection:** Letting someone know you care about them.

13 **Responding to others' feelings:** Trying to understand how another person feels and letting them know you are trying.

There are two ways in which you can tell how a person is feeling. Most obviously, you can listen to what they tell you about how they feel. Secondly, you can learn to 'read' the non-verbal clues which people give you – their body language. Whenever and wherever you are with other people, you can practise 'reading' how they are feeling (beware, this can become a fascinating hobby!).

Think it over

Try to picture a time when you were angry with someone. Write down a few notes about how you think you looked in that situation.

You may remember that:

- your face was screwed up and scowling
- your face was red
- you felt hot or cold
- your body was tensed, particularly in the shoulders
- you were leaning towards the person you were angry with
- you felt tearful.

This is not a complete list, but it is enough to show that anyone observing you would have been able to see you were not pleased or happy. This should remind you of Figure 1.4 on page 31.

Unless they are very good at covering their feelings, people show emotions in the following ways:

raised eyebrows = surprise
fully raised eyebrows = shock, horror or disbelief
fully lowered eyebrows = angry
frown = puzzlement or anger
nose wrinkled = dislike
eyes wide = surprise or happiness
mouth turned down = shock
mouth turned up = pleasure
tight thin lips = anger
wide full lips = sensuality
twitching muscles = nervousness
head in hands = sadness, boredom or deep concentration
biting or licking lips = fearful or expectant …

… and we have not yet considered below the neck!

You will no doubt already be 'reading' some of these signals people send out. As a care worker your aim must be to key yourself into non-verbal messages given out by clients at all times. When you are working with your group at school or college, train yourself to become super-observant.

Think it over

Write up some observations saying how you knew, without them saying so, when someone felt (a) anxious, (b) trusting, (c) bored, (d) attracted(!)

Someone who feels anxious is likely to have hunched shoulders and to be sitting on the edge of their seat. They may fidget (particularly with their hands or feet) without realising they are doing so. They may wrap their legs around each other or around the chair legs, and wrap their arms across their body. Their face is likely to be tense. Their face and palms (as well as places you can't see) may be sweating. The pupils of their eyes may be small and they may give little eye-contact.

Someone who is trusting and confident is likely to sit back in their seat. They will have an 'open' body position, with shoulders, arms and legs relaxed. Their mouth and face will appear relaxed. The pupils of their eyes may be dilated, and they will give good eye-contact.

Someone who is bored is likely to slouch in their seat. They may fidget and become preoccupied with small matters (e.g. examining their pen, or their hair for split ends). They may give little eye-contact because they want to show that they wish the episode to come to an end. (You will note from this that the author has had much experience of observing boredom!)

Someone who is attracted is likely to place themselves physically close to the person they admire. We all have an invisible space around us into which we allow only certain people. If someone moves into this space and we are not comfortable, we move back, sometimes without noticing.

A person who is attracted will try to extend periods of eye-contact. Physical contact may be sought: for example, taking slightly longer than needed to pass an object, to prolong the contact. It is quite easy to see when a relationship becomes more intimate, even when the people concerned hope they are keeping their mutual attraction secret.

DEMONSTRATING SUPPORTIVE BEHAVIOUR

It is not possible for care workers to solve all their clients' problems for them. What is possible, however, is to **support** people through their everyday life difficulties.

Carl Rogers identified three ways of making relationships supportive. They are to show:

1 acceptance/warmth
2 understanding/empathy
3 genuineness/sincerity.

So, in order to be able to support clients, you need to develop these skills. As you already know, they are demonstrated by what you say and how you say it (verbal messages), as well as by how you look and behave (non-verbal messages). The development of understanding, acceptance and genuineness depends on the skills you have been learning about – good listening and conversation management.

Acceptance and warmth

As a care worker you will come across a wide range of clients, many of whom will have ways of thinking and life experiences completely different from your own. When choosing friends we usually pick people who have views similar to your own, but you will not be able to choose your clients.

Think it over

Even within a group of friends or a family, there are likely to be areas of disagreement. Write down three areas in which you disagree with your friends or your family.

You have probably found that you have differences of opinion in areas such as:

● choice of clothing and hairstyles
● choice of foods – vegetarian, non-vegetarian, dietary etc.
● choice of leisure activities
● responsibility for household chores.

So, even our family or people we choose as friends do not *always* think or feel as we do ourselves.

In developing the skill of showing acceptance or warmth, you must learn not to judge, not to compare yourself with others. You need to accept that they have the right to be the way they are, to make their own choices. While you may disapprove of their behaviour, you must show that you do not dislike them as individual people. This is particularly important when working with clients with difficult behaviour which may need to change. It is important that they know it is the *behaviour* which is disliked, not them as a person.

Understanding and empathy

In order to understand someone it is necessary to give them **attention**. One of the qualities which makes a good care worker is the ability to understand people as individuals and not just as one of a client group.

Think it over

We all have the need to be liked for what we are, ourselves. But how does someone let us know we are valued? Try to think of how someone you don't know very well let you know they valued you.

It is likely that they remembered something about you from your last meeting and took the time to talk about it. Maybe you were planning a holiday or had a cold and they asked how things were going. When this takes place it shows that the person has been actively listening, giving attention, not simply hearing.

Think it over

Now ask yourself the following questions (cover up the scores – there is no point in fooling yourself!).

When someone tells you something, do you:

1 **a** note the content of what they say?
  b watch their face, gestures, posture etc.?
  c think of the context in which they are saying it?

Score: a = 1; a and b = 2; a, b and c = 3

2 **a** pick up on something that interests you, and reply straight away?
  b listen to all of what is said, then reply?
  c think of what the speaker is wearing?

Score: a = 0; b = 2; c = 0

3 **a** start thinking of a reply before the speaker has finished?
  b allow the speaker to finish before beginning to think of a reply?
  c interrupt with your own view?

Score: a = 0; b = 2; c = 0

4 **a** look around you?
  b nod and give eye-contact?
  c position yourself appropriately to the speaker?

Score: a = 0; b = 2; c = 2.

Interpreting your score

If you have scored between 7 and 9 in total you have a high level of conversational skill. The questions covered some of the most common listening problems.

In part 1 it is important to take account of all the clues the speaker has provided. This means taking notice of the *context* in which the conversation takes place and the non-verbal clues available, as well as what is actually said. (You will realise from this that communicating by telephone means it is much more difficult to get a full 'picture' of what the speaker is meaning.)

Part 2 deals with the way we can allow ourselves to be side-tracked into picking up mainly on what interests us, by hearing only what we want to hear. This is sometimes called 'selective hearing'.

Part 3 identifies a tendency to start thinking of a reply before the speaker has actually finished saying everything. This is a very common fault and we can all remember the frustration of talking with someone who finishes our sentences for us!

'If only he'd stop talking I could think of something really good to say!'.

Sometimes we do this because we want to avoid silences or gaps in the conversation. Sometimes we are more interested in what we ourselves want to say than in what the speaker is saying. Sometimes we are bored and want the speaker to get to the point. However, the point is that we must give the speaker space to make their point and say what they mean, not assume we know what they mean.

Part 4 deals with the importance of letting someone know you are listening to them, by looking at them and being in an appropriate position. If you are gazing around and not giving eye-contact, it is difficult for them to judge what your reactions are.

This is a point to remember when communicating with clients with sight disabilities. If a client is partially sighted or blind, he or she may not be able to give eye-contact. It is important that you realise this and are not 'put off' by not having the eye-contact they cannot give.

Clients from different cultures may have different uses of eye-contact. For example, people from Africa sometimes feel that the British are unfriendly because they look away from strangers. However, Britons are taught from childhood that 'it is rude to stare'. People from Asian cultures are taught not to look directly at people to whom they should show respect (e.g. teachers, older people, young men to women). If these cultural differences are not taken into account, the non-verbal signals sent out may be misunderstood.

Genuineness and sincerity

This is the third quality necessary to make a relationship supportive. It means letting a client know they are of significance and means more than just using the right words.

Think it over

Consider this situation: A woman goes into a shop, where the two assistants are having a conversation about a programme they saw on television the night before. The woman selects her purchase and takes it to the till. One assistant takes the item from her, rings the price into the till and holds out his hand for the money. He continues talking with the other assistant. The shopper hands over the money and is given the correct change and her wrapped purchase. The assistant is still talking with the other assistant, but as the shopper leaves says briefly: 'Thank you, have a nice day'. How would you feel if you were the shopper?

You would probably feel indignant, insulted, rejected or angry. If you decided to complain to the shop's owner, what would you say?

● Could you say that the assistant had not served you?
● Could you say you had been made to wait?
● Could you say the change was wrong?
● Could you say he had been rude in what he had said to you?

You could not in fact complain about any of these things, because the assistant carried out his job and had wished you a good day. Why then, should you be feeling rejected, angry, indignant or insulted?

The answer is that, although your need has been met (in that you were served), you were treated as if you were of no real significance in comparison with the other person. You were ignored as an individual.

It is all too easy for a care worker to carry out his or her job efficiently without bothering to treat the clients as individuals. The carer might, for example, bath a client carefully, dry him, dress him and make him comfortable. However, if this was done while still carrying on a conversation with another worker and not including the client, the experience would not be emotionally valuable to the client. He would be clean but under-valued as an individual.

The use of stock phrases such as 'Have a nice day' do not help to convey sincerity. It is much more effective to relate what you say directly to the person. For example, a care worker might say to an elderly client: 'I hope you enjoy the entertainment tonight. You're a pianist yourself aren't you?' The comment thus becomes much more meaningful and sincere to the ears of the client.

Physical contact

Any of Carl Rogers' three ways of making relationships supportive can be enhanced by some appropriate physical contact. A comforting arm around the shoulders, for example, can 'say' a lot.

You must be aware, however, that some people are not happy with close contact. Much of how we feel about touching people depends on how we were brought up. Families and cultures vary in how much physical contact their members have.

It is a good idea, then, to touch a client tentatively (perhaps on the arm) and watch the reaction. If they draw back it may mean either that they are simply not happy, or that your relationship with them is too new for physical contact.

Difficult messages

Sometimes as a care worker you will need to spend time with clients who have very serious problems. You will not necessarily have the answers to their problems, but this does not mean you should avoid talking with clients about their worries in appropriate ways – with warmth, empathy and sincerity.

▪ BEING SUPPORTIVE IN GROUPS ▪

In everyday language 'group' can mean a collection or set of things, so people will say any collection of people is a group. For example, we might talk about a group of people who are waiting to cross the road. These people have not spoken to each other, they may not have communicated non-verbally – they are simply together in the same place and time. They are a group in the everyday sense of the word, but not in the special sense of 'group' that is often used in health and social care work.

In caring, working with a group of people implies that the people belong together and would identify themselves as belonging to a group. Groups have a sense of belonging which gives the members a 'group feeling'. Sometimes this might be described as **group identity**.

Usually, a group will have some task or some common purpose or social role which acts as a focus for meeting. A group of people studying for a GNVQ might meet to try out practical ideas together. They would be a group in the care sense if they feel that they belong together. The learning tasks might contribute to getting the group to feel that they belong together in the first place.

How groups get started

Usually, a collection of people will come together because they have a **common goal**. If the group is going to get started, its members will need to have good communication skills and may need a 'leader'. The individual skills associated with providing emotional support will be a good foundation for assisting in group development, or in becoming a leader in the group.

To get a group going, people have to feel that they will belong to the group. To start with, the group will need a clear task or purpose which all the members feel they want to join in with. A playgroup for children will need to be organised around particular games. A reminiscence group for older people will need to be organised around photos or objects from the past. The organisation for these groups needs to be planned in advance. A discussion group (perhaps to discuss GNVQ skills) would need to be planned. Who would introduce the topic, what material would be needed, would the discussion be recorded on video, etc.?

Use of space

An important aspect of a discussion group would be how the group would sit. When working with a discussion group it is very important that everyone can see and hear one another. Non-verbal communication will be important, and if people can't see one another's faces this won't be possible. Usually, chairs are placed in a circle when planning a discussion group. In a circle everyone can get non-verbal messages from everyone else.

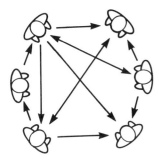

Organising a group to sit in a circle sometimes suggests that everyone is equal, that everyone is expected to communicate with everyone else. This freedom to communicate is also linked with creating a feeling of belonging: 'We can all share together – this is our group!'

Other patterns of seating send different messages. Teachers might sit in the middle of a half-circle. This sends the message: 'We are all equal and we can all communicate with each other, but the teacher is going to do most of the communicating!'

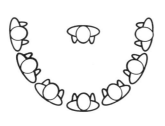

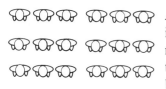

At a formal lecture, people sit in rows. This sends the message: 'The lecturer will talk to you. You can ask questions but you should not talk to one another!'

Some less formal seating arrangements are chosen to create blocks. In this diagram the table acts as a block. Perhaps the two people behind it were too tired to move it, but they might be sending the message: 'We aren't sure we want to be with this group'. The table can make them feel separate: 'We'll join in only if we feel like it'.

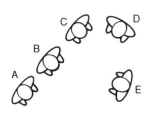

Sometimes space is used to create a gulf. In this arrangement, person A can't see person C properly – so they can't exchange non-verbal messages. Person A can sit 'square-on' to person F. Perhaps A doesn't want to talk

At Lincoln prison in the nineteenth century they built a chapel so that the prisoners were each shut in a cubicle and could see the person giving the sermon – but not each other! The theory was that they could be controlled better if they couldn't be in a group. They couldn't be in a group because of the partitions which blocked them off from one another.

to C. Perhaps F and A don't trust each other. The layout of seats does make it look like there could be tension or reluctance in this group.

Space can also signal social distance. A and B are keeping their distance from the rest of the group. There could be many reasons, but perhaps they are sending the message: 'We don't really belong with you other four!'

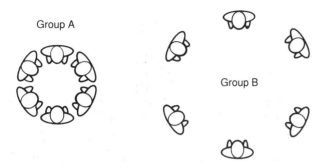

Group A

Group B

How tight or spaced out a group of people are is also worth thinking about. Here, group A are huddled together, whereas group B are very spaced apart. Why do people get closer or further apart in groups? Some answers include: being close can signal that it's noisy – the group have to get close to hear. It can signal that the members like each other and are very interested in the discussion topic. It might signal that group members don't feel very safe, and that being together gives more confidence that everyone will be supportive.

Whenever you meet a discussion group, study how people sit and where they sit. You may be able to guess a lot just by watching how people choose to arrange the seats.

Turn-taking

Working in a group can be more difficult than holding an individual conversation. If a group is going to be worth belonging to, people must take turns in listening and speaking. Once everyone is speaking, no one is listening! Turn-taking between individuals is easy; even young children are quite good at it. Turn-taking in groups is not easy. Sometimes people think of something that comes into their mind and then just dump it on the group. Usually no one really listens, but people imagine that they are making a point.

Turn-taking involves complicated non-verbal behaviour. When a speaker is finishing they usually signal this by lowering and slowing their voice and looking around. Who gets to go next depends on eye-contact around the group – not just with the speaker. Group members have to watch the faces and eyes of everyone else in order that just one person takes over and speaks in turn. If people get excited or tense, then they usually add gestures to their other non-verbal messages to forcefully signal that they want to speak next. Sometimes people will put their hand out or nod their head to say (non-verbally): 'Look, it's my turn next!'

Eventually turn-taking goes wrong, and two or more people start talking at once. This is called a failure to

'mesh'. **Meshing** means that conversation flows easily around the group, between people. People interlink together in conversation, like interlinking in 'wire mesh'. When two people talk at the same time, one person has to give way. The two should take it in turns.

A **group leader** can act as a 'conductor' to check that turns are taken. If there is no leader, then individuals in the group have to sort the order out. Supportive behaviour in groups requires that people don't speak until others are ready to listen. Meshing or turn-taking is an important feature of a group that is working well.

Get together with a small group of five or six people. Take four matchsticks each and agree on a topic for group discussion. Next, agree the following rules for the discussion. Only one person may speak at a time. Whenever that person speaks he or she must place a matchstick down on the floor. When a person runs out of matchsticks they can't say anything. No one may say anything unless others have finished and then he or she has to put a matchstick down. Non-verbal communication is allowed. People should not speak for more than one minute.

This exercise should emphasise the importance of turn-taking and the non-verbal messages which might help it. It should also be fun to do. Notes about the exercise might contribute to 'Monitoring own learning' grading and core skills criteria.

Reflecting before speaking to the group

When you try the matchstick game above you will find that conversation becomes difficult. Sometimes people discover that they have forgotten what they wanted to say by the time they have put their matchstick down! This is because we often get used to just joining in with the conversation in a group. We respond to what other people have said, but we haven't thought out our own ideas to the point of being able to say them clearly. If the group goes quiet and people look at us, we forget what we were going to say!

Being good at caring skills involves being able to hold a supportive conversation with other people in small groups.

It is important to be able to say what you think, when you have others' attention. One of the best ideas to help with this is to think out your ideas before speaking. You need to check what you are going to say before you come out with it! This might sound easy or simple, but it can often be a very difficult thing to do.

People sometimes just say anything that they feel. You have probably been in groups where a person will speak and another person will say something like: 'That's rubbish!' This kind of behaviour is not supportive and it can disrupt the group. Instead of just dumping such feelings on the group, the person should have reflected: 'Why do I feel that they are talking rubbish, what can I do to challenge this in a supportive way which shows respect for the other person?' The answer might have been to ask a question, rather than make a judgement. The person could have said: 'Did you just say … ? Why do you believe that?', or 'What evidence do you have for what you just said?' These questions can lead to a supportive discussion of the issues without causing the group to break up in an argument. Follow the rule: *'Think before speaking'*. In care work, you need to think to yourself: 'How well does the other person understand what I am saying?' Ask yourself questions if you are not sure what to say.

• MONITORING OWN AND • OTHERS' BEHAVIOUR

Part of good care skills is to be able to listen to others and understand what they really mean. We have to be careful not to make assumptions about other people. To improve our listening skills in a group we need to be able to reflect on what they have said and ask questions to clarify things. Skilled group discussion needs a lot of mental work. This mental work involves monitoring our own and others' behaviour.

Task

Learning to monitor might start with sitting out from a group and watching them discuss something.
Alternatively it might start by watching a video-tape of a discussion and monitoring the behaviour. If you can work with a group of people, use the 'fish-bowl' method of observation.

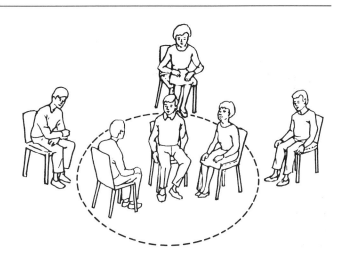

Figure 1.12 *The fish-bowl method*

The people in the middle are being watched – they probably feel like goldfish in a bowl! They will need to trust you if the observation is going to work. They discuss something important whilst you sit on the outside and listen and watch. What will you monitor? A wide range of things can be monitored, but to start with you might like to watch:

1 *Non-verbal messages – How do people organise the turn-taking? How does eye-contact work?*
2 *Questions – How good are people at asking other people for their ideas?*
3 *Giving opinions – Do people ask one another for their views and share ideas?*

After five minutes or so of listening and watching, the group should stop and people should share what happened. Did the people in the group remember what the people outside saw and heard? After discussing the monitoring, it's your turn in the fish-bowl, to give the others a chance to do some uninterrupted monitoring!

Keeping notes on this discussion might contribute evidence towards the grading criteria and core skills of 'Working with others' and 'Improving own learning and performance'.

Although learning to monitor group behaviour can be started by watching groups at work, the importance of the skill is to use it *to check your own behaviour when working in a group*. Carers have to think about the effect their words and non-verbal behaviour will have on others. Keeping records of observation of others might help you to reflect on your own performance.

Behaviours to avoid

Certain behaviours have to be avoided in groups because they can destroy the ability of people to communicate. Some behaviours can destroy the sense of belonging that people need if group conversation is to work. It is important to check that you don't display the behaviours listed below, when you want to get a group to work.

Dominating the talking

A person who talks too often or for too long may think that they are powerful. Very often they simply stop the group from working. They are not leading the group because they don't listen to the views of other people. Other people don't follow their lead, they just 'switch off' instead.

Putting other people down

Sometimes group members can be sarcastic or aggressive to others. When this happens it can destroy any sense of belonging. The aggressive person might be putting themselves 'above' other people in the group – saying that they have a right to criticise or judge.

Excluding others

Some groups break into little groups, with some people talking only to their friends. Sometimes a particular person might be excluded from discussion. The sense of 'belonging' in the group will be lost.

Talking only to the leader

A group that has a real sense of belonging will involve everyone. Members of a group that isn't working so well may talk mainly to one person – the recognised leader, or another whom they trust.

Where people talk mainly to one individual or leader they will probably not get the same satisfaction from being in the group as when everyone can communicate.

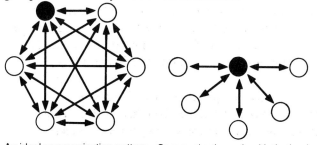

An ideal communication pattern   Communication only with the leader

Figure 1.13 *Two extremes of communication in groups*

Think it over

Sometimes people behave very differently when they are part of a group. Can you think of a time when you have said or done something as part of a group which you would not have done if you had been alone?

You may remember speaking in a certain way in a situation with others which was different from if you had been alone. Perhaps you have drunk more alcohol as a member of a group than you would have done as an individual. You may have dressed differently when with a certain group of people than you would have done alone.

Group power

There are many possible ways in which being with a group may affect the way we behave. A group of people together can become very powerful. Group power is sometimes used to achieve undesirable ends, which the individuals within the group would have rejected as part of their normal behaviour. For example, a crowd at a football match may become over-excited or violent. The people as individuals may not normally behave violently towards others, but in this situation they have stopped acting as themselves and have gone along with the combined fervour of the group.

It is as well to realise, then, that when you are part of a group you may find yourself behaving differently, uncharacteristically. It is important to keep a check on what you say and do. Ask yourself if what is being said or done is really what you feel should be happening, or if the group power has taken over and people are not thinking as individuals.

Speaking out and raising your worries can be really important if a group is to keep going. You do have to be careful, though, how you raise your concerns. If you think someone else is dominating the conversation you could speak up by firstly acknowledging their point of view, but then firmly saying that you have a view to put to the group, something like: 'You're saying that we don't have to do this work, OK, but I would like to put my view now'. If the person starts talking again, you could be even firmer with: 'I haven't finished my point yet, are you listening to me?' You should never say: 'Shut up, you've had your say, it's my turn now!' This is too aggressive.

Think it over

You can sometimes tell people to shut up in care work! You can tell them that they've said too much! You can only do this when you have a special relationship and you know that you are actually showing respect and value by using such language.

You might also be able to tell a friend to 'shut up'. This is OK because you know you both respect one another anyway. Being rude or aggressive is a chance to break the rules when you know that no one is going to get hurt. The important thing is not the words that you say, but the way the message will be understood. Saying 'shut up' to a client may make then angry or upset, whereas you can say a lot worse to friends and they will only laugh.

▪ INDIVIDUALS AND GROUPS ▪

If a group is going to develop a 'feeling of belonging' then the individuals who make up the group will need to feel that they 'belong'. To achieve this feeling you will have to learn about others, remember what you have learned and use the learning to convey warmth and interest, exactly as with individual conversations.

When starting to work with a group of people, you will need to be interested in each group member's 'sense of self'. You must check that you don't make false assumptions – be careful to ask others for their thoughts and feelings. Never live in your own private world and just put your thoughts on the group.

If you don't know much about the others in the group, conversation skills and listening skills will help. Over

Figure 1.14 *Switching on to the individuals in the group*

time, the important thing is to build up a memory of knowledge about the individuals and use this knowledge to make members of the group welcome.

You can convey a sense of respect and value by remembering important things about group members' interests and lifestyles, and asking about them. Groups often need to chat at the beginning before getting going. This is a good time to ask questions: 'How did you get on last night? Where did you go? Did anyone else go there?' Such questions pick up on what you know about the individual.

Values

When a collection of people first get together there isn't usually a sense of 'belonging'. To begin with, people just talk about general things or else they introduce themselves and begin to learn about one another.

After people have settled in there is often an uneasy stage when people are tense. Having to be in a group can be a threat – the sense of self and self-esteem can be threatened. People sometimes compete with one another for leadership. Sometimes people try to dominate the group or control the group to protect their own sense of self-importance.

At this stage the group may become either difficult or unpleasant to be in. It may, on the other hand, develop a sense of unwritten rules for working together. Then everyone can trust the others to work together in a particular way. This sense of trust might come about because the members of the group share a sense of **values**. Once a group has shared values, there is a sense of belonging and the group is a worthwhile thing to belong to.

Demonstrating respect and value for others and demonstrating supportive behaviour are not just skills; they also provide the value base for creating the sense of 'belonging' among individuals in a discussion group.

Task

Can you recall the start of a group, where you felt uncertain of what to expect? Can you, for example, remember starting a programme of study at college? How did the group settle in? What values did the group come to share?

You can gather evidence for the grading criteria if you are part of a group and find out what the other members think are the shared purpose and values of the group. To do this, the people in the group should write down one shared belief or value they have about the group. All the bits of paper are collected and put together in a box. Next, each group member takes out a piece of paper and reads it out loud. People can write what they really think, because no one knows who thought it!

All individual conversations, group work and professional care work have to demonstrate these values:

- *Support individuals through effective communication.*
- *Acknowledge individuals' personal beliefs and identities.*
- *Promote individual rights and choices.*
- *Maintain confidentiality.*
- *Promote anti-discriminatory practice (which includes identifying and challenging discrimination based on race, gender, culture, religion, age, physical appearance, physical ability and mental ability).*

Are you in a safe working place?

Groups can form around all sorts of purposes and values. Some people just want to belong to something and will go along with anything. Some groups create a sense of belonging by breaking social rules (taking drugs and so on). Other groups unite around values, like opposing fox hunting – they share a common value in being opposed to something.

In care work it is important that groups respect and value individual group members. Valuing individual people is part of the unwritten rules for working together. The Care Sector Consortium who designed the professional standards for NVQ qualifications have written out the values for care work.

Group work for the GNVQ should also reflect these values. (See box opposite.) 'Promoting individual rights and choices' and 'maintaining confidentiality' may not always be easy to demonstrate, but the other areas of the NVQ value base should come into all individual and group communication.

• GETTING CARE GROUPS TO WORK •

Most care groups have a purpose or task to work on. Children get together to play games, adults may get together in recreational groups. Groups often need a focus – a game to play, an activity to join in or a topic to discuss.

1 If individuals are going to join in a supportive group meeting, then someone will need to introduce the activity – start the conversation. From time to time when the conversation wanders, someone will need to steer it back to the right topic.
2 Occasionally group members will need to clarify, or make sense of, what is being said.
3 Throughout the group meeting people will need to exchange ideas on the activity or topic being discussed.
4 Towards the end of a meeting, group members will need to agree on what has happened (who won in some types of game) or what the group has decided. The group will come to some kind of conclusions.

As well as performing their tasks, groups have to be 'maintained'. Group maintenance consists of encouraging a sense of belonging and keeping the whole meeting enjoyable. The following are some behaviours to maintain group discussion in a caring setting:

a A bit of laughter can help to relieve tension and create a warm, friendly feeling that everyone can join in.

b Show interest in the people in the group – learn about the 'individuality' of group members.

c Be 'warm' and show respect and value when listening to people who are different from yourself or who have had different life experiences. This behaviour makes it safe to be in the group.

d Express feelings honestly and with sincerity. This will help others to understand *your* individuality. Help others to understand you as well as trying to understand others.

e Take responsibility for everyone having a chance to speak and contribute. Some people may need to be encouraged or invited to speak, some people may need organising, so that turn-taking works!

f If necessary get people to explain what they have said, and to talk through disagreements. Group members need to feel that their shared values will make it possible to arrive at solutions when people disagree.

A group leader must keep reflecting on what is happening in the group. Does the group need to come back to the task? Is this the right time for a funny story? Should I make it clear that I am listening and that I value what is being said by this person? Every other group member who really wants the group to work will also monitor how the group is getting on with its task.

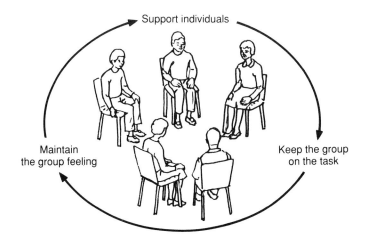

Figure 1.15 *The dynamics of a care group*

To summarise: care groups need to provide a task, keep a sense of belonging going and make sure each individual is supported and valued.

Task

The best way to learn about supportive behaviour in groups is to take part in practical group activities. Try to organise a discussion group with colleagues or friends. If you can, arrange to have the meetings video-taped or tape-recorded. Naturally you will need to check issues of confidentiality and plan the discussion task before doing any recording.

Once you have recorded a group discussion, analyse your own behaviour. How good were your listening skills? Did your questions and non-verbal behaviour convey respect and value for others' individuality? Did you learn anything about others' self-esteem needs? Did you contribute to group maintenance, by showing interest, conveying warmth or sincerity? Above all, was the group a pleasant experience, was there a sense of belonging?

Check your evaluations with another group member. What did he or she make of the group and your part in it? Reflect on what happened, then organise another group meeting.

Doing several observations should help to develop your own self-awareness and understanding of supportive conversation techniques in groups. The final observations should help to produce much of the evidence you might need for an assignment on 'Provide emotional support'. This work will also provide evidence for the core skill of Communication.

Self-assessment test

1 If a child came to nursery school and told the nursery nurse that their guinea-pig had died that morning, what would be the best response?

a 'Oh dear never mind, come and play with the sand'.

b 'Well, if you ask your mum nicely she'll maybe get you another one'.

c 'Oh, that's sad, come and tell me what happened'.

2 How might you show someone that you are listening to what they are saying?

a By asking them lots of questions.

b By telling them all about your own thoughts.

c By having good eye-contact and reflecting back things they had said to you.

3 If a client was unable to see, what non-verbal messages could you use to provide emotional support?

4 What non-verbal messages could you offer to provide emotional support to a client with impaired hearing?

5 What type of eye-contact might someone who was very angry use?

6 How could a care worker use voice tone to offer emotional support?

7 If someone sat in a stiffly upright position during a care worker group meeting, what effect might this have on the other people?

8 Suggest three types of communication which would help you learn to understand your clients more effectively.

9 What is the difference between an open question and a closed question?

10 You are having a conversation about lunch. Which of the following questions is open?
   a 'What, you like salad then?'
   b 'What do you think of today's menu?'
   c 'How much did that cost you today?'

11 You are having a conversation about lunch and the other person says: 'Cor, I had to pay £2.58 for this!' Which of the following are probes and which are prompts to follow this statement?
   a 'Is £2.58 expensive then?'
   b 'Not worth it?'
   c 'I'd ask for my money back if I were you'.

12 What problems might arise from behaving in exactly the same way to everyone to whom you try to provide emotional support?

13 A person is supposed to be joining in a group discussion, but he is sitting behind a large desk that he could have moved, and is a distance away from the others.
   a What messages might he be sending with this behaviour?
   b How could another member of the group check what non-verbal message he really means to send, without making assumptions?

14 What differences are there between demonstrating supportive behaviour in a group and supportive behaviour in individual situations?

15 What is reflective listening? Explain what reflective listening can be used for in care situations.

16 Which of the following ideas might help people to understand the self-esteem needs of others?
   a Discussing a person's past, listening and asking questions about their life (assuming that the person enjoys this discussion).
   b Remembering details of a person's chosen interests, achievements and life-style and using them in conversation with that person.
   c Going up to someone and asking them to tell you what their self-esteem needs are.
   d Reflecting back details of what someone has just said about their bus being late.

17 Why is it important to display respect and value for others' individuality?

18 Which of the following is true, if you keep on repeating exactly what someone else has said?
   a You sound like a parrot.
   b You help the other person to sort out their thoughts through reflective listening.
   c You make them angry or annoyed.

19 There is a story that says that in the 1940s a famous British prime minister called Winston Churchill visited some Greek soldiers in Greece. On meeting them he made his famous victory 'V' sign, which is two fingers palm-out to others. This sign is like the full hand out sign and is used as an insult in Greece. The soldiers knew he wasn't trying to be insulting, but they didn't know how to sign back. If they made the 'V' sign back it would be an insult in their way of thinking, but if they turned their hand round to make a 'V' sign it would make an insulting gesture to a British way of thinking! Why do gestures mean different things to different individuals? What did Churchill perhaps not think about when he tried to communicate with this non-verbal gesture?

20 Which of the following behaviours best sends a message of being interested in the other person when sitting down and facing them?
   a Staring at them.
   b Leaning forward a little, head at a very slight angle, varied eye-contact.
   c Sitting with arms crossed, legs crossed and head back.

21 Which of the following behaviours might best

communicate warmth when talking to a colleague?

a 'Oh, you didn't see that film again, I couldn't see it twice – why would you do that?'

b 'Well it's a very good film – I expect that's why you saw it twice'.

c 'So you saw it again – I remember you said that you really liked it and you thought you might see it again'.

22 What is meant by being 'sincere' when providing emotional support?

23 How can non-verbal messages be used to meet others' self-esteem needs?

24 What are organised question sequences?

25 How can tone of voice influence how others understand a verbal message?

Fast Facts

Assumptions These are ideas which we assume to be correct but which we haven't checked. In care work it is very important that we do check our ideas about other people and their needs. Wrong assumptions can lead to the breakdown of conversations and to the breaking up of groups. They can also be discriminatory. (For discrimination, see Chapter 2.)

Body language This is the language of non-verbal communication, messages we send with areas of the body. It consists of signs that other people can read in the way our body looks, or the way it moves. Non-verbal communication has a slightly wider meaning than body language. 'Non-verbal' covers everything which is not actual words (e.g. tone of voice). Body language focuses on the way the body, face, eyes, hands etc. look and move.

Body movements The speed and type of people's movements can send a vast range of messages. We can interpret tension, anger, attraction, happiness and many other emotional feelings by watching how people move their hands, eyes, head and body.

Caring This describes being concerned about, interested in, and giving attention to others. The *caring professions* all require respect for the individuality, the rights and dignity of others. The ability to use conversation to 'value' and support other people is a central caring skill.

Culture The customs and ways of thinking that people learn define their culture. It is the social learning that influences how people understand themselves, and so has a very important influence on how people explain their own individuality. Differences in culture lead to non-verbal messages being interpreted in different ways.

Distance Distance is one of the things to look for when trying to interpret other people's non-verbal messages. Distance has no fixed meaning, but in some cultures, standing or sitting close can mean: affection or love, anger or aggression, fear, or difficulty in hearing one another! Standing or sitting back might mean feeling comfortable or feeling separate. The cultural setting and other communications help us to work out the best interpretation.

Emotional support A general term, used to include listening and conversational work to support other people's individuality and self-esteem. Supportive behaviour – showing warmth, understanding and sincerity – is also covered in the broad area of 'emotional support'.

Eye-contact This happens when people's eyes 'contact' each other and send non-verbal messages. Eye-contact is important in both individual and group communication. Turn-taking in conversation often relies on eye-contact. Messages of interest, attraction, affection, hostility and many other emotions can be sent by eye-contact alone.

Facial expression The face is an important area of the body for sending non-verbal messages. Even line diagrams can convey instant meaning to people. Facial expression is often easier to control than our eyes. Much non-verbal communication using the face is conscious if not always deliberate. People think about their face and control it.

Funnelling This involves planning questions so that they narrow or 'funnel down' to the central question you really wanted to ask. Funnelling is an advanced skill which is useful to perfect at Level 3 and beyond. Funnelling is very useful when planning questionnaires because it enables the questioner to get the other person to think carefully before coming round to answer the real, important questions.

Gestures These are non-verbal messages sent (mainly) with the arms, hands and fingers. Gestures are especially sensitive to cultural interpretation. A hand-signal can mean 'everything is fine' in one culture, and can be a serious insult in another.

Groups   In social care a 'group of people' means that the people feel that they belong together. They will share some common purpose, common culture, or common values.

Group formation   Groups take time to build a sense of belonging. A collection of people will probably be very cautious at first. There is often tension until people feel that they belong – that they share common values. Once people feel that they all belong together, the group may work well.

Group values   These are shared beliefs which everyone agrees with or supports. Respect and value for other people's individuality, using supportive communication, preventing discrimination and encouraging choice and control in others are caring values. These care values have to be demonstrated at work to gain NVQ qualifications.

Individuality   This is a general term covering the sense of self that people develop from culture, religion, gender, age, race, social circumstances and their own physical and intellectual nature. Individuality is everything that makes the individual special. Individuality includes self-esteem, but is a broader concept than that. Recognising individuality is a necessary starting point for creating equality or a feeling of being equal. Recognising individuality involves not making assumptions about people.

Interest   Communicating interest is a step on the way to building an understanding of other people during conversations.

Meshing   When the contributions to a conversation link in a smooth and effective way, they are said to mesh. They fit together like links in a 'wire mesh' fence!

Mirroring   Don't confuse this with reflecting! Mirroring is when a person copies another person's non-verbal messages. A person who is attracted to someone may copy their way of sitting or standing when talking to them. For example, a person may cross their legs if the other person has crossed theirs. Successful mirroring sends the message: 'I'm like you', or perhaps 'I like you'.

Monitoring own behaviour   This is a really important skill for developing caring abilities. Monitoring involves reflecting on your own behaviour and on the reactions of other people. It involves thinking about what is happening within group or individual communication. Learning to support other people involves monitoring or attending to what you are saying or doing.

Muscle tension   This is one type of non-verbal message. Tension can communicate messages about the other person's emotions, especially when linked with body posture. It is something else to look for when trying to understand other people.

Personal space   This space is an area out of which an individual tries to keep other people. It can be seen as the distance between people when they communicate with one another. Like many non-verbal messages, distance is used in different ways by different cultures. How close people stand will depend on their culture, their feelings for one another and the physical and social situation.

Posture   This is the way a person positions his or her body. Posture usually sends messages about the individual's degree of tension or relaxation. It can also send all sorts of social messages, such as: 'I'm really interested', 'I'm bored', 'I don't want to be here', and so on.

Probes and prompts   A probe is a very short question like: 'Can you tell me more?' which follows an answer to a previous question. Probes try to dig deeper into the person's answer, they probe or investigate what the person just said. A prompt is where you suggest a possible answer: 'Was it good?', 'Did you enjoy it?' Prompts try to keep the other person talking and get them to add to their answers. Probes and prompts are both useful ways to improve skill in asking questions.

Questioning   This is an important skill for keeping a conversation going. Questions can be open or closed. A closed question is where the kind of answer required is simple and fixed. 'How old are you?' is a closed question because the answer has to be a number – once you've said it there is little else to say. 'How do you feel about your age?' is open because the other person could say almost anything – how long they speak is 'open'. Giving a short quick number is a 'closed' reply. Closed questions are of limited use in working with people. Open questions are often much more valuable for building an understanding.

Reflective listening   This is a care skill which involves either using your own words to repeat what another person said, or repeating their words exactly, or using non-verbal messages with silence. The idea of reflection is to use conversation like a mirror, so that the other person can see their own thoughts reflected. They can then alter them more easily.

Self-esteem   This expresses how good or bad a person feels about themself – how the person values their own individuality. High self-esteem may help a person to feel happy and confident. Low self-esteem may lead to depression and unhappiness.

Self-disclosure   This happens when we tell other people about our own experiences, thoughts and feelings. Some self-disclosure can be useful when trying to understand others. It can create a sense of trust if we share our own individuality with others.

Silence   Silence is a useful part of some conversations. Sometimes silence is better than just talking to fill a gap. It can provide an opportunity for feelings to be expressed non-verbally.

Sincerity   This involves being real and honest in what we say to others. Without sincerity, warmth and understanding usually break down or 'go wrong'. Honesty with clients is an important part of relationship and supportive work.

Tone of voice   Voice tone is the sound of the voice, rather than the words that are spoken. The tone of someone's voice can send messages about attraction, anger, sympathy and other emotions. Because voice tone is separate from spoken words, it is classed as 'non-verbal'. The sound of our voice is separate from the word messages we send.

Touch   This is another way of sending non-verbal messages. Touch can be a very important way of saying 'I care', or 'I am with you'. Touch can be interpreted in various ways. It can send messages of power and dominance, and can be sexual as well as caring. The important thing is how a client understands touch, not what you intend.

Understanding   An important goal of caring is to learn about other people's individuality. It is necessary to build some understanding so that you correctly communicate respect and value. Supportive conversations require some understanding of other people's individuality.

Verbal communication   Spoken messages – messages which use words – are 'verbal'. The opposite is non-verbal communication, which means messages sent without words. Non-verbal language is often harder to understand than verbal language, but skilled carers need to be able to learn their client's non-verbal ways of communicating.

Warmth   This expresses the feeling that exists when people do not evaluate and judge one another's individuality. 'Warm' feelings develop between people who respect and value each other.

chapter 2 INFLUENCES ON HEALTH AND WELL-BEING

▪ SOCIAL INFLUENCES ON ▪ INDIVIDUALS

It is an obvious fact that no two human beings are exactly alike. We differ from each other in physical appearance, in age and sex, and in our attitudes, personalities and behaviour. We are all individuals with our own particular needs and desires, and yet at the same time we are not completely unlike everyone else.

People with things in common often see themselves as members of the same **group**. Each of us belongs to a number of groups with which we feel ourselves to be linked, such as our family, our friends, our fellow students or people living in our neighbourhood.

There are also larger groups that we belong to, such as people living in Britain, or in Europe, and many other groups in between.

Some groups are quite **formal** and may be linked to a job or an organisation; for example the group of players that make up a professional football team, or the group of nurses working on a particular hospital ward.

Many other groups are more loose and **informal**, such as our circle of friends or a popular personality's group

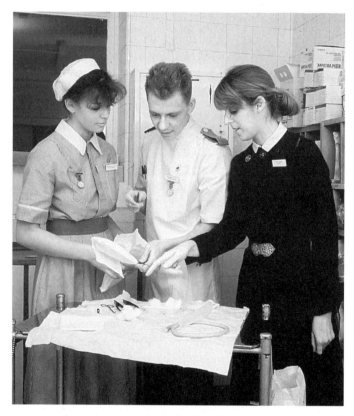

A group of nurses – an example of a formal group

of fans. Society can be seen as being made up of a multitude of groups which interrelate and overlap each other, both in membership and in area of operation.

Everyone has their own range of group memberships, of which some are more familiar and more important than others. In small groups like our family and our close friends we are often aware of our membership, whereas our membership of larger groups is not always as important to us in our daily lives and our links with other members are less strong.

For some more formal groups it is clear why we are a member and who the other members are. For example, when you started studying for a GNVQ you became a member of a group of health and caring students. You may also be a member of a group of care staff. Often group membership isn't so straightforward.

Think it over

Think about your own family and decide who you include as members, then write down a list of who belongs to your family.

Look at your list and think why you consider them to be family members, and why you left out other relatives.

Think about another group that you belong to. Try to decide what makes you a member of the group and how you recognise other members.

Belonging to a group

You have probably realised how difficult it is to be precise about the rules of group membership where informal groupings like friends and neighbours are concerned. How do people know that they belong to a community, or to a gang? The answer is that all groups have their own form of organisation, and their own purpose for existence. Members have a knowledge of the rules operating in the group and can tell that they are included by the way other members behave towards them. These *unwritten rules for membership and behaviour* are called **norms** and they vary widely from group to group.

For example, it may be the norm for a football fan to wear the team colours and behave in a certain way when at a match alongside other supporters. The norms of dress and behaviour to be followed by the same person as part of the congregation at a religious ceremony are very different.

Norms give you a sense of belonging to a group, and the last chapter looked at this from the point of view of individuals within groups.

We are familiar with the norms of the groups to which we belong but usually never stop to consider what they are. We just 'know' what we are allowed to do and what is forbidden.

Think it over

Choose two of the groups that you belong to. For each group think about what it means to be a member and how you behave when you are with other members. On a sheet of paper list the things you have to do and the things you cannot do in each of the groups.

Look again at your lists. Do you think that other group members would come up with the same things as you?

Did you find that the behaviour expected of you was different between the two groups? You probably discovered that the do's and don'ts of the two groups varied quite considerably. You may also have felt that other group members followed slightly different rules from you. Groups are rarely equal partnerships, and members have their own parts to play within them. Some group members have more authority or prestige than others, and this is described as having a higher **status**. For example, in a family the parents and older children probably have a higher status than the youngest child who is seen as junior and has less say than the others. In a group our status will help to define our behaviour, as well as that of others towards us.

The behaviour that we adopt in social situations is called our **role**, and we all have a number of roles that we assume. We play the role that is appropriate for the situation we are in, and the person we are communicating with.

With your parents you are a son or daughter, at work you are a carer, and amongst your friends at a party you play a different role again. The collection of all the roles that a person plays is that individual's **role set**.

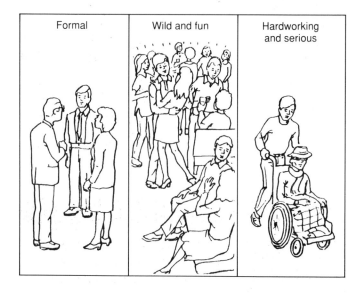

The roles that we play are not adopted artificially. They are a part of ourselves that we display quite naturally when circumstances call for it. We learn our roles while we are becoming a group member, and this process is known as **socialisation**.

Think it over

In the previous task you looked at two of the groups that you belong to. Now think about all the other groups to which you belong. Take a sheet of paper and write down your complete list of groups. It would be best to write down your list one below the other, to form a column down the left-hand side of the paper.

Now think about the roles you have in each group. Some are easy to name – like son or daughter – whereas you will have to think how to describe others. Remember that in some groups you have more than one role. For example,

in your family you may have the role of brother or sister as well as that of son or daughter. Write down the roles you play alongside the appropriate groups.

What you have created is a picture of your role set.

Now look at some of the roles you have taken on later in your life and try to think back to the period when you began to develop them. For example, you could think back to the period when you joined this course and began to develop the role of student. Can you recall how it felt to be a new student amongst many strangers in unfamiliar surroundings?

Think about the socialising influences upon you as you took on new roles. How did they operate to guide you into new patterns of thinking or behaviour?

Primary socialisation

Socialisation begins when we are born and continues to operate throughout our lives. However, we are far more responsive to influences when we are young, and our early socialisation within the family has more deeply rooted effects on us than experiences we have later. This period is so important that it is known as **primary socialisation** and is regarded as crucial in making us who we are.

During our early childhood we learn language, and the norms of behaviour that our families expect of us. We learn the customs and values of society as a whole, and are given indications of our own place within it. 'Primary' means first – primary school is our first school, and so primary socialisation is our first learning about norms.

It is during the period of primary socialisation that we learn what is expected of us in the roles we will play later in life. For example, children build up a picture of what it is like to be a man or a woman, or a parent or a child, and they act out their understanding of these roles in their play activities.

This preparation for future roles is also known as *anticipatory* socialisation, and it can be very influential in the development of people's lives. It used to be generally believed that girls and boys ought to be raised differently so that boys were prepared to lead and provide for a family and girls were content to become wives and mothers and look after the home.

Thus, girls were encouraged to play at motherhood, and boys to play at work and competition. This anticipatory socialisation taught children to accept and perform these roles in later life.

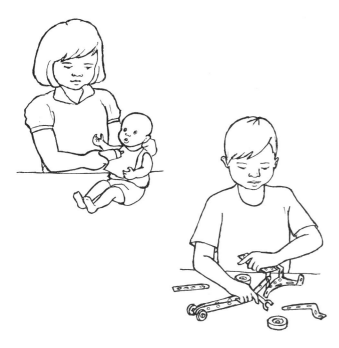

However, roles that boys were being prepared for were once thought to have a higher status in society than those offered to girls. Ideas about sexual equality have spread during this century and nowadays some families attempt to give similar experiences to both boys and girls so that

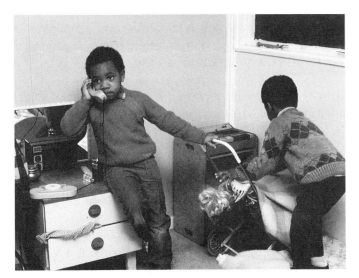

Children act out their understanding of their adult roles in their play activities

they are offered a more equal chance in life. However, children learn roles through *imitation*, and the behaviour of adults around them is a more powerful influence than the toys they are given to play with.

Task

Find an opportunity to watch young children at play – perhaps at a placement or in some other setting. Observe whether the boys choose different toys from the girls. Do they play differently with the same toys?

In role play games, do the girls take on different roles from the boys? See if you can spot the norms that the children have assumed about the roles they are carrying out.

Your observations can be included in a project and can help to demonstrate your understanding of socialisation.

Culture

During the period of primary socialisation children are learning about the ways of their family group and of the wider society in which they live. They learn what is regarded as good or bad behaviour, and develop concepts of right and wrong. Beliefs about what is good, important and worth striving for are known as **values**, and they are closely linked to norms of behaviour. Norms tell us how we should behave, and values help to explain why it is right to behave in this way.

The values and norms of a group, and the status and roles of its members, are all part of what is known as the group's **culture**. Culture is a very broad concept and it includes all aspects of the way of life associated with a group of people. The idea of a national culture is one that we are familiar with, and when we speak of Japanese culture or British culture we have in our mind a picture of all the features of behaviour and attitudes that we think of as being, say, Japanese or British.

It would be an impossible task to list all these features, because culture affects just about all aspects of the lives of the people who belong to it. Culture influences our dress, our diet, our speech, our religion and our ideas of right and wrong. Also, our cultural background is a fundamental part of our identity that remains with us throughout our lives.

Task

Think about the norms that exist in British culture. They could be norms about dress, diet, courtship and marriage, work, or any other area of life in British society. Take a sheet of paper, write the heading 'norms' and then write down five of the norms you have thought of, numbering them 1 to 5.

Now look at the first norm in your list and try to think what values the norm is linked to. Write down the heading 'values' and under it write the values you associate with norm 1. As an example, suppose you had written 'We try to dress smartly at formal occasions like weddings or religious ceremonies' as a norm in Britain. You may think that this is linked to the idea that it is right to show respect for others by looking your best on formal occasions – so you would write this is a value you associate with this norm.

The work that you have done can contribute to a project looking at culture and individual well-being.

Values are about what we believe to be good or bad. It is a basic value of society that we believe it is wrong to kill other people, and this is linked to the useful fact that it is the norm for us not to kill each other.

The concept of culture can be applied to any group and we could say that a particular culture exists amongst fans of jazz music, or members of the police force for example. However, these groups are part of the wider society and are an aspect of what we think of as British culture as a whole. It is this wider view of the culture of a nation or ethnic group that has the deepest impact on our lives.

Our culture influences our beliefs and behaviour in every area of life and is fundamental to making us who we are. It is during the influential years of primary socialisation that we learn the norms and values of the culture to which our family and ourselves belong. Britain is a multi-cultural society, like many other countries across the world, and people from a variety of cultural backgrounds live here.

Children are raised within the social environment of their family and community and learn the ideas and behaviour

at school that we begin to learn more about the world in general, and find out about groups that exist both within the school and beyond it.

School is intended to provide children with an education and prepare them for adult life, and there is a formal and organised side to the socialisation that takes place there. Teachers try to encourage behaviour that they believe will let their pupils get the most out of school, and the curriculum is intended to help with personal as well as academic development. School, like the rest of life, contains many different groups and it is there that we begin to form links with others who are in a similar position and whom we feel to be like us. In other words we make friends. This circle of friends is our **peer group**, and is a major socialising influence in our lives.

The informal socialisation that takes place within our peer group may lead to conflicts with the socialisation that the school is trying to impose. This is because the norms of behaviour expected from members of the peer group may include behaviour that is forbidden by the norms of the school organisation. This is one reason why some people do not enjoy being at school. Of course, some children form peer groups whose norms fit well with those of the school, but most of us spend our school years balancing between the conflicting influences of peers and teachers.

that make them a part of their own cultural group. This primary socialisation will affect their lives in many different ways. It will affect the kind of food they eat, the style of clothes they wear, how they choose a sexual partner, and how they raise their own children. In all our affairs our culture shapes our thoughts and behaviour. It will also affect the way we are treated by the rest of society.

Assumptions about a person's cultural background can affect your communication with them, as you have seen in the last chapter. This is an aspect of stereotyping which we will look at in detail below.

Peer groups

The process of socialisation is not limited to our early childhood years – it continues throughout our lives. School is another important socialising influence, and here our early experiences are built on and we learn more about the culture of the wider society in which we live. We learn new norms and roles, and revise and extend our role set, shedding the role of infant for a more grown-up status. It is

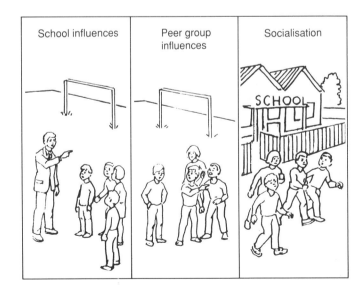

We are a part of peer groups throughout our lives, though we may change groups as we move from school to college, and as we go on to work.

So far we have seen how individuals are socialised as members of groups, and how society is made up of a multitude of formal and informal groupings. However, the idea of groupings can also be applied to society as a whole and used to divide the population into types or classes, as we shall now see.

▪ SOCIAL STRATIFICATION ▪

Social classes

Almost all societies see their population as split up into sections that are ranked in order of wealth and power. British society is often portrayed as being divided up into social **classes**, with the 'upper' class at the top, the 'working' class at the bottom, and the 'middle' class in between them. You may have seen diagrams like Figure 2.1 used in the media to picture these divisions.

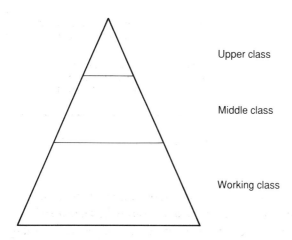

Figure 2.1 *The traditional British class structure*

The pyramid shape is cut into three to indicate the numbers of people in each class and the classes are placed from top to bottom to show the ranking of wealth and power. The diagram divides society into layers, as rock is divided into layers (or strata), and the process of splitting society up into layers is called **social stratification**.

The pyramid diagram is, of course, an over-simplified view of society; but the idea that classes exist in some form is a central feature of British culture. We all have an understanding of what classes there are and of the ways in which members are likely to differ from members of other classes.

Our primary socialisation may have left us with an impression of what class our family, and we ourselves, belong to. These ideas are developed later through other socialising influences such as our peer group and our life at work.

For classes, as for other informal groups, the qualifications for membership and the norms of behaviour cannot simply be written down. Our personal view of what upper class or middle class means is unlikely to be the same as everyone else's.

Think it over

Try to define your own views on class in more detail. Take a sheet of paper, divide it up into four columns and write the headings Upper, Middle and Working at the top of the first three columns.

Now think about the differences that might exist between the classes – in what areas do class differences show themselves? Your list could include education, lifestyle and income, and as many other categories as you wish.

The fourth column will be used to list the areas in which classes differ and you can begin by writing the first of your areas of difference near the top of this column. Now write down what you think the differences are in this area under the appropriate headings. Carry on doing this for each of the areas where you think differences between classes show themselves.

Keep the work that you have done for this task, and look at it again when reading the section on labelling and stereotypes.

Figure 2.2 shows how you could lay out your ideas on paper. Of course your own views about class differences may not agree with this example. This exercise should help you to sort out your ideas about class, and the characteristics and behaviours that you associate with members of different classes.

Upper	Middle	Working
Private education	Some private education Much encouragement	Low expectations Truancy

Figure 2.2

The concept of 'culture' can be applied to classes. We may speak of 'working class culture' or 'middle class culture' when we refer to the values and norms of behaviour associated with members of these class groups. You have been working on your ideas about class culture in the previous exercise, and though your ideas may differ in their details from those of others, there are certain areas where class differences are recognised by practically everybody. These areas include **income**, **wealth**, **occupation** and **lifestyle**, and they can be useful starting points if we want to try to divide the population up into classes and look at the consequences of class membership on the lives of individuals.

Class and income

Income means the cash received as wages, as interest on savings, or as profits from business or some other activity. **Wealth** refers to the value of the things we own, such as our car, house, or country estate. Income and wealth are certainly important factors to be taken into account but they don't tell us the whole story about a person's class. Some people, such as successful performers or professional sporting personalities, have very high incomes but we would not describe them as upper or middle class simply because of this.

Wealth may be a better indicator of class than income as we tend to associate ownership of land and estates with the upper class. But wealth alone, or the lack of it, does not guarantee membership of a particular class. Someone from a working class background who has become wealthy may never adopt the behaviour and lifestyle that we associate with middle class people, and we would find it hard to describe a poor member of the aristocracy as working class.

Class and occupation

Occupation is often used as a main indicator of a person's class. It is useful because it carries with it ideas of the standing or status of a person, as well as pointing to their likely level of income. The Registrar-General is in charge of the government's statistical office, and his **social classification** is based on

occupation and is widely used in government reports and other official documents (see Figure 2.3).

	Social class	Examples of occupation in each class
Middle class	*Class 1* Professional people	Doctor, lawyer, accountant, architect
	Class 2 Managerial and technical people	Manager, teacher, librarian, farmer, airline pilot
	Class 3A (non-manual) Clerical and minor supervisory people	Clerk, sales representative, office worker, policeman
Working class	*Class 3B (manual)* Skilled people	Electrician, tailor, cook, butcher, bricklayer
	Class 4 Semi-skilled people	Farm worker, postman, packer, bus conductor
	Class 5 Unskilled people	Porter, labourer, window cleaner, messenger, cleaner

Figure 2.3 *The Registrar-General's social classification*

The occupations given as examples for each class are chosen because they are linked to more than a level of income. They are ranked according to the general standing of the occupations within the community, which means that people in these occupations have a particular place or status in society and the behaviour and lifestyle associated with it.

This is illustrated by the way that Class 3 is divided into two, with 'non-manual' placed above 'manual' in the ranking of occupations. Though a skilled manual worker's income may be higher than a clerk's, he or she is still regarded as being in the working class. Non-manual (or 'white collar') workers are seen as tending towards the middle class and are expected to have many of the values and norms of behaviour associated with middle class culture.

Think it over

Write down ten occupations that don't appear as examples in the Registrar-General's classification. Try to fit your occupations into the Registrar-General's classes using your own judgement of the standing of the occupation in society, and the income level and likely class culture of people who work in it.

This exercise should have started you thinking about the lives of people in different occupations and classes. What is it, apart from income level, that separates the life of a barrister or accountant from that of a cleaner or a labourer? We may think of differences in such things as taste in clothes and food, political views, and preferred types of entertainment. People in the 'higher' classes are more likely to drive larger and/or newer cars, to eat out, to vote for the Conservative party and to travel abroad. People in 'lower' classes are more likely to drive older cars or use public transport, to eat in, to vote for the Labour party and to holiday in this country.

Of course, individuals do not possess *all* the characteristics of the class they belong to, and fictitious images in the media of a 'typical' working class or middle class person are *stereotypes* rather than descriptions of real people. But the life of a barrister *is* different from the life of a labourer, and in more ways than income and style of work. Other schemes of social stratification have been devised that attempt to reflect differences in lifestyle between members of different classes more accurately than the Registrar-General's, but occupation is still used as the basis for most of them.

Social class may seem to be difficult to define and hard to link to the different lives of real individuals. Nevertheless, social class is used by government, business and other organisations as a way of representing differences between people in society.

Class and life chances

The reason that so much effort has been put into defining social classes as accurately as possible is that research has repeatedly shown that membership of a particular class

has an effect on an individual's life chances. For example, the rate of infant mortality (the number of deaths of infants under one year old per thousand live births) is highest in Class 5, and gets progressively smaller as you look towards Class 1. The number of days taken off work through illness follows a similar pattern, and statistics on such things as educational attainment and life expectancy show that membership of a higher class improves your chances in many areas of life. There is no doubt that inequalities between classes exist, and the reasons for this are both social and economic.

One reason for these inequalities is that class cultures operate to affect the lives of the individuals within them. Differences between classes in diet and leisure choices can result in less healthy lifestyles for people in the lower class groups. People in the middle classes tend to take more exercise and eat a more varied diet, and are more aware of the importance of lifestyle in promoting good health.

The middle classes also make fuller use of the health and care services that are available to them, and the reasons for this are also linked to middle class culture. Because of the type of work that they do, people in the middle classes are usually accustomed to dealing with organisations so they find it easy to communicate with health and care staff, whom they regard as their peers. Also they are usually more assertive and determined in pursuing their rights.

Differences between classes in educational attainment are also partly due to the influence of class culture. Many working class families may not expect their children to do well at school, and their children often receive less encouragement and help at home than children from middle class homes. Children from working class homes may see formal education as useless to them, preferring to earn an income and 'get on with life' as quickly as possible. Also, children from working class homes may not be able to stay on at school because the family needs them to work and provide that extra income. Children from middle class homes, on the other hand, are more likely to see education as a way to get on in the long run, and they are prepared to study in the expectation of greater rewards later in life.

Class culture has an influence on the life chances of individuals that grow up within it, but it is certainly not the only factor operating. Economic realities play a major part in the lives of people in class groups, and the Registrar-General's scale reflects income as well as lifestyle.

Income and expenditure

The difference in income and wealth between social Classes 1 and 5 is very large indeed. At the top of Class 1 there are a few people earning more in one year than an average occupant of Class 5 earns during a lifetime. At the bottom of Class 5 are those on very low wages, and people dependent on state benefits (such as single-parent families and pensioners). There are also those with virtually no income in cash terms, and who live within the larger cities of Britain without a home.

If we rank the whole working population on the basis of income and then divide it into five equal groups, we find that the top fifth gets just under 40 per cent of the total wages paid nationally, and the bottom fifth gets just under 7 per cent (see Figure 2.4). This means that the average wage for the best paid fifth of the population is *over five times greater* than the average wage of the poorest fifth.

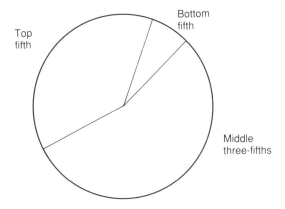

Figure 2.4 *How the income 'pie' is divided*

These differences in income have a great effect on the lifestyles of individuals and families, and on the opportunities open to them. All families have to meet the basic needs of their members but this can be hard to achieve on a low income.

The cost of providing food and shelter can absorb a large part of the income of a person on low pay, leaving little over for improvements in lifestyle or environment. Poorer people live in cheaper, and less well maintained housing than the better off, and in more crowded conditions. This may have effects on the health of individuals, and can have a social impact on them also. For example, another reason why children from working class homes do less well

academically is that they often don't have the room at home to find a quiet place to study.

The diet of poorer people tends to be less varied, and less healthy and balanced than that of the better off. People on low incomes buy a higher proportion of cheap foods and have fewer facilities for the storage and preparation of food.

Task

Families or households divide their income into different areas such as housing, food and transport. Try to think of other areas of spending that families have, and write your list, including the three above, as a column down the left side of a sheet of paper. Talk to your family and friends about your list and add any areas you may have missed.

Now imagine you are living on your own and are responsible for paying for the things you have listed. Try to estimate how much per week you would need to spend on each item and enter the amounts alongside your list. Total your estimates to see what level of income per week you would require to meet your needs.

If you were budgeting for a family consisting of two parents and three children, what extra areas of spending would you need to add to your list? Write down these extra areas, and then try to estimate how much this family would need to spend per week in all their areas of expenditure. Total your estimates and compare the result with your figure for a single person.

You could incorporate your findings into a project that looks at economic influences on individual well-being.

Unemployment

People who have been unemployed for a long time form another group within the system of stratification based on class. Though many members of this group have had an occupation in the past, long-term unemployment gives all of them a similar social and economic position in society.

In the hierarchy of professions, the victims of long-term unemployment form a 'dispossessed' class because they do not have the status of being able to work. The low status that goes with unemployment can have serious effects on the individuals who find themselves in this position. The process of seeking work yet being unable to find it is demoralising and can led to a loss of self-esteem. People may feel that they have been rejected from the working population, and that their skills and abilities have no value. Feelings of low self-esteem and rejection can lead to depression and a sense of hopelessness. In extreme cases the experience of long-term unemployment has caused people to attempt suicide.

The long-term unemployed are amongst the poorest groups in society. They receive only state benefits which are set at a low level and have no prospect of an improvement to their situation. This has major effects on all aspects of life. Unemployed people, particularly those with families, are only just able to buy the necessities of life and have no spare cash to spend on luxuries. Variety and quality of food is restricted and everyday products like televisions and washing machines become difficult to buy. The choice of leisure activities open to unemployed people is restricted to what can be afforded, and sports or pastimes which cost money are generally unavailable. Even the cost of transport can be a barrier which restricts choices.

Many unemployed people find that they spend a large amount of time at home because they don't really have anywhere else to go. For people who wish to be economically active this is a depressing and frustrating situation, and it can lead to strains on family relationships. Families who are forced into a home-bound lifestyle by unemployment and poverty face many pressures, and partners and children can be affected by long-term unemployment in ways that are not purely financial.

Long-term unemployed people therefore have to cope with the effects of poverty and the low status and hopelessness of the position they are in. Although they do not appear as a class in the Registrar-General's scale, they are numerous enough to form a large group within the population.

Commitments

Whatever level of income a person has, the amount left at their disposal will depend on what commitments they have. Financial commitments include things like mortgage repayments and hire purchase agreements, which need regular payments and are actually a form of debt. Most houses are bought on a mortgage and many people buy their cars using some form of loan scheme. Many people on low incomes find that hire purchase, or some other form of credit, is the only way that they can buy expensive items like furniture, washing machines and televisions.

Commitments can be taken on to the extent that even people in well-paid jobs find that they have little money to spare. The cost of a large mortgage, and perhaps other loans, can leave little money over for the other essentials of life. The pressure of finding the money to keep up payments can lead to social and physical problems, such as strain on family relationships and stress-related illnesses. If circumstances change – perhaps because of unemployment, or the arrival of extra dependants such as children or elderly relatives – it may become difficult or impossible to keep up payments. People in this position risk losing their homes or possessions if they cannot adjust their budget to meet their financial commitments.

Task

Think about the possible consequences for a family of being unable to meet the payments on their mortgage and other loans. Make a list of the kinds of help you think this family might seek from the health and care services.

The work that you do for this task could be incorporated into a project that looks at how commitments influence the lifestyle and well-being of individuals.

You have now seen how the lives of individuals are influenced by both social and economic factors. Membership of a class or cultural group affects how we spend our time and our money, and who we choose to spend them with. Our level of income and commitments can have a major effect on our lifestyle and spending patterns. For a carer it is important to remember always to treat people as individuals. It is also important to remember that their membership of a class and culture, and their economic situation, will affect how they see themselves and how they are viewed and treated by others.

▪ EQUALITY AND DIVERSITY ▪

One of the basic principles on which the health and care services operate is equality of provision for all, and this principle applies to access, quality of care and all other aspects of service delivery. Equality is a *value* in the culture of the health and caring professions, and the right of individuals to equal treatment is stated in the policies of all health and caring services and in the government's Patients' Charter.

However, statements by managers about equality, and good intentions on the part of staff, do not *guarantee* that all patients and clients receive the same level of care and attention. Many people find that they are treated differently from others and are discriminated against in their dealings with the caring services, and in many other areas of their life. As a carer you need to understand why discrimination happens, how it can affect the lives of its victims, and how you can work to identify and prevent discrimination in your own behaviour and in that of other people.

Labelling and stereotypes

Discrimination begins when someone is seen as being in some way different from other people. Of course we are all different from one another as individuals; but as we have seen, we are also members of groups sharing characteristics with other members.

Personal characteristics of physical appearance and behaviour are the things we first see when we meet another person, and we are quick to notice the differences and similarities between themselves and us. This is a natural part of the process of communication and is a skill which can help us to understand the needs of an individual more fully. Our perception of a person (i.e. the way that we see them) helps us to decide how best to meet their needs.

However, these features of appearance and behaviour may also be used to **label** an individual as a member of a particular group. People have no control over the ways others choose to label them, and they can even find themselves being seen as a member of a group that they don't feel part of. Once a person has been labelled as a member of a group they are no longer being seen as an

individual. They are assumed to have the characteristics that members of the group are believed to have, and are expected to behave and think in a certain way. They are expected to conform to a *stereotype* of how members of the group should be.

As you may know, stereotypes are not descriptions of real people. They are a collection of things like habits, dress, behaviour and attitudes that are put together and used to create a picture of a 'typical' group member. A stereotype is made of these scraps of personal characteristics which are put together to make up a picture, a sort of **social collage**, that is pinned on to an individual when they are labelled, and then taken to be a true likeness of them.

Task

In an earlier task (page 68) you may have linked personal characteristics to members of different classes. Look again at your work from that task and try to decide why you linked these collections of characteristics to particular social classes.

Write a paragraph explaining why you think certain characteristics are associated with certain classes. Where do you see these stereotypes used?

Your work can be incorporated into a project for this unit.

People who have been labelled with a particular stereotype can begin to find themselves discriminated against in different ways. Behaviour towards them will adapt to what

'I wanted you to feel at home, so I made a curry'

is regarded as the 'right way' to deal with people from that group, and the process of discrimination begins.

Who is discriminated against?

For some people, being labelled as a member of a certain group usually causes few problems. For example, being labelled as upper class, or as a film star, may affect how people are treated but it is unlikely to have serious negative effects on their life. In fact, here positive discrimination can take place, and special attention may be given to people who are seen as members of groups with a high status.

'Please madam – let me open the door for you'

For many people, though, the experience of being labelled as a member of a particular group is a negative one. Groups which are given a lower status and have less power

are likely to be in this position, and people labelled by their **race** or **ethnic group**, their **gender**, their **age** or their **disability** are particularly vulnerable to discrimination by others.

Race

One of the ways in which people are labelled is by their race, but what exactly is a race of people?

Human beings all belong to the same biological species whose members vary from each other physically in a wide variety of ways. We inherit our physical characteristics genetically (i.e. from our parents) and some of these features are more visible than others. Social stratification systems have been invented that are based on the fact that members of racial groups possess certain physical features in common, such as a particular skin colour or facial shape.

An example is the apartheid system of South Africa, which has used a complicated system of stratification based on race to define the political, social and economic status of members of the population. Since people come in an infinite variety of appearances it is impossible to draw a neat line so that everybody falls into one group or another, yet recent South African governments have put much time and effort into deciding what groups particular people belong to. This is an important decision for the individual because in South African society different racial groups have been forced to live apart. People classed as being white have considerably better conditions than are available to other racial groups. They have better housing and health care, and they have access to the better paid occupations. Also, importantly, they have the right to vote and hold political office. Happily, the apartheid system is in the process of being dismantled.

Quite apart from the moral questions raised by the apartheid system, it has met enormous difficulties when trying to draw clear lines between racial groups. Skin colour and facial features can vary infinitely, and trying to decide whether someone is African, Asian or Caucasian (white) can be so difficult that we begin to see how pointless it is to bother trying.

Biologically the makeup of individuals is basically the same, and the variations which give us the appearance we associate with the different racial groups are minute. Differences in hair and eye colour are inherited in exactly the same way as skin colour, and make just as little sense as a basis for social stratification. Differences in blood groups have far more biological importance than physical appearance and can be accurately measured so that people are clearly separated into different groups, yet this is not used as a basis of social stratification and discrimination.

This all points to the fact that the idea of race is a concept that has been developed socially and has little to do with the biology of human beings.

Ethnicity

Racial divisions based on biological differences may allow some individuals to be singled out easily for discriminatory treatment, but they take no account of differences in background, attitudes and behaviour. A person's **culture** or **ethnicity** may form the basis of discriminatory behaviour by others, whether they appear different in racial terms or not. The cultural or ethnic background of an individual may be indicated by their appearance, but clothes, accent and mannerisms may be more likely to indicate ethnic background than skin colour and facial shape. Ethnic groups have their own culture, and members following the norms of their culture are able to be identified.

Social stratification based on ethnic background is the basis of discrimination against many groups. Sometimes racism is directed at people who look black, but sometimes it is aimed at people's culture. Gypsies, and Irish and Jewish people, have a similar physical

appearance to the majority of British people but they are often discriminated against.

Gender

Gender is also used as the basis of discrimination. Though women are not a minority group and comprise more than half the population, they are usually given a lower status in society than men, and are discriminated against in both social and economic areas. Stereotypes of women abound in the media and they help to define the roles that are available to women, and how they are treated by men.

Women are discriminated against in education and in the labour market. Though their basic abilities are equal, few girls study to a high level in subjects like science, maths and engineering which have been seen as boys' subjects. At work women make up 40 per cent of the labour force, and yet there are very few women in senior positions. The average wage for women is only 75 per cent of the average for men.

Assumptions about a woman's role as a wife and mother are instilled into children of both sexes during primary socialisation, and are reinforced by media images and the influence of society at large. Many women become socialised into accepting traditional roles and never expect to compete with men at work. Women who do take on non-traditional roles and work in occupations that are dominated by men may be regarded as eccentric (i.e. odd) by members of both

sexes. There are very few female engineers or builders.

Women may be stereotyped as less serious *contenders* for jobs than men, who are regarded as the main breadwinners. Also, women may be expected to leave after a short while to have a family, presuming that childbearing signals the end of a woman's career.

Women who do try to develop a professional career may find that their chances of promotion are far worse than those of their male colleagues, even in areas where there are a high proportion of women. For example, around 90 per cent of primary school teachers are women yet over 50 per cent of primary school heads are men. This indicates the extent to which discrimination on the grounds of gender occurs. The low-status roles that are generally available to women help this discrimination to take place.

Task

Make a list on a sheet of paper of at least twenty occupations that you can think of. Talk to other students to make your list as large as possible. Now go through your list marking occupations that you believe are stereotyped as women's work with a W, and those you think are stereotyped as men's work with an M.

Are there equal numbers of professions associated with men and women? Do women's occupations have the same status as men's? Try fitting 'women's' occupations into the Registrar-General's scale of class.

Age

Another way in which society is stratified is on the basis of age. People are identified as belonging to a particular age group and treated differently from those seen as belonging to younger or older age groups. The processes of labelling and stereotyping cause the needs of the individual to be ignored and discrimination begins to take place.

Discrimination based on age particularly affects people who are seen to be old or young, whose status and power in society are lower than that of people in their middle years.

Though discrimination based on youth may be unjust, we do grow older. Adolescents may feel that they are being treated like children, but adjustment to the role of adult takes time for both the individual and those around them.

The rules and restrictions we place on younger children are not seen as discrimination, but are regarded as essential for their safety and development. But people labelled as 'elderly' are often stereotyped as dependent and helpless like small children.

Elders are likely to be less physically fit than others, and some will make increasing demands on family and the health and care services when illnesses of old age occur. Many cultures have great respect for age and if they stereotype elders it is as wise and learned. But in British culture the elderly are often stereotyped as big children whose opinions and feelings are not to be taken too seriously. This becomes the basis for discrimination in a variety of ways that the victims are powerless to prevent.

Even though many elders are fit and able, they are liable to be discriminated against by people who see them as belonging to a different group. In this case the discrimination comes from a younger generation.

Disability

Illness and disability in old age increases people's vulnerability to being stereotyped, but disability can become the basis of discrimination against people of all age groups.

People with disabilities come from all areas of society: from different classes, age groups and ethnic backgrounds. Despite this diversity it is often a person's disability that is seen as the most important thing about them. Some disabilities are easier to see than others and this makes stereotyping more likely. People who are wheelchair-bound are usually labelled as disabled, whereas people with severe dyslexia or asthma are very unlikely to be seen in the same way.

The stereotype of a disabled person is of someone who is dependent and helpless, and there may also be assumptions made about intellectual ability. People with physical disabilities frequently report that they are expected to have a learning disability as well. Physical disability has no biological relationship with learning disabilities, but the stereotype of disability links them together and can be the basis of discrimination in education and in other areas of life.

Don't assume we're at the same level

· FORMS OF DISCRIMINATION ·

So far we have see how individuals are sometimes labelled as members of groups, and how stereotypes of group members are applied to real people, resulting in discrimination against them. The word 'discrimination' means to treat differently, and it can be used to refer to any situation where a person is treated less well than others.

People who find themselves linked to one of the groups we have looked at may experience many forms of discrimination in different parts of their lives. It may range from being talked down to, or patronised, to being subjected to a violent attack. But some types of discrimination are more likely to be experienced by particular groups, and if we look at the types of things that happen to them we will be better equipped to identify discrimination and prevent it.

Physical and verbal abuse

One of the most extreme and brutal forms of discrimination is physical or verbal **abuse**. Members of ethnic groups are particularly liable to suffer this kind of treatment, and people have been killed because they were seen as a member of a particular group.

Some cases of physical abuse are the result of organised attacks by racist groups – there have been attacks on businesses and family homes, as well as personal assaults on individuals. Other physical abuse is not planned but is the result of people being regarded as 'fair game' because they have been labelled as belonging to an 'inferior' race.

Fear of assault by other groups in society is one of several reasons why members of some ethnic groups like to live close to each other.

Verbal abuse is suffered by members of ethnic groups, and the words used often show that stereotyping has taken place. The same insult may be used towards people who have no connection with each other except in the mind of the aggressor.

Verbal and physical abuse is also suffered by members of other groups who are commonly discriminated against. Attacks on women are often linked to their role and status in society. Women are often in a subordinate position in the family and have a lower status and power than males. Some suffer physical attacks from partners or male relatives who feel that their superior roles allow them to do this. Women may be unable to defend themselves either physically or socially from these attacks.

Images of women as sexual stereotypes may also be linked to verbal and physical abuse. Sexual attacks are sometimes explained by the comment that the woman was provocatively dressed, and this and similar arguments have been used in court to plead for light sentencing of offenders in rape cases. This shows how the blame for stereotyping can sometimes be shifted on to the victim.

Physical and verbal abuse towards elders or disabled people does occur to some members of these groups. As with women, violence is not likely to stem from *hatred* of the group, but is linked to the low status and power of elderly or disabled people. They may be stereotyped as less than full adults, and some are disciplined physically for behaviour that is regarded as bad. People who are dependent upon others for their care may also suffer physical abuse through neglect of their needs.

Exclusion

Verbal and physical abuse are usually easy to identify, but other forms of discrimination are less obvious, and more common. One of these is the process of **exclusion** of members of some groups from access to jobs, services and other facilities.

It is against the law to discriminate on the basis of ethnic background or gender in these areas, but discrimination can be very subtle and hard to detect. Job advertisements must be worded to allow everyone an equal chance to apply, but in practice the personal bias of members of the interview panel can exclude some applicants from the chance of appointment. We have already seen how women may be excluded from access to better paid jobs, and a similar situation occurs for people who are labelled ethnically. Many people have found that they are turned down for jobs for which they are well qualified because of their ethnic background or skin colour.

People from ethnic groups are also excluded from access to other resources. Another reason why members of ethnic groups live close to each other is that they are prevented from buying property in other areas. Again this is very difficult to prove in individual cases, but easy to see when statistics are examined.

Health and care services can also be denied to members of ethnic groups, or made more difficult to obtain. This could be through giving inadequate or incorrect information, or by ignoring any difficulties with the English language that they may have. The personal manner of an individual also conveys messages about how they see the other person and how they feel about them. These communications, both verbal and non-verbal, can be used to transmit hostility and act to put off further discussion. People from minority ethnic groups may be deterred from getting the help they need because of the way they are dealt with when they apply for it.

Elders and disabled people, too, can suffer from exclusion and avoidance of contact. Older people are generally excluded from the job market even though they may be fit, healthy and willing to work. Disabled people of working age often have useful skills and knowledge which would easily allow them to work effectively despite their disability. Nevertheless the stereotype of the disabled person as useless and dependent may be in the mind of the interviewer, so that the applicant is regarded as a potential liability rather than an asset. There is a legal requirement for larger businesses to employ a proportion of disabled people, but in practice many organisations fail to fulfil it. It is said that not enough disabled people apply, and that the facilities and environment are unsuitable for people with some disabilities, but these may be excuses rather than genuine reasons.

Exclusion because of environment is suffered regularly by some disabled people. This is a subtle form of discrimination which includes things like lack of wheelchair access to restaurants and other public places, and lack of suitable toilets. Transport is a particular problem for people who cannot use public transport or taxis very easily. This is a form of *discrimination by neglect*, in that the needs of disabled people are often forgotten in the design and planning of public places and facilities.

Task

Think about ways in which disabled people can be helped to gain access to facilities. Examples could include wheelchair ramps at entrances and designs that incorporate wider corridors. Write down a list of the features you think could be provided in public places to help disabled people to make full use of them.

Visit a local public facility such as a shopping centre or sporting complex. Using your list as a guide, assess the design and the facilities in terms of access and convenience for disabled people. Note where features on your list have been provided and where they have not.

Write a short report on your findings, including the changes you would like to make to allow disabled people full access. Your work could be included in a project which looks at disability and discrimination.

Devaluing

The forms of discrimination that we have seen so far have obvious social and physical outcomes for the victims, but there are other forms of discrimination that have effects which are less easy to see.

Individuals who belong to certain groups may find that their beliefs and opinions are regarded as worthless by some people. Though they are not subjected to physical abuse, or exclusion or avoidance, they find that they are held in low esteem and their views are not taken seriously. The norms of their culture may be criticised or ridiculed, and their beliefs devalued or denied.

This process works to undermine the confidence and self-esteem of the victims, which can have serious personal consequences for them. People treated in this way may come to share the view projected onto them and begin to see themselves as having less worth than others. Children growing up in an environment where they are constantly devalued can suffer serious setbacks in their personal development. They may see academic failure as inevitable for them and fail to develop their potential in other areas of life.

This form of discrimination is applied to all the groups we have looked at, and it is one of the ways in which the low status of members is reinforced. Women's opinions on many subjects are often regarded as less important than men's, and the areas in which they are credited with being accomplished are generally ones with low prestige, such as child-rearing and running a home. Many women are socialised into low self-esteem by this process and build up a picture of themselves which fits the subservient role they adopt in life.

Elders and disabled people can also find that their opinions and beliefs are not taken seriously by other people, and

---

that their power and status are lowered in the process. People whose self-esteem is damaged and who take on the belief that their opinions don't count have difficulty expressing their needs. They are reluctant to comment in case of ridicule, or because it seems pointless.

Stereotypes and self-concept

Though people may believe themselves to be free of prejudice towards others, practically everybody becomes involved with stereotypes of different groups. Jokes involving ethnic groups, or gender roles like mother-in-law, rely on the listener having the same stereotype ideas as the comedian. Stereotypes are very common in society, and many people use them to discuss other people and form judgements about them.

You saw in the last chapter how presumptions about a person's behaviour based on appearance may well be incorrect. *If you expect a person to behave or think in a certain way because you see him or her as belonging to a particular group, you are making assumptions based on a stereotype.*

This is very common throughout society and can work to influence the self-development of people who see themselves as part of the group being stereotyped. People can develop a concept of themselves which includes features of the stereotype, and then begin to behave in ways which fit this concept.

· PREVENTING DISCRIMINATION ·

To ensure equality of treatment you need to use your understanding of discrimination to prevent it taking place. Firstly you have to be able to identify behaviour that discriminates against any individuals. Some forms of discrimination are easy to see, but the more subtle ways in which people are excluded and devalued may not be. Look for signs of hostility to a person in the verbal and non-verbal messages they are being sent, and decide if you think they are being treated worse than others.

Try to spot the use of stereotypes in people's judgements of others, and see how it may affect the way they deal with people. If you think that you have identified an act of

discrimination you may wish to confront the person doing the discriminating. This is not always an easy thing to do but is important if equality is to be ensured.

Try to explain how the victim, as an individual, felt about the incident so that the stereotyped picture of the person is broken down. Some people may not realise that they are labelling others, and that the consequences of their behaviour can be so damaging to someone's personal development.

In a case of extreme discrimination, though, you may need to call in help to confront the situation safely and effectively. Use your own judgement and personal skills to decide how best to deal with an incident. *The important thing is not to ignore it.*

Think it over

One final aspect of preventing discrimination is your own behaviour, even though you may believe yourself to be free of bias. Think about your dealings with other people. Do you change your behaviour when communicating with people from other groups? Do you make assumptions about them based on stereotypes? Do your non-verbal communications convey warmth and interest or are you sending other messages? By monitoring your own behaviour, and that of others, you can contribute to ensuring that all people are treated according to their individual needs.

· A HEALTHY LIFESTYLE ·

Not everyone is lucky enough to have good health, and for some this is not their fault. However, for many other people good health is dependent on their **lifestyle choices**. Therefore, informed choices based on facts about the risks from chosen actions are important.

This section looks at three aspects of life which promote health – **diet**, **exercise** and **personal hygiene** – and the risks from poor choices in each.

Food for health

The type of food we eat contributes to the health of the body in two ways:

1 Nutrients provided by food allow the body to grow and function correctly.
2 Wise choices of food can help prevent some diet-related conditions

Many people eat a poor diet not because they cannot afford to eat well, or because there is a shortage of food, but because they *choose* the wrong types of food. They choose cakes, biscuits, highly processed and fried foods (and other 'convenience' foods) because such foods take little time to prepare and fit in with their busy lifestyle. However, these foods often contain few **vitamins**, **minerals** and **protein** but a lot of **fat** and **sugar**. Such diets can contribute to conditions such as tooth decay, obesity and heart disease. In many cases, symptoms are not immediately obvious but appear in later life.

As care workers are often responsible for preparing food for their clients, it is important that they are aware of an individual's nutritional needs and the best sources of food to provide these nutrients.

Nutrients in food

Figure 2.5 shows the five main **nutrient groups** in food. Each has a specific role in the body.

Besides the nutrients in the chart, *water* is also essential for life. You can live longer without food than you can without water.

Do all client groups need the same nutrients?

Everyone should have a balanced diet which contains all the nutrients listed in Figure 2.5. However, there are particular needs at various stages of life.

Childhood is a time of rapid growth, so children need plenty of protein and vitamin D and calcium to develop strong bones. Milk is important, so if they do not like to drink it, give

Nutrient	Functions	Sources in diet
Protein	• Growth and repair of body cells • Provides some energy	Animal protein – meat, fish, eggs, milk, cheese Vegetable protein – peas, beans, lentils, soya
Fat	• Provides energy • Keeps body warm • Protects vital organs • Makes food moist • Provides vitamins A and D	Animal fat – lard, butter, cream, suet Vegetable fat – olive oil, corn oil, sunflower oil
Carbohydrate	• Provides energy • Provides fibre from starch sources	Sugar – cakes, sweets, biscuits Starch – potatoes, rice, bread, pasta
Minerals Iron Calcium + phosphorus Sodium chloride	• Prevents anaemia • Strong bones and teeth • Prevents muscle cramp	Offal, dried fruit, eggs Dairy products, flour Cheese, ham, bacon
Vitamins A (retinol) B group C (ascorbic acid) D	• Helps sight in dim light • Promotes energy release • Helps absorb iron • Helps form bones and teeth	Carrots, fish oils Offal, yeast products Citrus fruits Dairy products

Figure 2.5 *The main nutrient groups*

plenty of milk in food. Give small portions of food and think about different ways to serve it attractively (e.g. faces in food might encourage the child to eat).

Do not encourage children to eat sweets and snacks between meals because they will fill up on these. Also, do not encourage eating sweet foods between meals as this can contribute to tooth decay.

Adolescence is another time of rapid growth, so plenty of protein, calcium and vitamin D are needed. Avoid too many snack/junk foods as these are high in fat and sugar and low in other nutrients. Plenty of iron is needed by young people (particularly by girls, to replace that lost in menstruation).

The energy needs of adults vary according to the job they do and the amount of exercise they take. Published dietary guidelines should be followed. In pregnancy, extra protein, calcium and iron is needed for the growing **foetus**.

As their activity slows, the amount of calories eaten by elders should be reduced to prevent **obesity**. The digestive system often slows, so food chosen needs to be easily digested (e.g. fish). Poor teeth often present problems in eating, so softer well-cooked foods might be chosen. Diets should be high in calcium and vitamin D to help prevent osteoporosis (reduction of bone density). Protein is important to maintain and renew body cells.

- Eat more fibre.
- Drink less alcohol.

The table in Figure 2.6 shows the health risks from not aiming for these goals. The chart also gives some suggestions about changes that could be made when planning or preparing food to provide a healthier diet.

Goal	Health risk	Change from	Change to
Eat less fat	• High cholesterol level • Heart disease • Obesity	Animal fats (e.g. lard)	Vegetable oil (e.g. corn oil)
Eat less sugar	• Tooth decay • Obesity	Sweet puddings	Fresh fruit
Eat less salt	• High blood pressure	Seasoning with salt	Using herbs or spices
Eat more fibre	• Constipation	White bread	Wholegrain bread
Drink less alcohol	• Liver damage • Stomach disorders	Alcoholic drinks	Low-alcohol drinks

Figure 2.6 *Health risks*

Task

Different people have different nutritional needs. Choose one client group and explore their needs further. Plan a day's menu for that client group.

Task

Complete the chart with other changes that could be made to the diet for each of the goals. Plan a healthy meal for a client group of your choice which also includes consideration of their nutritional needs.

Healthy eating

You now know which foods provide essential nutrients, and the particular nutrients needed by groups of individuals. You also need to find the healthiest way to provide the nutrients in meals.

There are five dietary goals to aim for:

- Eat less fat.
- Eat less salt.
- Eat less sugar.

Think it over

If changing to a healthier diet is so easy, and the benefits are so clear, why doesn't everyone do this?

People choose not to adopt a healthier diet for a number of reasons. They may not like the taste and texture of foods that have more fibre and less fat and sugar. Their taste and texture are certainly different.

Secondly, the healthier options are sometimes more expensive. Manufacturers need to recoup the money spent on developing the better product, and the market for such foods may remain small so that economies brought about by large scale production do not apply. The result is that the less well off in society may be less likely to adopt a healthier diet because their money for food will not go as far.

Where a person buys their food may affect their access to healthier alternatives. The large supermarkets often have a broad range of products, including the more healthy varieties. Those on a limited income might have to make their purchases at a corner shop, so again the opportunity to get healthy foods is reduced.

Task

Plan out a weekly shopping list for a family consisting of two adults and a young child. Estimate the cost of their food bill using healthy options where possible, and then again using less healthy options. What conclusions can you draw from the results? What does this imply for a family on a limited budget?

Exercise and health

Taking **exercise** is an important part of keeping healthy. There are many different and enjoyable ways an individual can exercise. Fitness can be achieved by taking some exercise about three times a week for 20 minutes. This exercise can range from walking to water-skiing, or from a gentle game of badminton to a hard workout in a gym. The important point is that the exercise should involve the heart, lungs and muscles and *should be suited to the individual's circumstances.*

It is important always to warm up before any exercise, no matter how fit the person. Cooling down is also a part of the exercise routine.

Most forms of exercise can be taken at different paces and levels. It is important to remember that the exercise should be taken at a pace and level to suit the fitness of the individual.

Most exercise is a combination of 'anaerobic' (which stretches muscles) and 'aerobic' (which works the heart and lungs).

The benefits of exercise

Regular exercise has many benefits. It usually makes an individual feel better – more relaxed, confident and able to cope with the strains of life. Exercise can be a way for people to meet new friends. It can also have a role in developing cooperative skills, especially in children.

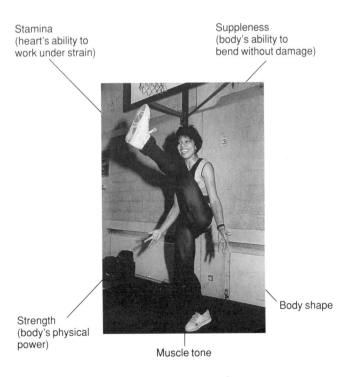

Stamina
(heart's ability to work under strain)

Suppleness
(body's ability to bend without damage)

Body shape

Strength
(body's physical power)

Muscle tone

Figure 2.7 *Some physical benefits of exercise*

83

The physical benefit of each form of exercise is often rated on its contribution to improving stamina, suppleness and strength, as depicted pictorially in Figure 2.7 and as a chart in Figure 2.8.

Exercise	Strength	Stamina	Suppleness
Badminton	**	**	***
Cycling (vigorous)	***	****	**
Golf	*	*	**
Disco dancing	*	***	****
Ballroom dancing	*	*	***
Swimming (vigorous)	****	****	****
Walking briskly	*	**	*
Climbing stairs	**	***	*

Figure 2.8 *The star ratings of some popular activities*

Costs of leisure

Unfortunately not all sports and leisure activities are easily or freely accessible to everyone. An individual's economic circumstances can thus dictate the possible leisure activities. However, this should not be an excuse for avoiding exercise as there are many cheap and even free ways. Walking suits most people and can be done at the individual's own pace. Cycling is free once you have a bike.

Belonging to expensive leisure and fitness clubs and wearing all the right gear will not mean you get fit any quicker!

Task

Draw up a list of interesting and beneficial exercises you think would suit a particular client group. Next choose one activity from your list, and state clearly the benefits that activity has for the client group.

Personal hygiene and health

Good **personal hygiene** is important for everyone. Understanding the importance of good personal hygiene and knowing routines to support this are important for people in care work because

1 You have to work closely with people, and poor personal hygiene has unpleasant aspects to it.
2 You are in a position to promote the personal hygiene of others.
3 Ill-health and disease can result from poor personal hygiene.

Using deodorants and perfumes will *not* hide poor hygiene. The body needs to be clean before these products are applied.

Remember:

Good personal hygiene includes:

- washing thoroughly every day (taking a bath or shower)
- washing after exercise
- using a cleansing product to remove sweat, dirt and sebum (oil produced by the skin)
- regularly cleaning teeth
- possibly using an antiperspirant or deodorant.

Task

Design an information leaflet about personal hygiene aimed at a client group of you choice. Keep it simple and attractive. Remember to be polite.

Think it over

How healthy is your own lifestyle? List aspects of your life which you would describe as health-promoting and those that are unhealthy. Think about another person's lifestyle. What differences are there between the two lifestyles? Explain the possible reasons for the differences.

▪ RISKS TO HEALTH AND WELL-BEING ▪

It is fairly easy to maintain a healthy lifestyle, but there are many risks to health in modern life. Sometimes the individual makes a conscious choice to take those risks. The risks covered in this section are related to **alcohol**, **drugs**, **smoking** and **sexual practices**.

Drinking alcohol

Alcohol is very much a part of the social scene in Britain. We may celebrate an achievement or good news by 'having a drink' or 'drinking a toast'. Alcohol is, however, a chemical substance and is really a drug, yet we often fail to see it as one.

The medical evidence seems to show that alcohol in *small amounts* is not harmful to most healthy people. There is some suggestion that a glass of red wine a day may actually have a health benefit.

Doctors have issued recommended maximum weekly intakes of alcohol. These are: for women, 14 units; and for men, 21 units. A unit is roughly equivalent to one glass of wine, one measure of spirit or half a pint of beer or lager. A person who frequently consumes over these recommended levels is thought to be placing their physical and mental health at risk.

The speed at which alcohol takes effect on the body after drinking it depends on a number of factors:

- If there is food in the stomach, this slows down the rate of absorption of the alcohol. (Of course, it will all be absorbed eventually.)

- The physical size of the individual has an effect. If two people consume the same amount of alcohol, the smaller person (having less blood) will feel the effects first as the *concentration* in the blood stream is higher.
- Women are generally smaller than men and have less fluid in the body. They therefore tend to feel the effects of alcohol quicker.
- The more alcohol taken and in the shorter the space of time, the greater the effect.

The adverse effects of alcohol

1 It slows the functioning of the brain. Things become fuzzy. You misjudge distances, which can result in **accidents**.
2 Very heavy drinking causes **inflammation of the brain**. The brain shrinks, reducing intelligence.
3 It is a **depressant**. Although at first alcohol seems to cheer people up, its depressant nature means that it eventually has the opposite effect, especially if drunk regularly.
4 **Liver damage** (cirrhosis of the liver) is a common effect of very heavy drinking. The liver enlarges as it tries to cope with the excess alcohol and eventually becomes inflamed. The liver hardens and the cells die, no longer able to function.
5 Heavy drinking weakens the body's **immune system**, leaving it open to disease.
6 Alcohol can damage the stomach lining and so can lead to **stomach disorders**.
7 Alcohol can cause **weight gain** because it is high in calories.
8 Alcohol interferes with nutrient absorption and can contribute to **nutrient deficiencies**.
9 Heavy drinking affects **sexual performance**.
10 Drinking in *pregnancy*, particularly in the early months, can damage the **development of the foetus**.
11 It is also important to remember that alcohol is a drug. A person can become **dependent** on alcohol.

As if the above list were not enough, alcohol also contributes to many lost working days due to sickness and headaches caused by a 'heavy' night out. It is connected with many road accidents where people 'drink and drive', with crime, and with violence both in public and within homes. Finally, people who are regular drinkers may find they do not have enough money for essentials.

Think it over

If alcohol is related to so many health risks and unhappiness, why is drinking alcohol so popular?

There are many suggestions why people drink. For a start it is regarded as sociable – it is common to go out for a drink or to have a drink with a meal. Furthermore, as alcohol is such an accepted part of society, some people believe it is difficult to refuse alcohol without being viewed as 'strange'. Therefore, friends may encourage you to drink and, to remain part of the group, you do so (this is **peer pressure**).

Some people start to drink alcohol regularly because they believe it helps reduce stress, and is enjoyable. However, the list of adverse effects above shows that the stress may eventually increase as health deteriorates.

How can the risks of drinking alcohol be reduced?

There are a number of ways to reduce the risks:

- Cut down on the number of units consumed each week (staying within the recommended limits).
- Consume low-alcohol or alcohol-free drinks, which are now available in both pubs and off-licences.
- Consume soft drinks occasionally instead of alcoholic ones.

Task

Design a questionnaire to assess the types and amounts of alcohol consumed in a week by your peer group. The survey should also cover their reasons for drinking or not drinking. Use the questionnaire and summarise the results. How do their responses compare with those mentioned in this section?

Tobacco smoking

Smoking is another health risk which has been very much part of our society. However, unlike alcohol, it is now less acceptable. This could be because the effects of smoking cigarettes, cigars or a pipe have been greatly publicised. Also, a number of court cases have been brought by employees against their employers, alleging that they have developed cancer from being in smoky areas. Employers have to provide a safe, healthy environment for their workers.

Thus there has been a reduction in the number of people who smoke and in the number of public places and work situations which allow smoking. Some areas are completely 'non-smoking' whilst other places have designated smoking areas.

Risks to health caused by smoking are increased according to the number of cigarettes smoked per day.

The adverse effects of smoking

1 Smoking can cause **cancer** of the nose, throat or lungs. Tobacco contains several substances which cause cancer, one of which is tar.
2 Smokers are more susceptible to chest and throat **infections**, including **bronchitis** and **emphysema** which is the destruction of the small bronchi in the lungs. Breathing problems are the end result.
3 Pregnant women who smoke produce **smaller babies** than the non-smoker. As they are smaller, they are also weaker and more prone to infections. It has also been suggested that there is a higher rate of stillbirths and miscarriages amongst smoking pregnant women.
4 Smoking contributes to the risk of having a **heart attack**. Smoking, combined perhaps with a diet high in cholesterol, leads to furring and hardening of the arteries (atherosclerosis). This causes the heart to work harder to pump the blood around the body. If a clot forms in one of these arteries it causes a heart attack.
5 Carbon monoxide is also inhaled from a cigarette. This can attach itself to haemoglobin and therefore reduces the **blood's capacity** to carry oxygen around the body. To compensate for this, the body produces more haemoglobin – but this increases the risk of blood clotting. At the same time, the heart works harder to

pump blood around the body to provide oxygen, putting extra **stress on the heart**.

6 Nicotine thickens the blood. This can contribute to **clotting in the arteries** if they become constricted. This condition is known as **thrombosis**, and can result in limbs having to be amputated.

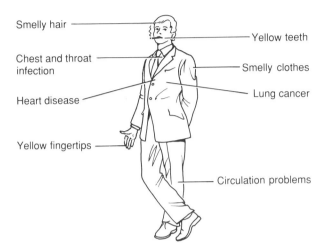

Figure 2.9 *Cigarette smoking drawbacks*

Besides these risks to physical health, the nicotine in cigarettes causes a yellowing of the teeth and fingertips which looks unsightly.

Smokers are sometimes thought to smell unpleasant as the smoke lingers in their hair and clothes. Also, a smoker's breath can smell, and physical contact may be unpleasant to a non-smoker. Besides all this, it is an expensive habit!

Think it over

If smoking is connected to all these drawbacks, why do people smoke?

Smoking relaxes some people. The nicotine in cigarettes is a drug which slows down nerve impulses – this gives the feeling of relaxation. As a result, it gives some people more confidence.

As with alcohol, there is **peer pressure** – particularly in adolescence when smoking often is first tried. It is interesting to note that more adolescent girls smoke than boys.

Nicotine, like alcohol, is a drug. People who have been smoking for some time find it difficult to give up.

Passive smoking

A lot of research has shown that non-smokers are also at risk, together with the smokers. The 'passive' smoker breathes in smoke which has not been filtered through the tip of a cigarette, and so the content of tar, nicotine and other substances is high. Evidence shows that only about one-sixth of the smoke goes into the smoker, the rest goes into the air!

The foetus of a pregnant woman is a passive smoker, receiving the drug by way of the woman's blood stream. This can produce dependency later on.

How can the risks of smoking be reduced?

Risk reduction has to be considered for both the smoker and the non-smoker.

For the smoker, the only sure way to reduce the risks is to smoke less or to stop smoking. This is only possible if the smoker really wants to do it. The smoker should:

- over a period, cut down on the number of cigarettes smoked per day (some people find it difficult to stop suddenly)
- use a substitute such as nicotine gum or 'patches'
- try 'low-tar' cigarettes
- tell friends and family and ask for support and encouragement
- smoke only in certain places or at certain times of the day (this will reduce the opportunity to smoke)
- give themselves rewards for achievement (e.g. use the money saved to buy themselves a treat).

Non-smokers must realise the risks they are taking by being in an atmosphere that is constantly smoky. They should avoid smoky areas as far as possible.

Parents, especially those who smoke, should avoid smoking around the children as it has been shown that children who are in constant contact with a smoky atmosphere are more prone to chest infections and pneumonia.

Task	The use of other drugs
Choose a clearly defined target group of people, and produce an attractive poster aimed at explaining the risks connected with smoking. The poster should give some pointers to a more healthy lifestyle.	As you have seen, alcohol and nicotine are both drugs. In Britain and many other countries they are available to those who can afford them, and they are, within limits, 'socially acceptable'. Other drugs are illegal to use (e.g. ecstasy, cannabis). Some drugs are prescribed by doctors as medicine (e.g. tranquillisers), but these can be just as dangerous to health *if used incorrectly*.

The use of other drugs

Drug	Form	How used	Effects	Health risks
Cannabis ('pot'/'hash')	Resin in form of solid brown mass	Smoked – usually crumbled and mixed with tobacco	• Relaxation and talkativeness • Lightheadedness • Possible hallucinations • Confusion	• Psychological dependency for enjoyment/coping with life • Bronchitis, lung cancer, heart disorders • Could lead to use of stronger drugs
Ecstasy ('E')	Tablet or capsule – white, brown, pink or yellow	Swallowed – effects begin in 20 minutes	• Calmness with raised awareness of colour and sound • Loss of coordination • High doses result in anxiety and confusion	• Prolonged use can reduce sleep • Those with high blood pressure, heart conditions, epilepsy or mental illness are at risk due to stimulant effects • Possible death
Amphetamines and cocaine ('coke')	White powder	Usually sniffed, but can be injected	• Stimulate nervous system • Breathing and heart rate increased, pupils dilated • Person feels alert, energetic, cheerful and confident • Tiredness reduced for a time • Appetite reduced	• Poor sleep, loss of appetite, bodily itching leading to scratching and anxiety • Lower resistance to disease • Damaged blood vessels • Heart failure • Damage to nose membranes • Depression and suicidal thoughts
LSD ('acid')	Impregnated into small sheets, like blotting paper	Dissolved on tongue	• Affects perception – can be visions of joy and beauty, or nightmares • Confusion and disorientation	• Accidents due to confusion • Can be a damaging experience to those with mental illness
Heroin ('H'/'horse')	White or brown powder	Sniffed or injected	• First alertness, then drowsiness and drunkenness • Overdose results in unconsciousness	• Dependency • Poor health due to inadequate diet • Risk of AIDS if needles are shared
Solvents	A range of forms easily available (e.g. paint, glue, lighter gas, petrol)	Sniffed	• Similar to drunkenness • Disorientation and loss of control • 'Hangover' effects following use (e.g. headache, tiredness, paleness) • Possible unconsciousness	• Injury/death due to accidents whilst confused • Can be weight loss and depression • Physiological dependence possible

Figure 2.10 *Analysis of some common drugs*

It is also important at this point to distinguish between **drug abuse** and **drug misuse**. Drug *abuse* relates to the taking of a drug that is not socially acceptable. Drug *misuse* relates to the taking of a socially acceptable drug but in an unacceptable way.

Prolonged use of any drug can be dangerous to health. The way the drug is used can also vary in safety; for example, injecting can be more dangerous than smoking a drug. Also, people vary in their reactions to the same amount of the same drug. This is due to individual factors such as body weight, tolerance of the body to the drug, and state of health.

As an individual's body becomes dependent on a drug, the money needed to finance the habit increases. In turn this has adverse effects on diet, housing, and the ability to cope in a job. A vicious circle of dependency and lack of coping is set up. It has been shown that people often turn to crime to finance a drug habit.

Figure 2.10 outlines some of the common drugs and their effects on the body.

Think it over

Why do you think people become involved in drug abuse?

There are many reasons why people take drugs, and again these include some of the social influences covered earlier in this chapter. Drugs are seen as a way to escape temporarily life's problems. They may be a way to relieve boredom, which may itself result from lack of opportunities.

Drug taking is seen by young people especially as daring and exciting, partly because of the risks involved. There is peer pressure, and opportunity.

People who lack confidence are less inhibited temporarily when they have taken drugs (as with alcohol).

Finally, and perhaps most seriously for the individual, people take drugs because they have developed a dependency.

How to spot drug taking

There are a number of signs which are linked to drug taking, but they can also be linked to other causes (e.g. stress or worry). These signs include:

- loss of interest in hobbies, friends and job
- mood changes
- irritability
- disorientation
- loss of appetite
- over-excitement or over-relaxation
- odd tablets, powders or smells.

Task

Design a questionnaire to assess your peer group's knowledge about the risks involved in taking illegal drugs. Apply the questionnaire and use a spreadsheet to collate the results using graphs, bar charts. Highlight any gaps in the knowledge and produce either an information sheet, display or leaflet to fill those gaps.

How can the risks from drug taking be reduced?

The only satisfactory way to reduce the risks is to stop taking drugs. It is not possible to ensure that a client never comes into contact with drugs, but as a carer you can follow certain guidelines:

- Education is important – the risks of drug taking should be understood and discussed.
- Avoid having too many prescribed drugs around as these can be a temptation.
- Ensure self-access to information for help/support if needed.
- If someone is taking drugs, talk calmly to them, try to discover why they take drugs and encourage them to seek professional help. Your role might be to provide emotional support.

Professional help is offered through a range of agencies in the health and social care services. These professionals often work together in a multi-disciplinary approach to help the client in a planned way. This ensures all needs are addressed – social, physical, psychological and emotional.

Think it over

Much of the health education material on drugs seems to give the message 'If you are going to take drugs, do it safely' and then informs the reader how to do this. Why do you think it is written in this way?

Sexual behaviour and health

Sex is a natural part of life. It is the way in which people reproduce themselves and this ensures that the species continues. It is also a way of showing love and affection as well as a way of giving pleasure and excitement.

Whether sex is part of a casual or a long-term relationship, infectious diseases can be transmitted. It is important to know how to limit the risks. The diseases are known as STDs, which stands for 'sexually transmitted diseases' (although doctors now call them GU or **genito-urinary** as they affect the genital area as well as the bladder and urethra).

It should be appreciated that anyone can contract an infection – men and women, heterosexuals and homosexuals. Getting an infection is not dependent on having a lot of sexual partners. Sometimes infections can lie dormant for a time and then come out. Some infections can be a result of poor personal hygiene. The more partners a person has, the greater the risk of catching or passing on an infection.

There are many different types of sexually transmitted diseases.

Gonorrhoea

Gonorrhoea is caused by bacteria which live in warm moist areas of the body. Symptoms include:

- a discharge from the vagina or penis
- burning pain on passing urine

- irritation or discharge from the anus
- pain in the lower abdomen in women.

This disease is treated with antibiotics that kill the bacteria causing the symptoms.

Thrush

This is caused by the yeast called *Candida albicans* which many people have on their skin. When it multiplies it causes an infection. The symptoms in women are:

- a thick, white discharge from the vagina
- soreness and pain on passing urine
- itching around the genital area.

Men get inflammation of the penis. The treatment is by pessaries and/or cream.

Genital warts

These are caused by a virus which produces skin warts. The warts appear around the genital area and are of varying sizes. Treatment is by application of an ointment.

Genital herpes

This is caused by the herpes simplex virus, and symptoms include:

- small painful blisters in the genital region
- tingling or itching in the genital area
- general flu-like symptoms (e.g. headache, backache)
- pain or tingling when passing urine.

Pubic lice

These are small lice which live in the pubic hair and are spread by close bodily contact. Symptoms include severe itching and small eggs appearing on pubic hair or in underwear. Normal washing will not kill the lice or eggs – a special lotion is needed.

Hepatitis B

This is caused by a virus present in the blood and other bodily fluids of an infected person. The liver becomes inflamed. Symptoms occur in two stages:

1 At between one and six months after contact with infection, flu-like symptoms appear, including a sore throat and cough. There is a feeling of fatigue and loss of appetite, and joint pain.

2 There follows the jaundice stage. Skin and eyes develop a yellowish tone. Stools become grey in colour and the urine turns brown. The abdomen is sore.

The treatment involves bed-rest and healthy food. Vaccinations are now available for people in some situations.

HIV and AIDS

AIDS (acquired immune deficiency syndrome) is caused by the HIV (human immunodeficiency virus). The virus survives in body fluids such as semen, blood, vaginal and cervical discharges.

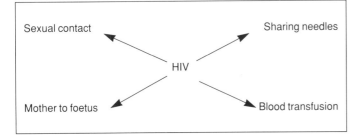

Figure 2.11 *How HIV may be passed on*

Who is most at risk?

- People who have a variety of sexual partners and have unprotected sex. The more people they sleep with, the more chance they have of contracting the virus.
- 'Gay' men. It was originally more common in this community in the USA and Europe, before the disease was understood.
- Drug-dependent people who inject drugs – if they share needles.
- Haemophiliacs (a condition where the blood does not clot). They have more frequent blood transfusions, which places them at risk. However, blood is now checked (screened) for the HIV virus before being put in the blood bank. Contracting HIV this way was much more common in the early days before society was fully aware of the illness.
- Prostitutes (male and female) if they do not practise 'safe sex' – because of the large number of sexual partners that they have.

What are the effects of HIV and AIDS?

An individual can carry the HIV virus and not have any ill-effects. It can be carried for many years before it becomes AIDS. Once it becomes AIDS it is fatal. An individual may show symptoms for anything up to six years, but most die within a year of diagnosis.

AIDS damages the body's natural defence mechanism so it is unable to fight infections effectively. People with the condition are more prone to serious illness and become progressively weaker as the body is attacked. Eventually many of the body's systems break down, resulting in death.

When the disease first came into the headlines a lot of incorrect information was spread around about the condition and how it could be contracted, because people knew little about it. Society is now much better informed, but some people still worry about contact with an HIV or AIDS sufferer because they are not fully clear about how the disease is passed on. HIV and AIDS *cannot* be passed on by:

- drinking from the same cup as an infected person
- hugging or touching an infected person
- kissing an infected person on the lips
- swimming in the same water as an infected person.

HIV and AIDS sufferers need a lot of support, and carers should fully understand the nature of the disease to be able to offer that support effectively.

Task

You may still hear a lot of false and inaccurate information about the HIV virus and AIDS. Obtain some literature on the subject. Design a leaflet for a chosen client group which explains accurately and clearly about HIV and AIDS.

Think it over

Think more deeply about how an individual can protect himself or herself from STDs.

In many cases the carriers of STDs, including HIV, are unaware that they have an infectious disease. They are healthy and seem perfectly well. This can leave a partner open to risk if he or she chooses to have unsafe, unprotected sex. There are ways to reduce the risk:

- Limit the number of partners you have.
- Practise 'safe' sex. Avoid penetrative sex – full sexual intercourse is not the only way of giving pleasure.
- If having full sexual intercourse, use a condom. This is the only method of contraception which will protect against the spread of HIV and other STDs. Both male and female condoms are available.
- *Do not* have full sexual intercourse unless your partner is willing to use a condom.

Self-assessment test

1 Which of the following are norms?
   a People form queues at bus stops.
   b People dress smartly at weddings.
   c People believe that it is right to wait for their turn to be served in a shop.
   d People send cards to family and friends on their birthdays.

2 The behaviour that people adopt in social situations is called a:
   a norm   c role
   b value   d status.

3 What is 'primary socialisation'?

4 List two groups within which socialisation takes place.

5 What is the name used for the collection of all the norms and values of a group, together with the status and roles of its members?

6 Who are a person's peers?

7 What does the Registrar-General's scale use as the basis of social stratification?

8 Which of the following may be influenced by the social class a person belongs to?
   a Type of car driven.   d Life span.
   b Type of food eaten.   e Educational attainment.
   c Voting behaviour.

9 Which of the following are income?
   a Wages.   c Profit from a business.
   b A house.   d Savings.

10 List four typical areas of expenditure for a family.

11 One possible effect of long-term unemployment is the development of low self-esteem in the victim. What is self-esteem?

12 What are commitments?

13 What is discrimination?

14 A person who is said by another to be a typical member of a particular group has been:
   a perceived   c identified
   b labelled   d devalued.

15 What is a stereotype?

16 Name four bases of discrimination.

17 What is the difference between ethnicity and race?

18 If someone is turned down for a job because of the colour of their skin, what form of discrimination is taking place?
   a Verbal or physical abuse.
   b Exclusion.
   c Devaluing.

19 What forms of discrimination are disabled people most likely to face?

20 How can a person's self-concept be affected by being labelled and stereotyped?

21 You should cut down on saturated fat in the diet because:
   a saturated fat products are expensive.
   b they are related to increased cholesterol levels in the blood.
   c they cause high blood pressure (BP).
   d they reduce the amount of protein absorbed in the body.

22 Smoking is the main cause of:
   a gum disease   c lung cancer
   b cirrhosis of the liver d heart attacks.

23 For young children, protein is important for:
   a growth and repair of cells
   b development of the bones
   c preventing anaemia
   d warmth.

24 State one way in which the HIV virus can be transmitted from one person to another.

25 State one health risk an individual may take if they regularly consume too much alcohol.

26 People can suffer from constipation. Suggest one way in which you could increase the fibre content of a person's diet.

27 Explain why it is important to 'warm up' before you do any form of exercise.

28 Services often use a 'multidisciplinary' approach. What does this mean?

29 What does the term 'passive smoking' mean?

30 State one reason why it is important to maintain high standards of personal hygiene as a care worker?

31 State one reason why an adolescent may take illegal drugs.

32 Swimming is said to develop stamina. What does this mean?

Fast Facts

AIDS Acquired Immune Deficiency Syndrome. A condition caused by a virus, where the body's immune system breaks down and is unable to protect the body from illness and disease.

Alcohol A chemical which causes intoxication (drunkenness) and can result in changed behaviour.

Atherosclerosis This is a medical name for hardening and narrowing of the arteries caused by the laying down of fatty deposits in them.

Bronchitis This is a medical condition in which there is an inflammation of the bronchioles – the small tubes leading to the lungs, through infection by bacteria.

Cancer A condition where the cells do not grow normally and result in a tumour.

Carbohydrate A nutrient in food which is particularly used for energy by the body.

Cirrhosis of the liver A condition caused by too much alcohol, where the cells of the liver are killed so preventing the liver from functioning as it should.

Class A group of people who share a common position in society. Class membership is linked to occupation, income, wealth, beliefs and lifestyle.

Commitments These are areas of expenditure which require regular payments. Commitments include mortgages, loan repayments, and any other areas where payment is planned and made regularly. Failure to meet commitments can result in loss of goods or access to services.

Constipation A condition where waste products move too slowly through the body, causing the individual discomfort.

Coronary heart disease A deadening of part of the heart muscle due to a blood clot blocking one of the arteries and preventing oxygenated blood reaching it.

Culture This is the collection of values and norms that are associated with a group, including the status and roles of individual members. Culture is intended to describe all features of a group that make it different and distinct from other groups.

Depressant Something which lowers or reduces nervous activity or an ability to function normally.

Devaluing Stereotyping the views and beliefs of others as worthless or ridiculous. Devaluing a person's culture and beliefs can undermine their personal development.

Diet The total food and drink an individual consumes.

Disability A physical or intellectual impairment which has an impact on the life of a person suffering from it. A person who is described as disabled may be prevented from doing only a few things by reason of their disability itself, but prevented from doing many more because of social factors.

Discrimination This involves treating a person or group in a different way from how others are treated. Discrimination can be either negative or positive; but when used on its own, the word is usually taken to refer to negative discrimination, which is to treat certain people less well than others.

Drug abuse The use of socially unacceptable drugs.

Drug dependency Being dependent on a drug, in order to cope with life. Attempting to stop using the drug can cause a 'craving' or a feeling that the person must take the drug.

Drug misuse   The 'improper' use of socially acceptable drugs.

Emphysema   The medical name for destruction of the bronchioles, causing a shortness of breath.

Ethnic group   A group whose members share a common culture which is broad enough to influence all areas of individual and family life.

Exclusion   A form of discrimination which operates to prevent certain people from gaining access to resources and services.

Exercise   Physical exertion which works the muscles.

Expenditure   The value of cash spent out. Expenditure includes all spending, in whatever area the spending takes place.

Fat   This is a nutrient in food which is used by the body primarily for energy as it is the most concentrated form. It also protects vital organs and gives the body warmth.

Foetus   The name given to the developing baby within the mother's womb, usually from three months after conception.

Fibre   Parts of food which are not fully broken down by the digestive process and so aid the movement of food along the digestive tract (mouth to anus).

Gender   The role associated with people of a particular sex. Sex is defined biologically as male or female, whereas gender is defined socially by the behaviour of individuals.

Genito-urinary   This is a term referring both to the genital organs and the urinary system.

Group   A collection of individuals who are seen as being linked by common characteristics such as appearance or behaviour.

HIV   Human Immunodeficiency virus. The virus which causes AIDS. Having HIV is not the same as having AIDS. HIV can cause AIDS later, but a person with HIV can look and feel well.

Immune system   The way in which the body protects itself from illness and disease.

Income   Money received as wages, interest on savings or profits from business activities.

Infectious disease   A disease which can be passed from one person to another.

Labelling   Identifying a person as a member of a particular group, whether or not they see themselves as members. Labelling is linked to stereotyping and people are expected to conform to the behaviour expected of the stereotype they have been labelled with.

Lifestyle choice   A choice made by the individual about something to do with the way they lead their life.

Minerals   Nutrients in food which are needed in minute amounts for the body to function correctly. There are a number of minerals, including iron, calcium and phosphorus.

Norms   Rules of behaviour which are followed by members of groups. Norms apply to members of the group only, and are usually different from norms of other groups.

Nutrients   Something that nourishes or feeds the body.

Obesity   The medical term for being severely over the recommended weight for the individual's height and size.

Passive smoking   Breathing in the tobacco smoke of others when you are not actually smoking yourself.

Peers   People who are like us in terms of group membership and status. Peers are our equals, and our peer group is often our group of close friends.

Peer pressure   Pressure placed on someone from their own age or friendship group.

Personal hygiene   This involves keeping yourself clean (e.g. through a washing routine and the use of deodorants).

Primary socialisation   The very influential socialisation that takes place during early childhood. This is when we are socialised into membership of our families and our culture.

Protein   A nutrient found in food which is used by the body for growth and repair of cells in children and repair and maintenance of cells in adults. It can also be used for energy.

Race   The idea of a group based on biological differences between people. In practice a person is assigned to a particular race on the basis of the subjective impressions of others, not on the basis of measurable biological differences.

Registrar-General's social classification   A method of stratifying the population along the lines of class. Occupational groups are used as the basis for deciding class membership.

Role The behaviour adopted by individuals when they are in social situations. Group norms and individual status help to define a role.

Role set The collection of roles that an individual possesses. The role played in a situation depends on the people who the role is being played towards.

Sebum The name used for secretions from the glands on to the skin.

Self-concept The way in which a person sees himself or herself as a whole. Self-concept includes not just physical appearance but also our understanding of the type of person that we are, and of our worth.

Sexually transmitted disease A disease which is passed on through sexual contact.

Socialisation The process of learning and accepting the norms and values of a group, and developing your own role within it. Through socialisation people become part of a group or culture.

Social collage A way of looking at stereotyping which describes the way that characteristics and features are put together to make up a picture which is not a true likeness of any individual.

Social stratification The process of dividing the population up into layers or strata. Society can be stratified on the basis of class, income, race, age, or any other characteristic by which people can be separated into groups.

Stamina The heart's ability to work under pressure.

Status A measure of the rank and prestige of a person or group of people. Status helps to define how people are treated by others, and how they see themselves.

Strength The physical power of the muscles/body.

Suppleness The body's ability to be flexible or bend without damage.

Unit A measurement used for alcohol. One glass of wine or one half pint of beer is usually one unit.

Values Beliefs about what is good, right and worth striving for. Values help to define and explain norms of behaviour.

Vitamins Nutrients found in food which are needed in small amounts for the body to function correctly. These include vitamins A, B, C and D.

Wealth The value of the property owned by a person. Wealth includes the value of houses, cars, savings and any other personal possessions.

chapter 3 HEALTH EMERGENCIES

This chapter will provide you with knowledge and understanding to help you overcome the worry most carers have, of knowing that accidental damage, injury and illness can occur quite suddenly to the clients in their care. For example, an elderly person, quite capable of moving about, can easily become confused and dizzy for a short while and fall when changing direction or stepping up to a different level.

Sudden events can happen in the workplace, at home, and when socialising or travelling. We accept these as inevitable parts of daily life. Most of us do not show the anxieties associated with sharing the responsibility for others.

The activities in this chapter will help you to prepare for an emergency, giving you the confidence and skills to enable you to do your best should these circumstances arise, bearing your own and others' safety in mind.

When you have worked through the material in this chapter you will have studied common emergencies and the care procedures linked to them. You will also be asked to think of materials you could use when you have not got the usual first aid equipment with you.

Task

In your school, work, college or work experience placement, find out what items are supposed to be in the first aid boxes. Then carry out a survey of their actual contents.

If there are many first aid boxes on the

premises, choose some at random. To choose at random, give each box a number and put folded numbered papers in a 'hat', mix thoroughly and draw out the required amount.

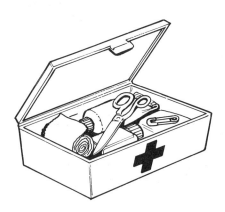

You will need to obtain permission to do this survey. Ask your supervisor for the name of the person responsible for first aid provision, and agree to make an appointment (or use the telephone to explain your purpose). At the same time, find out how often the first aid boxes are filled up and when the last refill occurred.

Next, design an observation sheet to note down your findings. You could also start preparing a spreadsheet to input the data on a computer, in which case you could present your results graphically.

Use the information you have obtained to decide whether the overall time intervals to fill up the first aid boxes are adequate. You could show all your working and present your investigations as evidence of core skill achievements (Application of Number). The first aid coordinator will probably appreciate a copy of your work, so send one in the internal mail and enclose a letter of thanks.

If you do the evidence task above you will become familiar with materials used in first aid and be more able to suggest substitutes when these are not available. There are some suggestions for improvised first aid materials in Figure 3.1.

Standard materials	Improvised materials
Triangular bandages used for arm sling	Elevate arm and either pin shirtsleeve or turned up hem of jacket to chest front
Bandages	Pieces of clean cloth or clean clothing
Cold compress	Bag of frozen vegetables, especially peas, wrapped in a towel
Plastic disposable gloves	Inside-out plastic bags
Dressings	Non-fluffy material (e.g. clean handkerchief)

Figure 3.1 *Some improvised first aid materials*

· UNCONSCIOUSNESS ·

Think it over

What is meant by 'unconscious'? How do you know when a person is unconscious? How is it different from sleep? Why is it so dangerous? What should I do to help if I find somebody unconscious?

By the time you have worked through this section you should feel able to answer all these questions.

An unconscious person is usually showing all of these three features:

- They are not **awake**
- They are not **attentive**
- They are not **aware**

In addition, they may or may not be breathing and they may or may not have a pulse. In this case the person is at risk of dying because there is no oxygen, vital to the survival of living cells, being carried around the body.

Ordinary sleep can be said to be a lower or reduced form of the normal wakeful state (which is full consciousness). When you lift a sleeping person's arm, it feels loose and floppy but it still has some firmness to the touch, because a few muscles are still contracting. In an *unconscious* person the limb is very soft and loose, like a rag doll's, because no muscles are contracting. This is very important to understand because it is the chief reason why, in unconscious people, the **tongue** tends to fall backwards and block off the air passages (see Figure 3.2). This obviously does not happen in ordinary sleep. Any unconscious person may need immediate first aid to unblock the air passage.

Figure 3.2 *The tongue may block the airway*

Reflexes are automatic muscular movements which occur as a result of some nerve stimulus (like a blink in response to a speck of dust in the eye). Reflexes are missing in unconsciousness, so any fluid or material in the throat cannot be cleared and may be breathed into the lungs, causing **asphyxiation** (suffocation). This serious effect is most often the result of bringing up the stomach contents (vomiting). When this happens the delicate linings of the lungs are intensely irritated. Watery fluids ooze out to fill the lungs, so stopping the oxygen in the air from reaching the bloodstream.

Remember:

DO NOT GIVE AN UNCONSCIOUS PERSON ANYTHING TO EAT OR DRINK

Your first aim is therefore to **keep the person's airway open**.

To do this, first put one hand underneath the person's neck and the other on their forehead. Then *gently* tilt the forehead backwards so that the chin moves upwards. Using the hand from the neck gently lift the chin upwards and forewards – the mouth will stay slightly open and the nostrils should be directly upwards. This position will pull the tongue away from the back of the throat, and straighten out the air passages.

Think it over

If you can, obtain and carefully examine a model showing a section through the human head and neck, and trace the passage of air from the nose to the lungs, noting the position of the tongue. Now turn the model face-up and horizontal, and look at the relationship of the tongue and air passages.

Even if you suspect any injuries to the head, neck or spine **you must still clear the airway**.

> **Remember:**
>
> *Many people die unnecessarily each year because they have been left face-up in an unconscious state.*

Your next important job is to check **breathing and pulse**.

Is the person **breathing**? Put your ear close to the victim's mouth and nose for a few seconds and :

> **LOOK** for evidence of the chest and abdomen moving
> **LISTEN** for sounds of breathing
> **FEEL** for the touch of breath on your cheek.

This sounds like the road safety drill you may have learned as a child. Perhaps you could learn it by repeating it over and over, just as you did with the road safety code.

If you find that the casualty is breathing , place the unconscious person in the **recovery position** (see page 101). Stay there and regularly check the breathing until emergency medical help arrives.

If the casualty is *not* breathing, check and quickly remove any obvious blockage from the airway. 'Look, listen and feel' again and if there is still no breathing start **resuscitation** techniques immediately (see below).

· ARTIFICIAL VENTILATION ·

When any casualty has stopped breathing and is turning bluish-grey you must get some oxygen from your own breath into their chest as soon as possible.

Approximately 20 per cent of the air around us is oxygen, and even when we have breathed this in and used some of the oxygen there is still 16 per cent left. This is enough to support another person and is the reason why **'mouth-to-mouth resuscitation'** works.

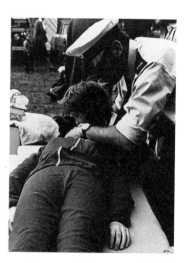

You cannot try this with another breathing person, so we have invented emergency technology to provide us with dummies (more correctly called 'manikins') on which to practise. Manikins usually have inflatable chests and compressible hearts. They are quite expensive so you will have to join a first aid class if you haven't one available for your use.

Procedure

1 With the casualty flat on his or her back, open the airway as described previously, taking care to remove any obstruction by sweeping your finger around the casualty's mouth.
2 Close the casualty's nose by pinching the nostrils with the thumb and forefinger.
3 Take a breath for yourself and seal your mouth around the casualty's mouth. Do not waste time putting handkerchiefs or tissues in between because they will only become soggy and interfere with resuscitation.
4 As you blow gently but firmly into their mouth, watch to see if the chest rises. Take your mouth away to breathe for yourself and watch the chest fall. Repeat

the process 10 times to load up the casualty's lungs with oxygen. The rate should be approximately 15 breaths each minute.

5 Check that the pulse is still there. If you can, call or telephone for help between series of 10 breaths, checking the pulse at these intervals as well.

6 If you are doing it properly you should begin to see a change in skin colour, particularly in the lips and tongue. If the colour does not improve, double-check your technique – especially the open airway and the pulse.

7 If the chest is failing to rise, check the airway position and your mouth seal. Is the nose blocked off and any obstruction cleared?

8 Continue until the casualty begins to breath unaided. Then place him or her in the recovery position.

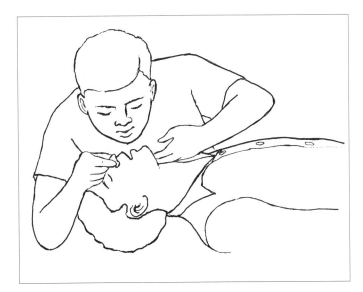

Figure 3.3 *Mouth-to-mouth resuscitation*

Mouth-to-nose ventilation

This is a variation which can be used if there is damage to the mouth or possible poisoning, or if the resuscitation is taking place in water.

Clearly, it is important to close the mouth with one hand. You are less likely to meet vomit or saliva using this method, but it is often more difficult to do.

Young children and babies

The procedure is slightly different for babies and children up to about 4 years.

Place the child on the floor or along your arm and seal your mouth around the child's mouth *and* nose. Give short, gentle breaths at about 20 per minute.

▪ BLOOD CIRCULATION ▪

If a person's heart stops pumping blood around the body, you will have to be an artificial pump until it restarts or until expert help arrives. The victim's blood has to carry oxygen around the body, and to the brain in particular.

The place to feel for a blood **pulse** is in the neck. Do not try to feel the wrist pulses, because the casualty's body systems are likely to have closed down the blood flow in the outlying blood vessels, to save the more important blood flow to the so-called vital centres – brain, heart and lungs.

There are two big arteries, one lying on each side of the windpipe (Figure 3.3) and it is here you should place two fingers and feel for the pulse for several seconds.

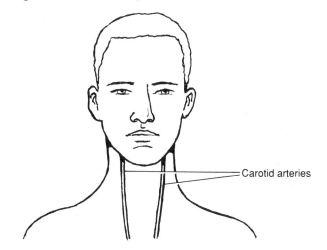

Carotid arteries

Figure 3.4 *Front view of the head and neck showing carotid arteries*

A person's heart may be pumping blood but they may have stopped breathing. In this case the heart will soon stop owing to lack of oxygen.

If you cannot find a pulse, you must start **heart massage** immediately (see below). Heart massage is more correctly termed *cardio-pulmonary resuscitation*, or sometimes *external chest compression*.

Chest compression (heart massage)

First check the **carotid pulse** (*not* the wrist pulse) in one of the two large arteries lying at the side of the windpipe in the neck. (Figure 3.3). Feel with two fingers pressed deep into the side of the neck.

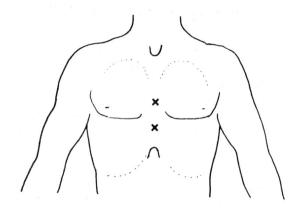

Figure 3.5 *Finding where to apply compression*

Think it over

Take your own carotid pulse, by counting it for 15 seconds and multiplying the number by 4 to get the beats per minute. Now take a friend's or a relative's carotid pulse to get practice in feeling for it.

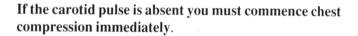

If the carotid pulse is absent you must commence chest compression immediately.

External chest compressions, if correctly performed, will artificially pump about one-third of the body's blood around the circulation, and if this blood contains oxygen it will keep the casualty alive for the time being.

The method squashes the heart between the vertebral column at the back and the rib cage/breastbone at the front. This action expels blood from the heart, towards the lungs and into the main artery (called the aorta). As you release the pressure, more blood is sucked into the heart from the big veins supplying it. You are therefore making the heart pump blood.

Method of chest compression

To be successful the pressure must be applied to the correct place.

1 Feel for the *notch* at the base of the neck between the two collar bones, and also for the *notch* where the ribs meet in the centre at the bottom of the rib cage (see Figure 3.5). Find the halfway point between these two notches, then find the halfway mark of the lowest of these halves.

2 Kneeling beside the casualty at the level of your marked spot, place the heel of your hand on this point and the heel of your other hand on top, interlocking the fingers together.

3 Lean forwards over the casualty with straight arms. Push firmly down until the chest is compressed at least 4 – 5 centimetres and then release. Keep your fingers off the chest, using only the heel of the lowest hand. Don't move the hands in between compressions.

4 You must aim for at least 80 pumps per minute. Experts agree that to help you keep to time, it is useful to say 'one and two and three and four …' up to fifteen, and then begin counting again.

Heel of your hand

Figure 3.6 *Applying compression*

Cardio-pulmonary resuscitation (CPR)

CPR is exhausting and if you are on your own you may not be able to continue for long. Therefore, before you start, shout or phone for some help.

While you are on your own carry out two breaths followed by fifteen chest compressions, followed by two breaths, fifteen compressions and so on. Don't stop to check pulses until you see some sign of blood circulation. If the heart restarts, check the breathing – if it is absent continue resuscitation. If there is breathing, place the casualty in the recovery position and recheck every 4 minutes.

If you have a helper, one of you can be at the head doing mouth-to-mouth while one is doing chest compressions. In this case one breath is given after every five compressions of the chest. Monitor the casualty's response as above. Exchange tasks every few minutes so that you can both keep it up for longer.

> **REMEMBER:**
>
> - *Don't practise on a living person!*
> - Join a class and get trained properly in the techniques. The best way to learn is to practise.
> - The ideas in this section will be easier to remember if you have tried them out in first aid training.

An unconscious patient who is both breathing and circulating blood must now be placed in the recovery position even if you think there may be injuries to the neck or back.

Remember to always use as many helpers as you can to keep the head, neck and spine in a line and well supported by helpers' arms and rolled blankets, coats etc. to lessen the movement.

· MONITORING LEVELS OF · CONSCIOUSNESS

The level of consciousness of a casualty can change over a period of time, and knowledge of these changes can be very important to a medical team when deciding on possible treatment. If at all possible the levels should be *noted and recorded by the first aider*. These levels can be assessed by examining the responses of the casualty to conversation, questioning and commands, and to painful stimuli. Figure 3.7 suggests a simple scheme.

Response level	Possible description
Responds well to normal conversation	'Fully conscious'
Responds only if asked clear questions	'Drowsy'
Gives wrong or muddled replies	'Confused'
Carries out only simple instructions (e.g. moving arm)	'Semi-conscious'
Body reacts only to painful stimuli (e.g. thumb pressure over a bone, pin prick)	'Unconscious'
No reaction to anything	'Deeply unconscious'

Figure 3.7 *Monitoring levels of consciousness by responses*

If the person is semi-conscious (only half conscious) or worse, always put him or her in the recovery position and check *airway*, *breathing* and *circulation* (pulse). You should monitor these vital signs every few minutes.

This is known to first-aiders as the **ABC rule**, and it provides you with the three important things to check for – and in the right order! Add to this – for an unconscious

THE RECOVERY POSITION

Experts agree that if more people knew how to put an unconscious person in the correct position, many more lives would be saved.

There is really no substitute for a trained person demonstrating the technique to you, who then watches you practise several times. You should try to do this with all first aid procedures, so if necessary join a local first aid class. Your local library will be able to tell you where.

The **recovery position** is a steady position which keeps the airway open, allows fluid (particularly vomit) to drain out of the mouth so that it does not enter the lungs. It also prevents the tongue from falling back and blocking the back of the throat.

Putting a casualty in the recovery position

The procedure is the same for a woman or a man

1. Open the airway.
2. Kneel alongside the casualty and straighten her legs.
3. Place the arm nearest to you at right angles to her body with the elbow bent and the palm facing skyward. (Some people like to tuck the nearest arm under the casualty's bottom.)
4. Take the other arm across her chest and tuck this hand palm downwards under her cheek to cushion her head. You will probably need to hold it there.
5. Cross the further ankle over the nearer one.
6. Grasping her hip, waistband and shoulder, turn her smoothly over to rest against your knees. Support her head as she rolls.
7. Adjust her head to lie on the hand so that it remains tilted backwards and the other bent arm gives stability (if you tucked the arm under the bottom, pull behind now to stop her rolling backwards – the two positions of the lower arm are equally acceptable, but slightly different).
8. Adjust the upper leg so that both hip and then knee are bent at right angles.

REMEMBER: IT IS BEST NOT TO LEAVE THE CASUALTY ALONE. IF YOU HAVE TO GO AND GET HELP, THEN RETURN AS SOON AS POSSIBLE.

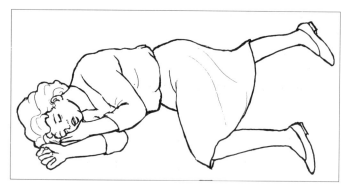

Figure 3.8 *The casualty in the recovery position*

patient – *monitoring* the levels of response and you are well on the way to coping with most serious emergencies.

You can now attempt a piece of work, which will also count towards core skills.

Task

Design an 'observation sheet' for recording the important observations you might make while dealing with a casualty at the site of an emergency. Decide how often you would make the observations and state exactly what and how you would be measuring/observing. What other information would it be sensible to include if you were making a thorough report, and what would you do with the information?

Keep your work on this task because it can count towards your core skills assessment.

Suspected spinal injury

In certain accidents or injuries the risk of **neck and spinal injury is considerable**. Such accidents include falls, road accidents and sports injuries.

You must, as explained above, make sure the airway is clear. It is possible to put the casualty in the recovery position, *but ensuring that head and neck are supported at all times* by at least one assistant. The head and neck are turned to be kept in line with the body at all times during the turn.

However, depending on the circumstances, it may well be wiser to watch and monitor breathing and pulse closely, and wait until the emergency services arrive. You will have to use personal judgement over this, depending on the state of the casualty's vital signs: is the pulse getting weaker, is the breathing becoming rapid and shallow etc. The decision will depend on how many assistants you can muster from the bystanders, and their experience. It will also depend on the likely time interval before the emergency services arrive.

This is all rather like trying to juggle four or five balls in the air when you have never tried to do it before – and now someone's life may depend on it. The most important thing is not to panic yourself. The principles of your action are really to try to weigh up the odds of keeping a seriously injured casualty alive whilst not making the injury worse.

> **Remember:**
> - *Approach*
> - *Assess*
> - *Act!*

TEMPORARY LOSS OF CONSCIOUSNESS

A **faint** is a temporary loss of consciousness arising from a lack of blood to the brain. The casualty falls to the ground and in doing so makes it much easier for the heart to get blood to the brain. This is, perhaps, nature's way of dealing successfully with the problem, and so an eager helper should not prop the person up again. In fact, people have suffered brain damage (and have even died) as a result of not being able to fall flat after fainting in a crowd (e.g. at a football match).

Figure 3.9 *Speeding the recovery from a faint*

Most people feel strange just before a faint – they experience a change of temperature, giddiness and confusion. Certain action at this point will usually prevent the faint – the person should bend right over so that the head hangs lower than the heart and take deep breaths until the blood flow to the brain improves and the victim feels better.

If the faint has occurred, leave the person lying down but raise the legs. Open a window to let in fresh air. Reassure the person as they recover. Sit them up gradually. Recovery is usually rapid and complete.

· A FIT, CONVULSION OR SEIZURE ·

These all mean the same thing and can be thought of as a feature of an over-sensitive brain. Some people have regular fits and are said to suffer from **epilepsy**, while others may have only one in their whole life.

After falling to the ground unconscious, the victim becomes rigid, breathing stops for a few moments so that the face and neck become purplish and the lips bluish. Then **spasms** shake the body – often quite violently. Frothing of saliva can occur and the person may urinate or pass a motion.

This is followed by relaxed muscles, normal breathing and a return of consciousness, often to be followed by a sleep or dazed period.

As the convulsion starts, make a space around the person and remove any objects likely to cause injury. Don't move the person unless they are in danger, and don't try to hold them down with any force. Allow the fit to pass away. *If you can protect the head then do so*, and loosen any clothing around the neck if possible.

After the fit, place the person in the recovery position and remain with them until fully recovered. Tell them tactfully what has happened. They may be embarrassed but should be reassured.

· ASPHYXIA ·

This difficult word, which comes from the Greek language, literally means 'no pulse'. However, in first aid it refers to any condition which results in a low level of oxygen being carried by the blood. Many accidents, illnesses or injuries can lead to asphyxia. Some of the most common are:

- smoke or gas fumes
- poisoning
- hanging/strangulation
- drowning
- crushing by soil, rock or crowds
- smothering by a pillow.

Recognition of asphyxia

- Quickened noisy breathing, often with gasping for breath.
- Bluish look to the lips, earlobes, fingertips and skin generally (called **cyanosis**).
- Widened nostrils and drawing in of the chest wall.
- Confusion, irritability, even unconsciousness.

Care procedure for asphyxia

1 Remove any obstruction to the airway quickly. The brain can only tolerate up to about 3 minutes without oxygen before its cells start to be damaged beyond repair.
2 If the person is conscious, provide reassurance and keep checking breathing and pulse.
3 If the person is unconscious, check breathing and pulse and resuscitate if these cease.
4 Call the emergency services. *Remember, speed is essential*.

· CHOKING ·

This may also lead to asphyxia and death. It occurs when breathing suddenly becomes obstructed, possibly by food stuck in the throat. It may also happen on drinking too much, and on taking a drug overdose. People witnessing the choking often fail to realise the seriousness of what is happening. Most deaths from choking could be avoided if people knew what to do, and did it!

With choking, the signs of asphyxia are present (see last section) and usually the victim is clutching at his neck, pointing or coughing. Do not let him run out of the room (if he does, follow and stay with him).

Care procedures for choking (except in a child)

Try this backslapping technique first.

1 Encourage calmness and give reassurance.
2 Bend the victim over so that the head is lower than the chest. This is so that gravity helps the obstruction to become loose.

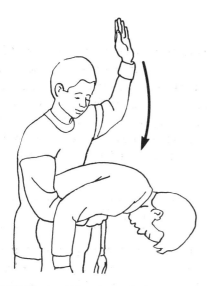

Figure 3.10 *The backslapping technique*

3 Give up to five strong, hard blows between the shoulder blades. Use the heel of your hand. The blows should be jarring as they are meant to force the obstruction out.
4 Encourage the casualty to cough at all stages.

If this doesn't dislodge the obstruction, then you must quickly try the **Heimlich manoeuvre** (the abdominal thrust). To do this:

1 Stand behind the casualty. Place your arms around the waist, make one hand into a clenched fist and grasp it with the other hand.
2 Your hand should be just under the ribs but above the tummy button (umbilicus). Now pull sharply *inwards* and *upwards* at the same time. What you are hoping to do is vigorously force air upwards to dislodge the obstruction. You should do this four or five times.
3 If the obstruction is still not released, then alternate the backslapping and Heimlich techniques and ask someone to seek medical help. Call an ambulance if you are in doubt.

The Heimlich manoeuvre or abdominal thrust should only be taught by experienced trainers.

Be aware that the casualty may at any time become unconscious. If this happens, check breathing and pulse. If they are present, give abdominal thrusts by sitting astride the casualty and using the heel of one hand covered by the other below the ribs and give several upward and inward thrusts.

If breathing and pulses are absent, commence resuscitation.

Care procedure for a child

Place the child over your knee with its head hanging down. Slap it between the shoulder blades *using less force than for an adult*.

Care procedure for a baby

Lie the baby along your arm, head and face downwards. Slap it between its shoulder blades *using much less force than for a child or adult*.

> **Remember:**
>
> *On a baby or child, only use abdominal thrust if you are trained, and then **only as a last resort**.*

• BLEEDING OR HAEMORRHAGE •

The body has efficient systems for closing off **wounds** and preventing **blood loss**. Unfortunately, when there is a massive bleed the systems don't get a good chance to work. Then help is required to stop the bleeding, prevent infection and the development of shock (which is dealt with in the next section). The first aider must know what to do.

The sight of blood can make some people feel faint, and it can be quite frightening if a lot of blood is lost in a short time.

There are three types of bleeding, just as there are three types of **blood vessels**:

- **artery damage** leads to arterial bleeding
- **vein damage** leads to venous bleeding
- **capillary damage** leads to capillary bleeding.

> **Arterial bleeding** spurts out at the same rate as the pulse. It is *bright red* in colour.
>
> **Venous bleeding** flows out steadily. It is *dark red* in colour.
>
> **Capillary bleeding** oozes out and clots readily. It is red in colour, neither bright nor dark.

Care procedure for bleeding

There are *two* main things to remember to do:

a *Raise* the bleeding part above the level of the casualty's heart. This simple procedure has saved many a person's life.

b Apply direct *pressure* to the wound for long enough to allow the protective systems to operate (about 10-15 minutes). If the wound is large, it may be necessary to actually hold the wound edges together with both hands.

Occasionally, it may not be possible to press directly on the wound because of the injury. Then indirect pressure is applied to the nearest point where an artery crosses a bone – called a **pressure point**. In an arm this is most likely to be in the upper arm on the inside surface. In a leg it will be halfway across the groin. Try feeling for these pulses on yourself.

After about 10 minutes release the pressure on the wound and observe whether the bleeding has nearly or completely stopped. If it has, bind a pad of **sterile gauze** over the wound with a bandage. If you have no first aid materials with you, tissues, handkerchief or similar will do, held in place with a tie, scarf, belt, tights etc. *Do not tie too tightly* because you do not want to cut off the blood supply. If the blood continues to seep through, put more *on top* of the existing. Do not attempt to remove your original dressing because you may disturb the clot and start the bleeding again.

If the blood loss is considerable, give the casualty first aid treatment for shock (as described in the next section).

With **internal bleeding** the symptoms of shock become apparent, and you might see blood appearing from a body opening (e.g. the mouth). Treat the person for shock and call immediately for an ambulance.

As usual, check and record **vital signs** – level of consciousness, breathing and pulse – and proceed as in Figure 3.11.

Breathing	Pulse	Conscious	Action
✔	✔	✔	Treat for shock
✔	✔	✘	Put in recovery position and monitor
✔	✘	✘	Cardiac compression
✘	✔	✘	Resuscitation
✘	✘	✘	CPR

Figure 3.11 *An action checklist for bleeding*

Nose bleeds

These are probably the most frequent bleeds apart from minor cuts and bruises. Sit the casualty with head forward and down, and get him or her to pinch the nostrils just below the bridge of the nose for 10 minute intervals until the bleeding stops. The person should not cough, sniff, spit or speak for fear of disturbing the clots. If the bleeding is excessive, take the person to a doctor or hospital.

▪ SHOCK ▪

This is a condition caused by the body tissues and organs not getting their normal supply of oxygen. It is often described as 'circulatory collapse'. Many conditions can produce shock, and it can lead to death.

Think it over

Study the diagram of causes of shock (Figure 3.12). Consider how each one leads to loss of oxygen to body tissues. If necessary consult a textbook of human biology.

Severe heart attack	Loss of body fluids Bleeding Burns Vomiting Diarrhoea	Toxins Infections Allergies Poisons

Shock

Figure 3.12 *Some causes of shock*

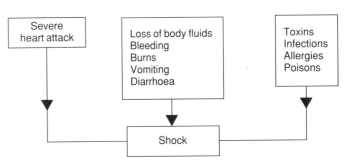

Task

An individual has between 5 and 6 litres of blood in their body, and when people donate some of their blood to the Blood Transfusion Service the amount usually taken is one pint. Convert the pint into cubic centimetres (cc) and into litres. Now calculate what percentage of (i) a woman's and (ii) a man's blood volume will have been donated. (Use the figure 5 litres for a woman and 6 litres for a man.)

There are very few after-effects from a blood donating session, so it is quite clear you can lose this percentage of blood without causing trouble.

Now convert the following volumes into litres and say which one is approximately half (50 per cent) of a person's total blood volume.

a 2 pints =

b 3 pints =

c 4 pints =

d 5 pints =

e 6 pints =

When between 2 and 4 pints of blood are lost, the signs and symptoms of shock are steadily increasing. By the time 5 pints have been lost the victim is usually unconscious.

Study Figure 3.13 very carefully – it shows the signs and symptoms chart. You will need to memorise the warning signs of developing shock.

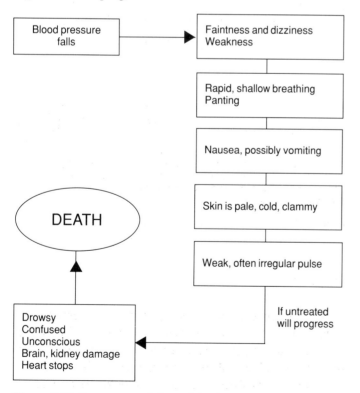

Figure 3.13 *Symptoms and signs of shock*

Care procedure for shock

1 Get help fast, but be cool and reassuring. If the casualty is anxious or in pain the shock will deepen.
2 Take action to stop any bleeding.
3 Lie the casualty down on a blanket, coat etc. with the head lower than the trunk and with feet raised. In this way, the heart will have less work to do. Raising the legs increases the blood pressure a little and helps drainage to the vital organs. Do not use a pillow.
4 Do not give anything to eat or drink in case an anaesthetic is required. If the casualty is thirsty, moisten the lips only.
5 Loosen all tight clothing, particularly around the neck, chest and waist, which may restrict blood circulation and breathing.
6 Keep the person warm by covering with blankets, coats etc. Do not use direct heat such as hot-water bottles.

Don't overdo the warmth. You do not want to divert blood away from the brain, heart and lungs or cause more loss of fluid by sweating.

7 Check and record vital signs every 10 minutes.
8 If consciousness is lost, open the airway and place the person in the recovery position.
9 If breathing or pulse stop, begin resuscitation immediately, continuing until medical help arrives.

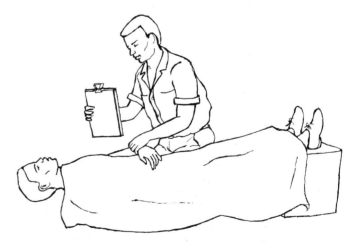

Figure 3.14 *Caring for a casualty in shock*

• ELECTRIC SHOCK •

Minor electric shocks may make you jump and do no permanent damage. Other electric shocks may give you severe burns (where the current enters and leaves the body) or painful muscle spasms. Electrical current affects the heart's rhythm and may make it stop. It also affects the breathing control centre in the brain.

> *Electricity can kill*

If somebody has had an electric shock, you too can easily become part of the accident *if you don't take precautions.*

> *Never touch the casualty until you are sure the electric current is turned off.*

If the accident involves high-voltage electricity (e.g. from a pylon or its cables) then you cannot go anywhere near until you have been told the supply is switched off. In fact high-voltage electricity can travel through the earth for a great distance.

In a domestic incident, switch off the supply at the socket or mains fuse box. Until this is done, avoid any wet areas or stand on insulating material such as wood, thick wads of paper (telephone directories are ideal) or a rubber or plastic mat.

If you cannot immediately switch off the current, under no circumstances should you touch the casualty directly. Use something (*not metal*) to pull or push the casualty away from the electrical source. Suitable materials are walking sticks, chairs, long-handled brushes etc.

Figure 3.15 *Make sure you don't become another casualty*

Care procedure for electric shock

Once the casualty is free of the electrical source, treat as for severe bleeding or shock. Consult Figure 3.11 for a memory check.

Treat any burns with clean dressings. If the accident appears serious, the casualty will need to visit a hospital because there may be unseen damage.

• CARDIO-VASCULAR PROBLEMS •

Heart disease is the most common cause of sudden death in Western countries. You have probably already studied factors which influence health and well-being, and found that the four most important factors influencing the development of heart diseases are:

- diet and obesity
- lack of exercise
- smoking
- stress.

There are many cardio-vascular conditions which could be described, but we shall consider here only those most commonly leading to medical emergencies. These, together with simple explanations of their causes, are shown in Figure 3.16.

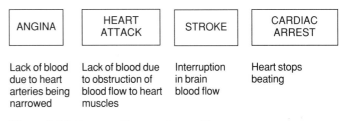

Figure 3.16 *Four cardio-vascular problems*

Angina

This condition is characterised by pain in the chest and arms brought on by exercise and/or excitement. The taking of special tablets (glyceryl trinitrate) which dissolve under the tongue, and resting, usually bring relief. If the victim does not improve then a heart attack should be suspected and appropriate action should be taken.

Heart attack

This is also known as a coronary or coronary thrombosis. Study Figure 3.17 which shows all the possible symptoms of a heart attack. A victim may suffer from some or all of them.

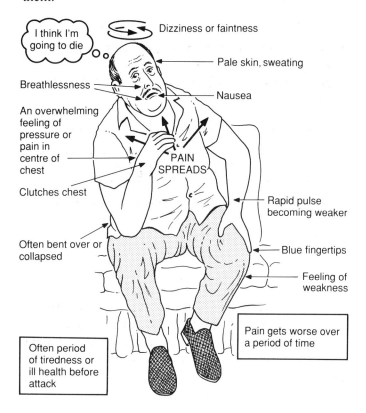

Figure 3.17 *The possible symptoms of a heart attack*

Consider making up your own figure using either paper, odd pieces of material, or papier-mâché. Think of an unusual way of displaying as many of the symptoms around it as you can. Then include the course of action you should follow when dealing with a heart attack.

You could aim to target the information at a particular client group, so that core skills can be obtained in communication. Include statistics and you are achieving even more!

Another idea might be to produce a leaflet or handout to leave with the members of your client group, so 'using images' could be achieved as well.

Care of a casualty with suspected heart attack

This will be presented in the form of a 'bullet' list so that you can rephrase and expand upon the points if you wish to undertake the task outlined above.

- Don't delay
- Dial 999 for an ambulance
- Reassure, keep calm
- Make comfortable and rest
- Put in half-sitting half-lying position
- Don't give food or drink
- Support knees and shoulders
- Check consciousness, breathing, pulse often

Now follow the decision diagram in Figure 3.18.

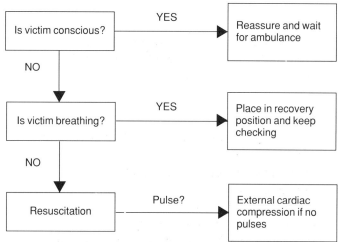

Figure 3.18 *A decision flow chart for suspected heart attack (or stroke)*

Recently it has been shown that if the conscious casualty is able to slowly chew on a single aspirin tablet, this will help the condition. Paracetamol and codeine will *not* do as substitutes. Remember not to give any water.

Remember:

It is important to know that survival from a heart attack is increased if help is given in the first hour.

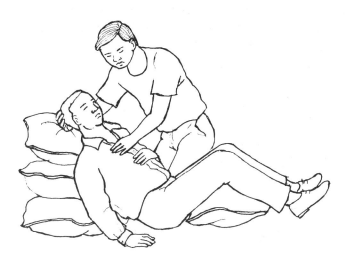

Figure 3.19 *Caring for a heart attack casualty*

Stroke

Stroke is the common name for a cerebro-vascular accident or CVA.

In a stroke, the casualty has symptoms related more obviously to the nervous system of the body. This is because the brain is suffering a lack of blood through a clot or bleeding. The precise symptoms depend on exactly which part of the brain is affected, but those most common are:

- being unable to move a limb or limbs on one side of the body
- being unable to speak or slurring of words
- a confused mental state
- a sudden severe headache
- uneven size of the pupils of the eyes
- loss of bladder or bowel control (called incontinence).

In addition the casualty may become unconscious.

Care of a stroke victim

Follow the same decision chart as for a suspected heart attack (Figure 3.18).

This time lie the victim down, supporting the head and shoulders. Turn the person's mouth to one side to divert any saliva dribble.

Cardiac arrest

The heart can stop beating as a result of a heart attack, electric shock, drug overdose, hypothermia (drastic cooling of the body) or asphyxiation. Clearly, there will be no breathing and no pulse.

- **Begin resuscitation right away** – *there must be no delay or the patient will die.*
- *Send for help immediately and keep resuscitation up until it arrives.*

· HEAT STROKE ·

There are two similar conditions which occur when the body temperature starts to rise because the natural regulating mechanisms have failed. These are:

- **heat stroke** and
- **heat exhaustion**.

It important to distinguish between them, because heat stroke is much more serious than heat exhaustion. Heat stroke can threaten someone's life, so it is important for you to know about both and how to spot the difference.

Features of heat stroke

- Illness with high fever, or long-time exposure to high temperatures.
- Temperature control centre in brain fails.
- Onset can be sudden but may be preceded by period of discomfort.
- Life-threatening
- Headache, dizziness, restlessness and confusion.
- Hot, flushed and dry skin.
- Full, bounding pulse.
- Response levels diminish rapidly.
- Body temperature above 40°C.

Care procedures for heat stroke

1 Get help quickly.
2 Remove to cool place.

3 Take off clothing and wrap in a cold wet sheet or garment until temperature falls.

4 Observe very carefully for signs of deterioration.

5 If unconscious, put in recovery position.

6 Check breathing, pulse, responses, and be prepared for resuscitation.

Features of heat exhaustion

- Comes from working/exercising in hot, humid conditions, or fluid-losing illness.
- Excessive sweating, loss of water and salt.
- Gradual onset.
- Usually less serious than heat stroke.
- Headache, dizziness, confusion.
- Pale, clammy skin.
- Rapid, weakening pulse.
- Muscular cramps.
- Breathing rate quickens.

Care procedures for heat exhaustion

1 If unconsciousness develops, send for help quickly, otherwise send to GP after treatment.

2 Remove to cool place.

3 Lie down, raise legs.

4 If conscious, give weak salt solution to drink (1 teaspoon to 1 litre of water).

5 Observe.

6 If unconscious, put in recovery position.

7 Check breathing, pulse, responses, and be prepared for resuscitation.

· BURNS AND SCALDS ·

Do you know the difference between a burn and a scald? If you don't, think carefully about the occasions when you, or someone close to you, has burned or scalded a part of their body, and then what caused the accident.

In fact, a burn is caused by a dry source of heat, such as a fire, while a scald is produced by hot fluids.

Think it over

In either your own home or your work placement, make a list of all the possible sources of (i) dry heat and (ii) wet heat which, if care is not taken, could lead to burns and scalds.

Task

1 *Either examine official statistics, or (with permission from the care supervisor) examine the accident records of your placement. Construct a pie chart to show the major causes of reported accidents (cuts, falls etc). What percentage of the total number are burns and scalds? In case of difficulty see Chapter 6.*

2 *In 1988, 915 people died as a result of fire accidents and 80 per cent of these deaths occurred in domestic fires. Work out the actual number of people who did not survive a fire in the home, and the mean number of deaths per fire accident, if there were 365 000 fires and 19 per cent of these were in the home.*

3 *Get in touch with your local Fire Brigade and, using your communication skills, find out how many people had fire accidents in their homes in your area during the last five years. Investigate the causes of the fires, and how many people needed first aid. You could also investigate another very important part of the role of the Fire Service, that of fire prevention.*

Fire officers regularly give talks to groups of people, ranging from Girl Guide groups to the elderly, including people with learning difficulties and those with physical handicaps. *You could invite a fire prevention officer to share with your group the methods used for delivering the fire prevention message to different client groups. Plan and arrange to give a display to a target group either in school or college, or to a special group in the community. After the event, write a brief description of your own performance including your strengths and weaknesses, and after discussion with your group state how you could improve the performance next time.*

You will have realised that safety is a very important aspect of this health emergency, because burns, particularly, are very often complicated by hazards of fire, explosion, smoke, fumes, road traffic, electricity, chemicals etc.

> **Remember:**
>
> *You must always make sure of your own safety before trying to treat the injured person.*

Care treatments for burns and scalds

Burns and scalds can vary in thickness as well as area. Generally speaking, only superficial burns of a small area will not need a doctor's attention – provided that adequate first aid treatment is given.

The skin is a waterproof, bacteria-proof layer on the outside of the body. If it is damaged then body fluids can escape, possibly resulting in shock. Also, bacteria can invade, causing **infection**. The cells of the body are made mainly of protein and water, and these two chemicals **retain heat** for quite a long time. These few facts determine the care treatment for burns.

It is usually not difficult to *recognise* a burn, but with minor injuries and with people who have communication difficulties you may have to inspect the area very carefully for signs of redness and swelling, and note stinging or pain symptoms.

There are just as many 'Dont's' to remember with burns as there are 'Do's'. Figure 3.20 is a convenient checklist.

DO	DON'T
✔ Cool the burned area with cold liquid for at least 10 minutes (20 minutes for chemical burns)	✘ Don't let hypothermia develop if the burnt area is extensive
✔ Remove tight items of jewellery or clothing	✘ Don't apply any creams, gels or ointments
✔ Cover with sterile dressing; use clean non-furry material with no sticky surface	✘ Don't remove anything sticking to the area
✔ Treat for shock	✘ Don't interfere too much or break blisters
✔ Dial 999 or fetch medical help quickly, if the size of the burn warrants it	✘ Don't use adhesive dressings

Figure 3.20 *First aid for burns or scalds*

Regardless of the *cause* of the burn or scald, the same general principles of treatment can be followed provided common sense is applied as well. For instance, eye burns must only have water poured on *gently*. Remember that you must protect yourself from chemicals by wearing gloves, and at all times be aware of the danger of water near to electricity.

Finally, if necessary, resuscitation and treatment for shock must be carried out immediately the initial cooling has been done.

• MUSCULO-SKELETAL INJURIES •

The **skeleton** is a framework made of **bones** to which **muscles** are attached by their tough extensions known as **tendons**. The place where two bones meet is called a **joint**, and this is strengthened by tough strands of material called **ligaments**.

A blow, fall, twist or wrench may cause a bone to break, crack or split. In a healthy body the force needed to do this is quite considerable. Sometimes the bone may instead become displaced. This is known as a **dislocation** (see page 114).

It is almost impossible to damage a bone in any of the ways described without also causing damage to the so-called **soft tissues**. Soft tissues are muscles, tendons, ligaments, blood vessels and nerves, and these surround the bones.

First, you need to be able to recognise the signs and symptoms that point towards bone and joint injuries. A **sign** is something the carer would notice – this is why observation skills are so important. A **symptom** is something the casualty complains about.

Signs	Symptoms
• Distortion	• Pain at or near the injury
• Signs of shock	• Tenderness at site
• Swelling	• Difficulty in moving
• Bruising	• History of blow or fall

Figure 3.21 *Recognising a fracture*

Most of the signs and symptoms in Figure 3.21 will be present if a bone is fractured. If you are in doubt, *treat the injury as a fracture*.

Remember, too, that a casualty may require an operation later, so you must *never* allow them to have anything to eat or drink.

Care for suspected fracture

Your responsibility is to arrange for the person to be transported to hospital safely, and to prevent any further damage to the injured part by stopping movement of the bones, as they may damage blood vessels and nerves.

The casualty will need your constant reassurance to cope with the pain (and often shock). You should try to remain still and calm.

An **open fracture** is one where the skin is broken and the injury is exposed to the air. There is therefore the possibility of contamination by bacteria from surrounding skin, air or dirt. There may be considerable bleeding which needs controlling first.

A **closed fracture** is not open to the air because the skin is unbroken.

- Step 1 (open fracture care begins here)
  Control the bleeding by covering the wound with a sterile dressing or clean pad. Be careful not to touch the wound with your own fingers, and gently apply pressure to control the bleeding. Doing this will also help to prevent infection. Do not press on protruding bone ends.
- Step 2
  Pad the wound (with soft padding such as cotton wool) over the dressing and secure both firmly, taking care not to hinder the circulation of blood beyond the dressing.

Think it over

You can test for circulation of the blood beyond the dressing by pressing on the nail of the finger or toe, releasing and checking to see that the pink colour under the nail returns quickly. Try this for yourself on a fingernail.

- Step 3 (closed fracture care begins here)
  Support the injury above and below with hands until the part is immobilised.

Lower limb (leg) fractures

Secure the injured part to an uninjured part wherever

possible – unless a better alternative can be found. Move the injured part as little as possible, so take the 'good' part to the 'bad'!

Pad all bony points and fill hollows to prevent movement. Then tie the two parts together above and below the break in the bone, as many times as practically possible.

Give emotional support and send for the emergency services. Treat for shock if necessary, and check circulation beyond the break about every 10 minutes.

Figure 3.22 *Using the good leg to support the injury*

Give emotional support and treat for shock if necessary. It may be possible to take the casualty to hospital without calling for an ambulance.

Figure 3.23 *A sling support for a broken arm*

Task

Carry out a simple survey of 50 or more people across stated age bands to find the incidence of bone fractures they have had and their age at the time of the injury. Remember that the older people are, the more life stages (and therefore age bands) they have passed through, and vice versa. You may need to consider this in your study if you wish for a higher level core skill.

Display and tally these results in a chart and complete with a graphical display. Discuss the trends shown by the figures and predict the likelihood of sustaining bony fractures at various life stages, and the probability of having a bone fracture in a lifetime.

Upper limb (arm) fractures

The principles are the same as for a suspected broken leg. Carefully place padding around the injury and in any hollows. Using a **sling** to support the arm across the chest, in as comfortable a position as possible while elevating the part as much as you can. Remember, raising any part helps to drain fluid, so reducing swelling and helping to stop bleeding.

Then with a broad folded bandage, tie the injured limb to the body. Tie the knot at the front on the uninjured side and allow the casualty to maintain a sitting position. If the arm cannot be brought across the chest because the injury is to the elbow, then carefully and gently tie the unbent limb to the trunk, above and below the injury to secure it comfortably.

Injuries to the backbone or spine

The **spine** is a bony column which consists of many small bones called **vertebrae**. Each vertebra has a hole through its centre to allow the **spinal cord** to pass through as it travels down the trunk delivering nerves to different areas of the body (see Fiigure 3.24). *The danger with spinal injuries, and fractures in particular, is the possibility of damage to this main nervous pathway.* Such damage can result in loss of sensation or mobility, either temporarily or **permanently**.

You might suspect a spinal injury if the accident was a fall, or a sudden forceful movement to the head, neck or back (such as in a motor vehicle or sports accident), or something heavy falling on the spine.

The symptoms and signs shown in Figure 3.21 will still apply, but you might also see a bend or twist in the normal curves of the spine and the casualty might tell you about lack of feeling or being unable to move properly. They are likely, if conscious, to become upset, so you will need to reassure them quietly and calmly. They may describe the change in feeling as 'heavy' or 'strange', so you will need to listen carefully. You must send for the emergency services immediately and prevent further damage.

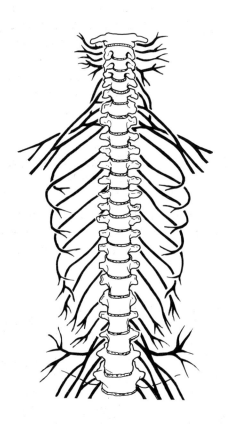

Figure 3.24 *The spine and spinal nerves*

Care of a conscious casualty

- Step 1
  As always, check your own safety first and then that of the casualty. If the casualty is not in danger and is conscious, then *do not move him or her from the position in which they are found*. Reassure and instruct them to keep still.
- Step 2
  Support the head by placing your hands over the ears. Keep supporting the head until help arrives.
- Step 3
  If you are not on your own, get a helper to place rolled supportive materials–clothes, blankets etc. around the subject's head, neck and trunk. It is possible to improvise a neck collar if you suspect neck injury, but this can only be done if you have assistance as *you must not remove your supporting hands*.

Care of an unconscious casualty

- Step 1
  Resuscitation has **priority** over the spinal injury. (Priority means it comes earlier and is more important). Check for breathing and pulse and proceed as follows:
- Step 2
  If breathing and pulses are present, the airway must be protected and you are back to juggling those balls in the air (see suspected spinal injury and the recovery position).
- Step 3
  If, however, breathing and/or pulses are **absent**, then CPR performed gently must take priority over the injury. The casualty may die while you worry about a fracture and clearly this comes second.
  It is important to consider the injury when undertaking CPR. If you have to turn the casualty on his back then you must get as much help as you can, keeping the head, body and legs in a straight line for the turn (which will be more of a roll). You must be very gentle in tilting the head but this must still be done or the airway will not be open for your life-giving air to enter their lungs. For details refer to Artificial Ventilation and CPR.

Dislocation

This happens when a strong force pushes a bone out of place. It may also cause muscle and other tissue damage in the same way as a fracture. It is often very difficult to tell a dislocation from a fracture.

Do *not* try to replace the bones in their normal positions, Treat the casualty as for a broken bone. Restrict movement as previously described, and arrange for transport to hospital.

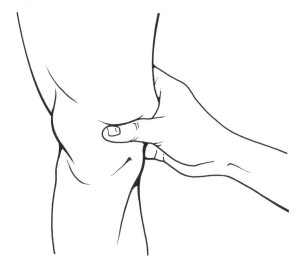

Figure 3.25 *A dislocation*

Sprains and strains

This type of injury occurs when a ligament, tendon or muscle has been stretched and torn. Such injuries can be surprisingly painful and take a long time to heal. If you are sure no bone is broken, then treat the injury as follows.

- Step 1
  Remove any tight clothing, including shoes. There is likely to be considerable swelling because fluid leaks into the damaged tissues. Now raise the part to help in the drainage of fluid from the injury, and of course rest the area.
- Step 2
  Wrap something cold fairly tightly around the injury. This can be an ice pack, cold wet towel or even a bag of frozen peas wrapped in a clean cloth. Then stop the part from moving by wrapping over the cold material (often called a **compress**) with bandages and soft padding.

The casualty should seek medical help as soon as possible, to make sure there are no broken bones.

Think it over

Try applying a compress to yourself, using one of the above suggested cold materials or anything else you can think of. Bandage it firmly to a leg joint to stop movement. What does it feel like?

What would you now do if you were out hill-walking and a long way from a telephone? Most sprains are at the ankle, due to the foot turning suddenly on rough or slippery ground. Might this be a time when you would try to leave the shoe on? What might you do as a half measure (compromise)? So what do you think would be the best sort of footwear for this type of walking?

Task

Design a simple leaflet suitable for giving out to people with learning difficulties, to explain the right clothing and footwear for a day out walking in the country. Specify a simple first aid kit to put in their bags, remembering that many people will not be able to carry anything very heavy.

CHEMICAL AND POISONOUS SUBSTANCES

Poisons are substances that, when taken into the body, can cause damage. They may be breathed in, swallowed, absorbed through the skin, splashed in the eye or injected.

It is often obvious from the smell or the presence of containers what the poison is likely to be. Keep any evidence to go with the casualty when the ambulance arrives, and you may need to keep any vomit!

Care procedure for poisoning

1 First make sure you will not get contaminated with the poison yourself.
2 Quickly assess the casualty. Notice any special signs which may tell you something (e.g. vomiting, burns, blisters, fits, unconsciousness).
3 Check breathing, pulse and consciousness level.
4 Resuscitate if appropriate, but be careful not to get affected if the person has swallowed a poison. This is an occasion when mouth-to-nose resuscitation might be more suitable.
5 Dial 999 and say you think it is poisoning.
6 Do *not* make the casualty vomit, particularly with corrosive or burning substances. Throat tissues will get damaged a second time. It is better to try to dilute the poison by giving quantities of water or milk to drink, *but only if the casualty is conscious.*
7 If the person is unconscious, but breathing, place him or her in the recovery position to reduce the risk of inhaling vomit.
8 Monitor level of consciousness, breathing and pulse.

When the poison has been *inhaled* rather than swallowed you should follow the same basic treatment. However, protect yourself from fumes, and remove the casualty to fresh air as quickly as possible.

When the poison has been absorbed through the skin, again follow the same basic treatment. In this case wash chemicals off with large quantities of water, allowing it to drain away.

· PROTECTION FROM INFECTION ·

When a part or whole of a person becomes contaminated by disease, we say he or she is **infected**.

Such disease is caused by tiny organisms (*micro-organisms*) called 'pathogens'. Micro-organisms are too small to be seen properly without a microscope, and many need special types of microscope to be seen at all.

Micro-organisms are commonly **bacteria**, **viruses** or **fungi**. They multiply quickly under the right conditions – moisture, warmth and a food supply. The human body can supply all of these, hence the dangers and ease of transferring infection from person to person.

You may feel worried about 'catching' a disease when you are caring for someone, and particularly if you are carrying out first aid in difficult circumstances, in dirty places, and with spills of body fluids around. However, if you use hygienic practices and sensible precautions you should not increase the likelihood of catching something after dealing with a health emergency.

You may be particularly worried about two virus infections that have received much publicity – hepatitis B and HIV (the AIDS virus). It is very comforting to know that no recorded cases exist of first-aiders getting either of these infections from carrying out care procedures in emergencies. However, it must be stated that there *is* a risk with any contact with body fluids, *and correct practice should be followed.*

Unbroken skin is an excellent barrier to most micro-organisms (also known as 'microbes' and 'germs'). It is *broken* skin which is most susceptible to infection. The situation is particularly unsafe when a wound is dirty, exposed to the air and touched by fingers.

Bleeding helps to 'wash' wounds naturally, and the body has some internal defence mechanisms. Medical science has developed immunisation programmes. All of this helps us to avoid many of the infections to which we might otherwise surrender.

> **Remember:**
>
> *When you are caring for others, it makes sense to ensure that all your own immunisation programmes are up -to-date.*

Task

*Research the health and safety policy of your school, college or work placement. Find out the clauses (sections) relating to the prevention of the transfer of infection from one person to another (known as **cross-infection**).*

Are these sections easily understood by non-scientists? How many staff know of the existence of such clauses? Are the guidelines followed? If not, why not? Are resources adequate?

This research could provide you with the opportunity for a survey and interpretation of results.

Good practices to prevent infection

1 Always use disposable gloves, if they are available.
2 If they are not available, try to improvise (e.g. put your hands inside plastic bags).
3 If the casualty is conscious and able, instruct him in dealing with his own wounds, especially if gloves are not available.
4 Wash your hands before and after dealing with wounds.
5 Handle everything as little as possible, particularly the wound.
6 Try not to breathe directly on to a wound, or *sneeze etc.*
7 Cleanse a wound from the centre outwards, because normal skin is full of micro-organisms.
8 Cover any broken skin on *your hands* with waterproof plasters before handling wounds.
9 Wash any surfaces which have been in contact with spills or body fluids with a solution of bleach or disinfectant (1:10 dilution).
10 Dispose carefully of all used, dirty materials by sealing in a plastic bag and then burning.

Task

1 If you need to make up 4 litres of bleach cleaning solution, how much undiluted bleach would you use to make a 1:10 solution? How much water would you add?

2 Someone has a bleeding duodenal ulcer, vomits blood, and the area the blood spill covers is a circle approximately 0.45 metres in diameter and 5 millimetres in depth. Calculate the approximate quantity of blood lost.

Tetanus

Some types of bacteria thrive in places where there is not much air. The bacteria which cause **tetanus** or **lockjaw** are like this, and they normally live in soil and dirt.

Tetanus used to be invariably a fatal disease – very few people recovered if they developed it. Even today it is still a very serious condition, so most people are vaccinated against tetanus at an early age. However, they still require further injections every 10 years, called 'boosters'. Unfortunately the majority forget to do this.

To protect a casualty against this dreadful disease, you should encourage them to see a doctor if they are not up-to-date with their injections and have suffered an open wound. This advice is very important for long, penetrating wounds such as those from garden forks, rose thorns or dog bites, because the bacteria get left at the end of a 'tunnel' where the air is scarce and multiply readily.

A good first-aider, then, will always ask a casualty about tetanus injections and recommend as needed.

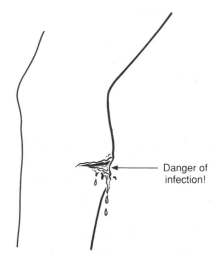

Danger of infection!

Figure 3.26 *What a dog bite might look like*

GENERAL CONSIDERATIONS IN HEALTH EMERGENCIES

When you suddenly meet an accident or are called to help someone who is ill, it is important that you don't just leap in and start to react without thinking. It only takes a few moments to consider your options carefully, and weigh up the possible results of what you might do.

Use the flow chart in Figure 3.27 to help you decide in what order to treat injuries.

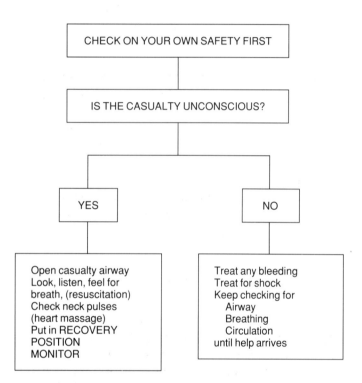

Figure 3.27 *Chart to show priority action*

Road traffic accidents can be very frightening. The blood, broken glass, bent and twisted metal and possibly fire all serve to increase the horror of the scene. One of the simplest things anyone can do in this case is turn off the car's ignition switch to reduce the fire risk. Leave any trapped casualties where they are unless they need urgent resuscitation, because of the risk of neck and spinal injury. Even if you cannot move a trapped casualty you can still protect the airway *by lifting the head gently and pulling the chin forward and up.*

Think it over

Do you remember Approach, Assess and Act (suspected spinal injury)? Look back to page 102 then read on.

APPROACH carefully, look around and be sure that you will not put yourself in danger and increase the number of people ill or injured. Look at Figure 3.28 and work through the possible dangers you might come across in some situations.

Road accident	• Being run over especially in the dark or fog • Fire – petrol being set alight by cigarettes or sparks • Chemicals – fumes, fire, poisons
Drowning	• Currents – carried out too far • Cramp – too close to meals, and coldness • Being dragged under by casualty in panic • Hypothermia • Lack of experience in life-saving
Fire	• Burns • Fumes – difficulty in breathing • Becoming trapped in fire as well • Parts of building may collapse
Gas	• Risk of being in an explosion • Risk of fire • Suffocation • Poisoning
Electricity	• Electrocuting yourself • Risk of fire

Figure 3.28 *Types of dangers which may be experienced by first-aider*

ASSESS the situation carefully. Can you see all the people who are hurt? Sometimes people are thrown from moving vehicles over hedges, or are carried by a fast current downstream.

Do you need the emergency services? You certainly will need to call the fire brigade if there is any danger of fire or if anyone is trapped or stuck. This service has all the equipment for such jobs. The police will usually be informed in road traffic accidents, suspicious circumstances, and where there is injury and death. However, this is not your responsibility as a first-aider. Any problems associated with the sea and boats will involve the lifeboat service.

You will definitely need to call the ambulance service in cases of:

- unconsciousness
- absence of (or difficulties with) breathing
- absence of pulses
- haemorrhage (serious bleeding)
- suspected heart attack
- severe burns or scalds
- fractures of skull, back or legs (other fractures need hospital treatment but don't necessarily need an ambulance).

Sometimes it may be more appropriate to call the local doctor if you know he or she is much closer (such as in a small village). This is an occasion when you must include common sense in your 'first aid box'!

Having assessed the situation you should ACT. *Who will you help first if several people have been injured?* Give about 30 seconds to each one, while quickly assessing

their condition. Go to the quiet ones first – if someone is screaming, groaning or crying you can be sure that they are breathing at least!

Now the question is: are there other people around (bystanders) who can help you or who are more experienced than you – people *you* could assist? Try shouting for help as you work because there may be someone within hearing distance who you cannot see.

BUT DON'T WAIT. The most serious cases cannot be left while you go to get help. You need to be there to keep the airway open, carry out resuscitation and external chest compression if required.

This poses a very difficult problem if the first-aider is on his/her own. In cases of serious heart attack, for example, the longer the delay in getting the person to hospital the smaller the chance of survival. However, you must not leave a patient in a condition which seems likely to change for the worse (an **unstable condition**). If the patient is conscious, breathing well, has controlled bleeding if any, is in the recovery position and appears unlikely to change, it may be permissable to seek help. Otherwise, stay with the patient until help arrives.

Summoning an ambulance

If you are going to summon an ambulance you must know what to do and say. If you are taking charge and sending someone else you must be capable of telling *them* what to say. Make sure they can tell the message and ask them to return to let you know how long the ambulance is likely to be, and whether there are any special instructions to follow.

Find a place where you can use a telephone. Don't look only for public call-boxes, use common sense. Houses, shops and public houses usually have telephones.

*Dial 999 and ask for an ambulance.
It is a free service.*

This is what happens:

a The operator asks you which service you require.

b Ask for 'ambulance'.

c The operator then asks for the phone number you are calling from. This can be found on the phone dial or on a notice in the box.

d The ambulance control officer will then come on to the line and ask for:

- the location of the accident
- the nature of the accident
- how many people are hurt
- what their condition is (e.g. unconscious, bleeding)
- what other risks there are (e.g. fire, fumes).

Give your answers as distinctly as you can. If necessary provide landmarks to help the ambulance crew. Put lights on and post lookouts if you have assistance.

e Sometimes, aid instructions are given by the ambulance controller. Listen carefully.

Task

Contact the local ambulance depot to see whether a speaker can come to talk to your group. Alternatively, if you are carrying out self-supported study, can you make an appointment to talk to a controller?

Find out how many calls a day the service has, and the main reasons for the calls. Present the information in the form of a bar chart, and present this by using a statistics software package. Find out how much an ambulance costs to buy, maintain and staff for 24 hours. Ask the ambulance staff what, in their opinion, is the most useful first aid measure and what is the most harmful thing that people do, thinking they are helping.

Safe lifting

First, a word of warning. In some care establishments, unpaid volunteers (particularly young people) are not allowed to lift clients. This is to protect both the volunteer and the client against personal injury and to meet the insurance requirements.

Within your GNVQ work you are required to describe and explain safe lifting techniques and to give a practical demonstration with supporting notes. This does *not* mean that you have to lift clients to achieve competence, although many health and social care students may lift in other activities. It is important for your own protection that you are correctly taught and expertly supervised during your demonstration.

Recently, the European Community has introduced new regulations for manual lifting which updates an existing UK law called the Health and Safety at Work act. The new law means that both the employee and employer have responsibilities for safe practice while lifting and moving clients. Figure 3.29 gives a summary.

Think it over

*It is sometimes difficult to tell the exact difference between skills and procedures. You may know the procedure for lifting but be unable to carry out the lift. This can be a dangerous situation because you may, in fact, **be skilled in an unsafe practice**. Think about this for a moment. The carrying out of a safe lift is a skill which requires practice and coaching by an experienced trainer, who has the ability to notice and correct any faults you may have.*

Principles of lifting

1 *Assess the lift*

- Can the client help themselves?
- Are mechanical aids available?
- Is there enough space?
- How many lifters should be involved?
- Is suitable clothing being worn?

2 *Plan the lift*

- What is to be done?
- Is everyone informed?
- Who will give instructions?

3 *Carry out the lift*

- Never lift with your back twisted.
- Make sure you keep balanced.
- Where possible, avoid stooping.
- Get close to the load – never lift at arms' length.
- Always start with your knees bent.
- Use your buttock and thigh muscles to take most of the weight.

Employer responsibilities
- Provide training at start of job and each year
- Record training and ensure it is satisfactory
- Supply mechanical aids to lifting
- Make sure employees are medically fit to work
- Develop a code of practice for lifting clients
- Assess the risks and take action to reduce risks
- Record the assessment
- Avoid lifting by humans whenever possible

Employee responsibilities
- Take reasonable care for your own and others' safety
- Co-operate with employer in developing codes of practice and reporting risks in lifting

Figure 3.29 *Summary of EC regulations when lifting*

Your trainer will tell you the different types of lift. They must not be practised simply from following pictures in a book. The trainer will watch you and give you *feedback* on your performance.

Remember:

Never lift a client if you are not allowed to do so and if you have not been trained by an expert.

Apart from in the care setting, you may also be required to lift in a first aid situation. However, the same principles of lifting apply. If you can make a casualty comfortable on the floor and *there is no danger*, it is usually better to leave them there until expert help arrives. If this is impossible, and lifting is essential, you will have to assess the speed required. If it is not very

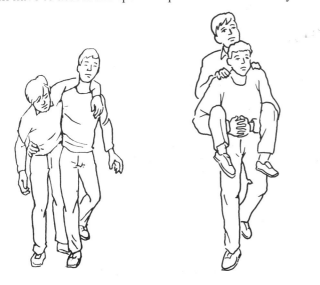

Figure 3.30 *The human crutch and piggy-back techniques*

urgent, try to plan using stretchers. These may be improvised with stout poles through buttoned jacket sleeves if nothing else is suitable.

If the casualty is conscious and able to walk, use the **human crutch technique**. Pass the person's arm on the injured side around your own neck and put your arm around the person's waist. Walk slowly with small steps. This method can also be used with two people, one on each side.

If the person is not able to walk, then a 'piggy-back' is useful. Tell the casualty to hold on tight!

Self-assessment test

1   Which of the following is not a symptom or sign of a fractured bone?
   a   Pain in the injured part.
   b   Distortion or deformity of the injured part.
   c   Blistering over the injured part.
   d   Swelling around the injury.

2   Abdominal thrusts are used in cases of:
   a   Constipation.
   b   Poisoning.
   c   Heart attacks.
   d   Choking.

3   Which of these is a symptom?
   a   Pallor.
   b   Skin colour changes.
   c   Lowering of consciousness.
   d   Complaint of pain.

4   You have just started your journey down the motorway, when two vehicles crash in front of you. What is your first action after getting out of your own vehicle now safely parked?
   a   Look for all the casualties.
   b   Resuscitate the nearest casualty.
   c   Check that it is safe for you to approach the crashed vehicles.
   d   Telephone for assistance.

5   In an emergency situation, concerning an unconscious casualty, you should check the pulse by feeling for:
   a   the radial pulse
   b   the carotid pulse
   c   the thumb pulse
   d   the wrist pulse.

6 In first aid, it is important to understand the ABC rule. What do these initials mean?
   a Any Blood Circulation.
   b Any Breathing and Circulation.
   c Air, Breathing and Circulation.
   d Airway, Breathing and Circulation.

7 A faint is:
   a temporary loss of consciousness
   b temporary loss of unconsciousness
   c permanent loss of consciousness
   d permanent loss of unconsciousness.

8 Your next door neighbour calls for help and when you rush round her ten year old daughter is having an epileptic fit on the sitting room floor. You assist the mother by:
   a holding the little girl down
   b moving the daughter into the kitchen
   c making sure the daughter does not injure herself
   d sitting her up.

9 Mouth to mouth resuscitation works because:
   a you are warming the casualty up
   b you are cooling the casualty down
   c you are giving carbon dioxide to the casualty
   d you are giving oxygen to the casualty.

10 It is important to compress the chest in the right place for effective external chest compression. This place is to be found by feeling for the notch between the two collar bones and the notch between the lowest joined ribs and:
   a halving the distance between them
   b doubling the distance between them
   c halving the distance and halving the lowest half
   d halving the distance and halving the upper half.

11 With two emergency helpers, the ratio of breaths to chest compressions should be:
   a one breath to every five compressions
   b one breath to every ten compressions
   c one compression to every five breaths
   d one compression to every ten breaths.

12 The brain cannot survive without oxygen under normal conditions for:

   a more than five minutes
   b more than three minutes
   c more than thirty minutes
   d more than thirteen minutes.

13 You are required to treat a person for shock at the scene of an accident. Would you:
   a lie the person completely flat
   b raise the head and lower the legs
   c lower the head and raise the legs
   d sit the person up and keep warm.

14 When approaching a victim of electric shock you could stand on insulating material such as:
   a a metal sheet like a tray
   b wads of paper like a telephone directory
   c wet carpet
   d wet cloth.

15 A substance which, when chewed slowly, helps when a client has a heart attack is:
   a aspirin
   b paracetamol
   c glyceryl trinitrate
   d pure glycerin.

16 You happen to find yourself one of the first to arrive on the scene of a very nasty motorway accident. Describe how you would recognise someone suffering from shock.

17 You went to another person in the same accident and immediately suspected his heart was not beating. Describe the signs you would have noticed to reach this conclusion.

18 Describe the steps you would take to maintain an open airway in an unconscious person.

19 A 45-year old smoker in the establishment where you work suffers a heart attack, explain how you would react.

20 What must you take care NOT to do when treating burns?

Fast Facts

Airway The passageway which includes the mouth, nose, throat and windpipe (trachea).

Angina (Pectoris) Pain brought on because the heart is deprived of oxygen carrying blood in the right quantities.

Asphyxia Suffocation, a lack of oxygen in the blood.

Burn/scald Skin damage due to heat – burn by dry heat, scald by wet heat.

Coma Unable to be roused.

Consciousness A state of mental awareness in which a person asks and replies to questions in a normal manner.

Coronary thrombosis A heart attack, a blockage in a blood vessel supplying the heart causing death of a piece of heart muscle.

CPR: Cardio Pulmonary Resuscitation Reviving both heart and lung function.

Dislocation Displaced bones at a joint.

Fracture Broken or cracked bone.

Heat exhaustion Salt and water deficiency of the body.

Heat stroke The brain is unable to control the temperature of the body.

Poisoning A substance which damages health on entering the body.

Recovery position A recommended stable sideways position of the body which minimises the risk of inhalation of vomit and protects the airway.

Resuscitation A method of reviving or bringing back to life.

Shock A condition which arises through a lack of circulating blood volume.

Signs Observations made by a first aider.

Sprain Damage to ligaments and tendons surrounding a joint.

Symptoms Sensations or feelings which the casualty describes.

Unconsciousness Lack of awareness of surroundings and inability to give reliable responses.

HEALTH AND SOCIAL CARE SERVICES

chapter **4**

This chapter is about people, their health and care needs, the services available to meet those needs, and the 'rights' of people when using the services.

The chapter starts by explaining the organisation of health and care services at central, regional and local levels. Then the focus is on *people* – as individuals, as service users and as care workers. The 'rights' of clients as consumers of the services are then covered.

· THE CARE INDUSTRY MAZE ·

The care industry is vast. On its own, the **National Health Service** (NHS) is the biggest employer in Europe. But the NHS is only one strand of the industry. Local Authority social services departments form a second strand, thousands of voluntary organisations a third strand, and private health and care services a fourth strand. Consider where health and care services are provided: in hospitals, residential homes, clinics, doctors' surgeries, dentists' practices and in people's own homes, amongst others. Think of the towns, cities and rural areas where these establishments are found and the number of people who work in these settings. *This is the care industry.*

On completion of this first part of the chapter you should be able to:

- give an account of the health and care services available to meet people's needs
- describe the organisation of health and care services at central, regional, and local levels
- discuss the purpose of the main services
- explain the ways in which the services are connected to each other.

When people need to use the care services because they are ill or their social circumstances have changed, it helps if they are able to understand where to go for help or assistance. Most people know at least how to contact their general practitioner (GP) if they are sick and, if they require other forms of health care, the GP is one of the people who can refer them on to the appropriate person or source of help.

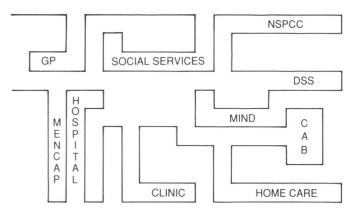

The health and caring maze

It is particularly important for all workers in the health and care field to know and understand the organisation of the health and care services, because it is highly likely that clients will ask for information about them.

Think it over

Can you think of any other reasons for needing to know about health and care services?

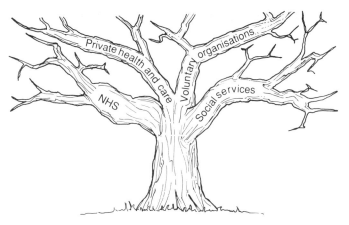

The field of health and care

The two main services in the field of health and care are the NHS and the social services. These are provided by organisations of different types, with different responsibilities, and operating at different levels.

There is a *hierarchy* of organisations, which means that some of these organisations have control of others or are seen to be more important than others.

Many of the organisations are **statutory** – that is, they have been established because Parliament has passed a law which requires them to be set up to provide a service or a range of services for citizens.

Health and care services are also provided by private and voluntary organisations. A **private** organisation is one run by an individual person or group of people, often on a profit-making basis and on the lines of a business. A **voluntary** organisation, too, is run by private individuals. The main aim is to provide a service for people in need of help where there may be a gap in existing statutory provision. Voluntary organisations are run on a not-for-profit basis.

Task

Look in textbooks, magazines, a telephone directory or use other sources of information such as TV and radio to identify:

- *private health or social care providers*
- *local and national voluntary*

organisations providing similar services.

Create your own mini-directory of services using the information. Divide your directory into three sections, for voluntary services, one for private services and one for statutory services. List the names, addresses and telephone numbers for the services. Give a brief summary of what each of the services provides. If you have access to one, use a computer to produce your directory.

The *central government departments* responsible for services are shown in the chart in Figure 4.1. Within each department there may be services which are administered centrally or locally. Some examples of how health and social care services are administered are:

- CENTRALLY
  NHS
  Benefits
  Pensions
- LOCALLY
  Housing and public health
  Children's services
  Schools
  Elder welfare
  Services for special needs.

Name of department	Areas of responsibility
Department For Education (DFE)	Schools, colleges, universities, research
Department of Social Security (DSS)	Provision of benefits (e.g. income support, child benefit)
Department of Health (DoH)	Health services (e.g. primary health care, hospitals, social services)
Department of the Environment (DoE)	Housing, planning

Figure 4.1 *Central government departments in health and care*

There is a further division that you should know about when considering services provided by statutory organisations. While statutory services *must* be provided, **permissible** services *can* be provided if there is sufficient funding available.

Task

Within the range of voluntary services in your area, choose one agency and investigate its work. How does it fit into the provisions provided by statutory and private agencies in the area?

· THE HEALTH SERVICES ·

The provision of health services can be seen as dividing into two separate strands: primary services and district/regional services.

Primary health services

Primary health services are provided by professional people who are often the first line of call if there is a problem. General practitioners (GPs), dentists, opticians and pharmacists are the most obvious examples. This provision is overseen in an area by the Family Practitioners Committee, which keeps a register of services and monitors the complaints of service users.

The GP's surgery is usually the first point of call if you feel unwell. The GP will, if necessary, refer you to the other services you need. For this reason, the staff at the surgery are often known as the **primary health care team**. The 'team' consists of the GP, the district nurse, the health visitor, local practice nurse and the community psychiatric nurse. Sometimes a social worker is included. They are all based full-time or part-time at the local surgery.

Each member of the team has a specific role, and each one **complements** the others to provide overall care. Nowadays a GP's surgery offers a wide range of services, including 'well man' and 'well woman' clinics and possibly some minor surgical treatments. They are interested in preventing illness as well as curing illness.

All citizens can be registered with a particular GP to get treatment, although someone can register as a temporary patient if visiting another area.

You register with a dentist in the same way as with a doctor. Dentists often recommend that you should make six monthly visits for check-ups regardless of whether there is anything wrong. If you do not do this you may find that the dentist will only treat you subsequently as a private patient. All children under the age of 16 (or under 19 if in full-time education) are treated free by the dentist under the NHS system. Others have to pay something for treatment, but for NHS patients the prices are reduced.

Opticians, too, have patient registers. Once you are registered you should have your eyes tested regularly (usually every two years) because they change with time. For some, eye tests are free, but others have to pay something towards the service. Those entitled to free eye tests can also obtain cheaper frames and lenses.

Regional and district services

There are 14 Regional Health Authorities in England, and three separate authorities for Wales, Scotland and Northern Ireland (see Figure 4.2). There are 192 District Health Authorities in England. These are part of the Regional Authorities.

Regional Health Authorities

Each Regional Health Authority (RHA):

- develops strategic plans
- allocates financial resources to the District Health Authorities in its region
- evaluates the policies and performance of District Health Authorities to make sure that provision is consistent across the region as a whole
- develops regional plans for specialist services (such as radiotherapy treatment for cancer)

Figure 4.2 *The Regional Authorities*

1 South Western
2 Wessex
3 South West Thames
4 South East Thames
5 North East Thames
6 North West Thames
7 Oxford
8 East Anglia
9 Trent
10 West Midlands
11 Mersey
12 North Western
13 Yorkshire
14 Northern
15 Wales
16 Scotland
17 Northern Ireland

- is responsible for building hospitals
- operates the Blood Transfusion Service
- provides an ambulance service (although responsibility for the day-to-day operation may be delegated – handed over – to larger District Health Authorities.

The provision of health services such as hospital care (e.g. general operations and medicine, gynaecology, outpatients, X-ray, casualty, mental health services), and day care and community services (e.g. care of the elderly, child health, family planning, health visitors and district nurses) are organised by the District Health Authority which is in turn part of the Regional Health Authority.

Each RHA has a Community Health Council related to it. These Councils are independent bodies that monitor the provision of health services and represent the views of the service users.

Figure 4.3. shows the way in which the primary services

and district/regional services in England relate to each other. The organisation of health services in Wales, Scotland and Northern Ireland is slightly different.

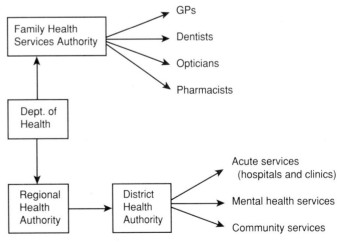

Figure 4.3. *The relationships between health service authorities in England*

In Scotland, the Secretary of State for Scotland is answerable to Parliament for the health services there. Health services in Scotland are administered by the Scottish Home and Health Department, and local Health Boards are responsible for providing services at district level (Figure 4.4).

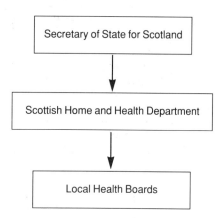

Figure 4.4 *The structure in Scotland*

Northern Ireland's health services and social services are organised as a single agency. This is called a 'unified structure'. This unified structure is outside local political control. Four Health Boards are responsible for providing the services at local level. The Department of Health allocates resources for the services to the four Boards (Figure 4.5).

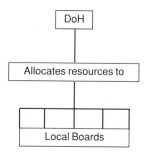

Figure 4.5 *The structure in Northern Ireland*

Organisation of the health services in Wales is similar to that in England except that there are no Regional Health Authorities, only District Health Authorities (of which there are nine). The Secretary of State for Wales is accountable to Parliament for health services (Figure 4.6).

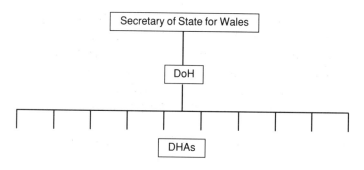

Figure 4.6 *The structure in Wales*

Whilst the organisation of health services in Scotland, Northern Ireland and Wales may be different from that in England, the range and provision of services is much the same.

Task

Using the map in Figure 4.2, complete the following activity.

1 Identify the region in which you live.
2 Look in a local Yellow Pages directory, where you should find the name, address and telephone number of your Regional Health Authority and District Health Authority if you live in England (District Health Authority if you live in Wales, local Health Board if you live in Scotland or Northern Ireland). Also look up the Family Health Services Authority (FHSA).
3 You will probably already know the name of your own GP, but find your GP's address and telephone number.
4 Organise all this information into notes under the three headings: statutory, voluntary or private services.

The 'NHS and Community Care' Act in operation

As a result of this recent Act, there have been changes in the way some areas operate.

Some hospitals have chosen to become **NHS Trusts,** which means that they operate their own budgets independently of the District Health Authority and the Regional Health Authority. They can use their funding as they feel it is best used within the hospital. NHS Trusts might not always take account of the services offered in other hospitals in their region, which means that some services could become doubled and some not covered at all. Also, some people are concerned that hospitals may offer only cheaper operations to keep within their budgets.

Figure 4.7 shows the changes that *could* occur within a health authority as a result of the new Act. In 'Newtown' all the **provider** services and staff have become a part of the Trust. The situation in 'Uptown' is different – here only the hospital has become a Trust, so that the District Health Authority retains control of the other services.

Where a Trust hospital has been established, the District Health Authority is no longer responsible for providing hospital services or for employing hospital staff. Instead, the Trust hospital becomes the **provider** of the services and the employer of hospital staff. The DHA changes its function to become a local **purchaser** of care services. This two-fold arrangement is referred to as the 'purchaser/provider split'.

Trust hospitals remain within the National Health Service but they are self-governing. This means a Trust hospital has the power to control its own budget and to determine the working conditions and rates of pay of its staff. In some areas the community health services have also become part of a Trust.

Think it over

Complete the following statements:
* *Newtown District Health Authority now*
  a *is the . . . . of hospital and community services*
  b *no longer has . . . . over hospital or community health services.*
* *Newtown Trust hospital*
  a *is the . . . . of hospital community services*
  b *is . . . .-. . . . . but remains within the framework of the . . .*
  c *. . . . . . . hospital and community care staff except for . . ., ..., ... and . . . ., who are contracted by the FHSA.*

Use these words to complete the sentences: opticians,

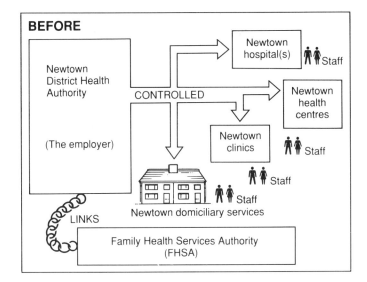

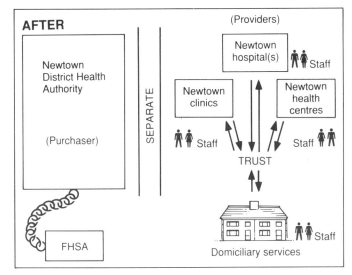

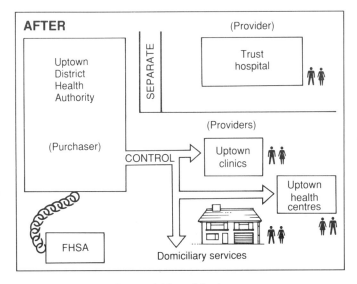

Figure 4.7 *The Before and After of the Act*

pharmacists, dentists, GPs, employs, NHS, self-governing, provider, control, purchaser.

The local health authority therefore looks at the needs of local people and purchases health care for those in its district through contracts with providers. The provider may be one local Trust or it could be a Trust or non-Trust hospital from a different area, or even a different part of the country. The authority is funded by the government.

Since Trust hospitals are no longer in the control of health authorities their funding must come from another source. Trust hospitals have to compete with other Trust and non-Trust hospitals to treat patients. As an example, take the case of Zubadia who needs an eye operation. Newtown Trust hospital's waiting time is two weeks and the charge for the operation is £2000. Zubadia, of course, does not pay for her treatment. She also knows that the quality of services are excellent at Newtown, the premises are pleasant and the environment non-threatening. The cost of the operation at Uptown hospital is £3000 and the waiting time is six weeks. Newtown Trust hospital offers the best quality and value-for-money service, and allows Zubadia to exercise her freedom of choice. Newtown wins the contract.

But who pays the £2000? The answer is a GP fund holder or a District Health Authority.

A fund holding GP receives money directly from the Regional Health Authority in order to purchase services for clients, as in this example. However, had the cost of Zubadia's operation been a lot more expensive, the DHA would pay.

Think it over

Which RHA and DHA is responsible for health care services in the area in which you live? How could you find this out?

The cost of health

Health services are available to all. This doesn't mean that everyone has access to all services whenever they like.

Some services are available free to all, such as seeing a doctor or obtaining family planning. Some services (e.g. dental work, prescriptions) are only available free to particular groups. Sometimes services are mixed – for example, you can see a doctor without charge but may have to pay for medicines your doctor prescribes for you.

Some people choose to 'go private', which means they opt out of the service provided by the government and pay for a service. This private service may in fact be provided by the same person who does the work for the National Health Service, but it might mean that the individual is seen sooner.

The statutory and private provisions may be mixed. For example, you could see your GP with a problem and be recommended to see a specialist (a 'consultant'). If the consultant has a long waiting list of NHS patients, you could opt to go private (i.e. pay) at this point and be seen earlier.

Many people now take out health *insurance* which they can call upon when they need treatment that the NHS cannot provide quickly.

· THE SOCIAL SERVICES ·

Although the Secretary of State for Health is responsible for the *provision* of social services, it is the Local Authorities that administer them. Local Authority social service departments have responsibility for the coordination of all forms of social care in the community.

Each Local Authority has a Social Services Committee which has responsibility for the social services within its area. It must appoint a Director of Social Services. The director is in charge of the department which administers the services. Social Service Departments are often organised into area offices from which the services for that area are operated.

County Councils run Local Authority social services in England and Wales, as do Metropolitan Councils and the London Boroughs.

In Northern Ireland there are four Boards set-up to administer social and health services. This unified structure is outside political control. In Scotland, Regional Local Authorities control social work departments.

Social services must not be confused with the Department of Social Security (DSS), which administers benefits and pays out money. Apart from an occasional small sum in an emergency, the social services *do not* hand out money. Their main function is to offer advice, to provide access to services and to provide a number of services themselves. They provide community and residential services for all client groups.

Social service departments might be organised as shown in Figure 4.8.

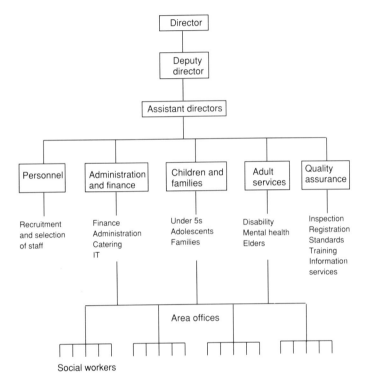

Figure 4.8 *One way of organising a Local Authority social services department*

Social workers are sometimes organised into 'patch areas'. Each patch has an office from which the social workers operate.

Much of a social worker's work relates to legislation such as the Children Act, which raises the rights of the child and makes social work an important part of childcare services. Social workers will also be involved with the Community Care Act which aims to provide care for individuals in their own home surroundings for as long as possible.

Children's services

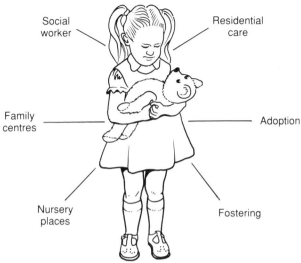

Figure 4.9 *Some of the care needs of a child*

Access to services

One of the main functions is to offer advice and help about the services available for children, ranging from nursery places to benefits the parents may be entitled to claim. Social services can find children priority places in a playgroup or nursery if they feel it is necessary. They can sometimes help to gain financial help for the payment of fees.

Child protection

The social services keep an 'at risk' register. This has details of any child they feel to be in danger from psychological or physical abuse. They monitor everyone on the list closely and are ready to act if the situation warrants it.

Family support

Social services aim, as far as possible, to support the family group. The help given often aims to keep a family together in their own home in their local area. A range of help and support could be offered by social services, which might include a 'home help' – a person who offers practical help in the home while a parent is ill. They may offer a 'family caseworker' to work with the family as a whole, trying to improve the quality of family life that a child is experiencing.

Some areas offer **family centres** where the parents and children can go each week for support. Here a variety of activities go on. They could include working with the parent and the child trying to improve communication and understanding, or working just with the parents on the skills of parenting whilst the children are looked after by qualified staff.

Fostering

Sometimes children need to be looked after temporarily away from their natural or adoptive parents for a number of reasons (e.g. illness, bereavement or being at risk). This is usually a short-term measure. The social services take on the role of organising a foster family which will suit the needs of the child. They also monitor the child in the placement.

Adoption

Social workers have a crucial role to play in the adoption of a child. They assess the suitability of those who wish to adopt and match them with a suitable child.

Residential care

Sometimes it is necessary to put children into residential care. Children's homes are usually run by social services staff, and they aim to provide a stable background for the children as close to home life as possible. They also operate residential homes for children with special needs. Each child is usually offered a 'key worker' who takes a special interest in them.

Services for elders

Social services can offer advice to elders and help them gain access to community services such as day centres. Social services can provide advice on claiming benefits they are entitled to. Social services staff can assess a client in their own home to see if they are eligible for some services such as home help and meals on wheels.

The Community Care Act aims to make it possible for people to remain in their own homes as long as possible, so the provision of support services has become even more important. The services provided or organised by each social services department will vary according to policy and available finance.

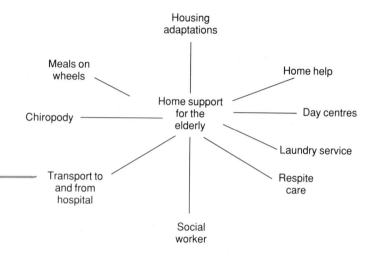

Figure 4.10 *Some of the care needs of elders*

Meals on wheels

Cooked meals are delivered to elders ready for reheating at home. The meals used to be 'cook–chill', but now they tend to be frozen owing to the scares over listeria infection in recent years (which were particularly linked to 'ready to heat' meals). Meals are delivered a couple of times a week and stored in the person's home until required. The elderly person only has to heat them up to the proper temperature. They provide nourishing meals which are thought suitable for the client group in terms of nutrition and texture. The service is often staffed by volunteers.

Day care

Social services often provide day care for elders. This gives people with mobility difficulties the opportunity to leave their house and meet others. A range of activities are organised, from mobility exercises to crafts. Many may enjoy the opportunity to chat. They are also usually given a hot meal.

Day care also provides a rest for carers who may otherwise have to provide 24-hour care for a relative.

Some authorities operate 'luncheon clubs' where elders attend only for lunch. This is very much a social occasion. This would also cover some of the aims of the day care service.

Home help

A 'home help' is a person who goes into a client's home and does tasks the client has difficulty with or cannot do adequately. This may include cleaning, washing, shopping or cooking. This gives a regular visitor who can monitor the elderly person's health whilst also providing a social contact for the client. The service is not free but usually charged on the basis of ability to pay.

Laundry service

This service is provided for elderly people with particular problems such as incontinence, where bed linen will need frequent changing. In such cases, social services can sometimes arrange for a home help to take care of personal laundry for the client.

Home adaptations and safety

The social services can sometimes help people who want to remain in their own home to get home adaptations as needed to improve their quality of life. This may range from structural changes to a few small gadgets for everyday tasks, such as opening tins when a person has arthritis. Social services might advise on both the kinds of adaptations needed and the cost. They may provide access to some money to support this.

Besides adaptations, social services could also advise on home safety, which might include alarms and telephones. This would enable an elder to call for help should the need arise.

Support services

Some elders are cared for by relatives (e.g. sons or daughters) or by partners in their own homes. This can be a very stressful task and until recently the difficulties of being a 'carer' were very much overlooked.

A number of support services are now being developed. They include 'sitting services'. Social services might arrange for a 'sitter' to come and sit with an elder whilst their regular carer has a break. These people are not always trained and they usually only sit for a few hours in the day or evening. It is rare to get sitters for the night. This service can be regular or just occasional. There is usually a charge for the service.

One essential role of the social services department is to organise **respite care** for the elderly. The older person spends a short period of time in residential care to allow the person who normally cares for them to have a break or a holiday. This service can be a tremendous support for a carer. Caring for an individual – even a family member who is loved very much – constantly over a long period of time can prove very stressful. Breakdowns in relationships can happen if respite care is not available.

Sometimes respite care is also used to support an elder living alone in their own home, as regular breaks from caring for themselves can help them remain in their own home for longer.

Sheltered housing and residential homes

When an elder feels they would like some more support with daily living, there may be a number of options available to them. However, sometimes the elderly person does not have a full choice. They may need so much support that sheltered accommodation is not a reasonable option. Sometimes an accident such as a minor fall can result in an elder being moved from their own home straight into residential care.

The person's own choice of accommodation is very important in these situations, and their wishes need to be carefully explored.

Sheltered housing is sometimes viewed as a mid-way solution by older people – between going into residential care and remaining in their own home. Sheltered housing consists of individual self-contained living units – either bungalows or flats – with some communal facilities such as a lounge and laundry. The units are usually unfurnished so that the older person can have a selection of their own things around them.

Sheltered housing allows the person to have the privacy they had in their own home and to live independently, but they have the support of a warden if necessary. The warden does not interfere with the residents' routines but keeps a check on the maintenance of the accommodation and ensures communal facilities are kept clean. The warden will also be aware of the medical situation of each resident and who their doctor is. They will know how to contact relatives in an emergency. Each unit usually has a good alarm system so the resident can raise the warden.

Besides having the warden, another advantage some elders see in sheltered accommodation is that they are near other people. If living alone, they are never too far from company. Some sheltered accommodation also offers day care facilities.

Sheltered accommodation can be run by the social services department or by the local council. Much sheltered accommodation is now privately owned or rented.

However, not all elders choose to remain in their own homes. Some need a greater level of support and this can be provided in the form of **residential care**. This care is for 24 hours a day. Social services is involved in two ways: They can provide and run homes. Alternatively they can register and monitor practices in private homes. They are responsible for checking that standards do not fall below a certain level, and they provide a list of approved homes.

Residential homes fall into two categories. **Rest homes** tend to be for the more independent person who perhaps chooses the support of an organised environment but is fully in control of their own routines. The focus is not on nursing, and these homes do not have to employ a qualified nurse. In fact, many rest homes are not equipped to deal with infirm or immobile people. **Nursing homes**, on the other hand, deal with the more infirm elders who may need care for up to 24 hours a day.

Residential homes run by social services are usually for people who have lived in the area. Social services staff will provide an assessment of a potential client. The cost of the care is dependent on the means of the individual. These costs cover accommodation, food and essential services. The client can sometimes claim allowances and financial help from various places, and it is a social work role to advise on that.

Think it over

An older neighbour has suffered a minor stroke and although able to cope with daily tasks, they need help with shopping. What form of housing and/or community support might you recommend to them, and why?

Services for clients with special needs

'Special needs' is a term used to cover any physical, social or emotional factor which prevents an individual reaching their full potential.

Many of the services provided for special needs or disabled people are similar to those provided for children and elders. They include community care services, residential services, respite care and day care. Their function is the same except that they provide for a different client group.

Day care services for people with learning disabilities can differ greatly. Some are still termed 'adult training centres' although mostly they are now called 'social education centres'. These services sometimes offer clients employment in a limited way as well as teaching life skills which aim to encourage independent living.

Some day care concentrates purely on the personal development of the individual and programmes focus around the needs of the individual. Activities may include life skills (e.g. personal care), leisure pursuits (e.g. swimming), physiotherapy to improve mobility, or work aimed at improving communication skills.

Services for special needs are very much a mixture of services provided by the health service, eduction and social services. The services complement each other.

There is a range of benefits available for individuals with special needs. Social services staff may be able to offer advice on which ones an individual can claim.

Think it over

Choose one client group and identify and describe the services available for them in your area. Check out the services using information gained from the Local Authority social services, Health Service information gained from GP and dentist's reception, or from Health Clinics. You could also get information from libraries or from the local Citizens' Advice Bureau. Information on benefits might come from the Post Office or from your local Department of Social Security.

What is the cost of care?

Whether or not you have to pay for services provided by the social services department depends on your circumstances. For the majority of services listed, you are assessed to check your needs as there is limited provision. If you are deemed in need of a service then the amount you pay is dependent on your income.

As with health services, you can sometimes choose to pay for services privately.

Mixed economy of care

Many areas operate what is called a 'mixed economy of care'. This means that the major agencies work together to satisfy the needs of the individual.

The government has a policy of promoting care in the community, which means that people should be cared for in their own homes or an establishment in the community whenever this is possible.

Under the NHS and Community Care Act, responsibility for services in the community lies with Local Authority social services departments. Each social services department appoints care managers who are responsible for purchasing services from the full range of statutory, voluntary and private providers.

In order to ensure the delivery of cost-effective health and care services of quality, the organisations responsible for

the services need to work together. Community care, on one level, involves a partnership between the District Health Authority, social services department and Family Health Services Authority (representing GPs). On another level it involves the practitioners who provide the care social workers, community nurses, support workers, informal workers and families.

The partnership between the District Health Authority, social services department and Family Health Services Authority is at a senior (or strategic) level. These three organisations work together to produce a plan for the district they cover. Publication of a yearly **plan** is required by law under the NHS and Community Care Act. The 'strategic plan' shows a strategy or plan of action for the area. The three organisations take an overview of the district's situation in relation to the health and care needs of people living in the area and the services needed to meet these needs.

Benefits

An individual's health and care problems may be linked to his or her social and financial situation.

With the exception of housing benefit (which is dealt with by the Local Authority), financial matters are dealt with by the Department of Social Security (DSS) via the Benefits Agency. The latter works for the Department of Social Security. The DSS produces a number of leaflets which set out people's rights and entitlements.

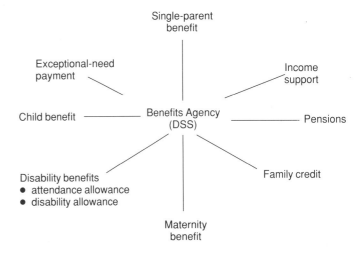

Figure 4.11 *The Benefits Agency*

Benefits can be the same for everyone (such as child benefit) or they may be **means tested** – that is, account is taken of any income or saving before a benefit is awarded. Sometimes no benefit is given because the person applying has too many savings. A reduced benefit is sometimes given when people have some savings or income. Some benefits are only payable if the individual has paid contributions to National Insurance. These include unemployment benefit, sick pay, maternity pay and pensions.

Education

Education services are provided by the Local Authority or by private or 'opted out' services. The Local Authority provides free education for those aged 5–19 years. The school structure will vary according to the Local Authority – some have a secondary school system whereby children attend the same school regardless of ability. Others still operate a 'grammar school' system whereby children can be streamed according to their performance.

Schools provide other services as well. Educational psychologists are available to help pinpoint why a child is not achieving and can recommend ways to improve the situation. Sometimes health services are provided in schools, including medical checks and dental checks. Within the immunisation system, there is an injection offered to children at a certain age (e.g. the BCG at approximately 13 years).

Schools can provide a vital role in identifying children who are at risk or who are not thriving. As they see the children every day, teachers often pick up small changes that they can then notify to the appropriate authority, so an attempt can be made to help. Early detection may prevent a problem getting out of hand.

Some local authorities provide nursery education, but it is not a statutory requirement and nurseries are very few and far between. Learning opportunities are also provided for those outside the 5–19 age group through local colleges, but these have to be paid for.

A public library is provided by the Local Authority and is a source of educational information. Anyone is able to use the library and registered people can borrow a number of books over a specified period of time. The libraries aim is to cater for all groups in the community and provide books for children and books with large print for those with poor sight. Libraries also provide a range of information on other issues such as benefits.

Information on benefits and health and care services can also be obtained from Citizens' Advice Bureaux. Addresses may be found in your local telephone guides or *Yellow Pages*.

Housing

Housing for rent is an important service for many of the client groups we have looked at. Housing is provided by the Local Council and by voluntary and private groups who provide a range of accommodation available to rent. If you wish to live in council accommodation, you have to apply to the council. Priority is given to elders and those with young families. The council may also have some specialist accommodation such as warden care flats for those in need of extra support.

Local councils may also provide short-term accommodation for homeless families.

Who pays for all of these services?

Although many of the services we have described appear to be free, we all pay for them in an indirect way. Public services are funded by local and national taxes – income tax, value added tax (VAT), National Insurance contributions (by individuals and organisations) and the Council Tax.

• PEOPLE AND NEEDS •

Regardless of their age, sex, race, ability or disability, each person is an individual with needs that are specific to him or herself. The needs of people vary according to age and stage of development and according to their own particular circumstances at any point in their lives.

For the GNVQ in Health and Social Care you should be able to:

- explain what 'being an individual' means
- describe the idea of 'needs' in social care work
- explain the terms 'service users' and 'clients' and discuss the needs of different client groups
- describe the roles of various health and care workers
- outline the key sources of information on the health and care services
- describe ways in which people can gain access to the care services.

Defining a need

What is a need? A need is a requirement of life that must be satisfied in order for people to survive, grow, develop, and reach their full potential.

Needs are not the same as wants. Consider, for example: 'I need a coat to keep me warm in winter, and I want a coat with a trendy designer label in it'.

Needs can be divided into general needs and specific needs. **General needs** include food, warmth, shelter, respect, independence, dignity. Everyone has general needs. The general needs of a four-year-old child living in a high-rise flat in an inner city area are the same as those of a child of the same age living in a country village. But each of the two children will also have **specific needs**. This is because the two children's *circumstances* are different.

Think it over

Consider the possible differences between the two children's circumstances, in relation to play, forming relationships, exploration, independence and safety. For each category think of examples of the specific needs of each child.

You will probably have identified different kinds of physical, social and emotional needs. We use an acronym (a word formed from the initial letters of other words) when looking at human needs:

PISCES =

P hysical needs

I ntellectual needs

S ocial needs

C ultural needs

E motional needs

S exual needs

Whilst we separate these different aspects of people for the purpose of study, in real life they cannot be separated because each aspect will have an effect on the others.

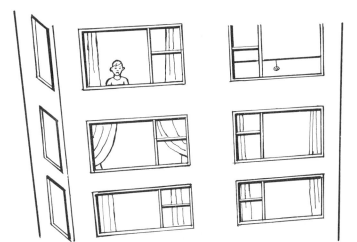

Imagine a situation where you have argued with your friend. You may feel upset. This is the emotional effect. You think about the argument, perhaps wishing you had not said certain things. This is the intellectual aspect. You will probably also have experienced a physical reaction, such as your heart beating faster. Friends may notice that you seem worried. This is the social effect. You may perhaps try to hide your feelings about the argument because in some cultures adults are not expected to show their feelings in crying, for example. This is a cultural aspect. If the relationship is a close one then the sexual aspect may be involved.

Task

Using the examples given in the guide below, list your own general and specific needs.

General needs		Specific needs
Oxygen	P	Hours of sleep
Stimulation	I	Knowledge for a GNVQ
Relationships	S	Number of friends
Beliefs	C	Religious practice
Love	E	Trust in others
Recognition of own sexuality	S	Friends of the same or opposite sex

Now try to imagine you have to remain in a wheelchair because of an accident, and relate this to the situations shown in the pictures.

Draw up a new list showing how your needs would change if you were confined to a wheelchair. Discuss the changes you have identified with a friend or another person who is interested in the subject.

Your answers could show the following:

1 What you give as your needs will be influenced by the views you already hold about yourself and the world you live in.
2 Each individual's specific needs are different.
3 It is difficult to imagine what it is like to be in a situation if you have had no similar previous experience.

Individuality

Because everyone is different we talk about **individuality**. Each person is an individual. Each person is also **unique.** No two people are the same, not even identical twins. Each twin has a set of fingerprints and a voice-print which is unique to him or herself. Neither is the experience of each twin the same. One twin is usually heavier at birth than the other, probably because of having received more nourishment whilst growing in the mother's womb. One twin is always born first, making it older than the other. The experience of twins, then, is different both before and during birth. The differences in experience continue throughout life. We are all unique and this means that our specific needs are also unique, that is, special to ourselves.

Treating each person as an individual is always important. For the providers of health or social care services it is essential, otherwise it would not be possible to deliver a good standard of care that meets each individual's needs. It is providing for the great range of individual need that creates the challenge for the caring services and those delivering the care.

What leads to people becoming clients?

We refer to people who use services as **service users** or **clients** regardless of their life-stage or what their particular need or needs might be. The clients are therefore children and their families, adolescents, people with a physical disability, people with learning disabilities, people with a mental illness and elders.

The term **children** refers to people between 0 and 18 years. However, the law has always sent out confusing messages about what children's rights are. For example, according to the law, children are able to assume grown-up responsibilities or behave in a particular way at different ages. At 16 years children are allowed to buy cigarettes. At 14 years children may go into a pub but may not drink alcohol on the premises. At 18 years they can drink alcohol and do not need to be accompanied. At 18 years people have the right to vote.

An **adolescent** is a young person at a stage of development between childhood and adulthood – a teenager in other words. For some people this can be a particularly difficult time, whilst others really enjoy life during their adolescence. The period is characterised by a marked change in physical appearance and development. Emotional development does not necessarily keep pace with the physical changes, so that outwardly the adolescent may give the appearance of being an adult but inwardly the child remains. This can be part of the problems that some adolescents experience.

The Children Act 1989 attempts to increase children's rights and the responsibility of parents in relation to the care of their children. Society recognises that it is usually in a child's best interest to be with its family. Of course, there are a range of family types, including the nuclear family consisting of two parents and a child or children; a single parent of either sex and children; and the wider family, consisting of parents, children, grandparents, aunts, uncles, cousins, known as the **extended family**.

Think it over

Consider your own family and that of friends and neighbours. Are they all the same? Discuss the various family types with a colleague and see if you can identify one consisting of members different from those in the categories outlined above.

The complexities of modern day living and the range of relationships that individuals may be involved in can lead to families experiencing problems. Since the interests and safety of children are of the utmost importance, a range of professional health and care workers are available to help families with any problems.

The health visitor can provide advice for a family experiencing problems with a young child's diet or development. A social worker can be involved if there are emotional difficulties in the relationships in the family, or where physical, emotional or sexual abuse is suspected.

Think it over

Paul Jones had a motorcycle accident which left him unable to walk. He spent 12 months in a specialist hospital dealing with spinal injuries. He was helped to make the best use of the remaining movement in his legs. Paul now drives a car to and from work but has to use crutches to help him walk.

Tim Smith was a pillion passenger on Paul's bike on the day of the accident. Tim suffered a severe head injury which led to brain damage. As a result, his intellectual ability was affected. Tim can read and write but only with difficulty. He can also learn and master new skills but it takes him a long time to do so.

Both Paul and Tim have a disability. Paul has a physical disability, Tim a learning disability. Look at the word disability. What does it mean?

Disability means 'want of ability'. People who have a disability are not able to do an every-day activity that the majority of other people can do. Some people are born with a disability. Others like Tim and Paul may become disabled as the result of an accident or an illness. Both Tim and Paul will have used a wide range of services during the course of their treatment and recovery.

Task

List the health and care services which may have been involved in Tim and Paul's care and treatment from the time of the accident to returning home to the community.

Rose Barton is 86, her daughter Jane, 65. Both are elders. Jane is fit and active and cares for her mother who has severe arthritis in her knee, shoulder and hip joints. Arthritis is a painful condition which makes movement very difficult. Both Jane and her mother are widows.

Elders like Jane's mother Rose present the greatest challenge to the caring services for two main reasons. Firstly, the likelihood of disabling conditions such as arthritis increases with age. Secondly, people are on average living longer, so there are an increasing number of elders. In the United Kingdom there are approximately 10 million people of pensionable age at present. That is 18 per cent out of a population of 56 million people. By comparison, at the beginning of this century only 6 per cent of the population was in this age-group. An average baby boy born in 1901 was expected to live to 48 years, and a girl was expected to live to 52 years. In 1981 average life expectancy had risen to 70 for men and 76 for women.

People over 85 years of age are most likely to need additional support and help from the health and care services. Of course there are many fit elders, and using age is only one way of defining what an elder is. How a person functions is far more important than how old they are.

Assuming that all people over 60 have exactly the same characteristics and needs is a form of **stereotyping**. Seeing service user or client groups as a category can carry the risk of individuals being stereotyped.

People with **mental illness** may also be the subject of stereotyping. Mental illness is a term used to describe a range of conditions which may affect the way people think, feel and behave. Iola, for example, has recently recovered from depression. Her illness followed the sudden death of her father. For a time, she was unable to function properly. She said: 'I felt I had nothing to live for. My appearance took a nose-dive and I had no interest in anything. I was unable to work for a time but thanks to the help of the psychiatrist, social worker and psychiatric community nurse, I am now back to my old self'.

Anyone can become mentally ill, but because of advances in treatment using drugs and therapy, most people can be helped to overcome their illness and lead a productive and fulfilling life.

Task

The blank chart on page 141 shows the different types of need and the categories of service users or clients. Complete the boxes to show examples of the general needs of the service users, and the services which might be required for each category user.
With a colleague or friend identify and discuss the possible specific needs of the users in the different categories.

Service users	Types of need					
	Physical	Intellectual	Social	Cultural	Emotional	Sexual
Children						
Adolescents						
Elders						
People with physical disability						
People with learning disability						
People with mental illness						

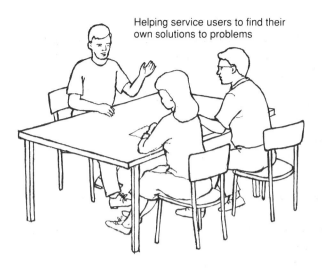

Helping service users to find their own solutions to problems

Residential and day care staff

Some social care staff provide physical and emotional care on a daily basis for the full range of service users in either day care or residential care settings – including, for example, elders in residential homes and day centres.

An increasing number of residential social care staff will hold NVQs in Care. Others may have the CSW, DipSW, Certificate in Social Services (CSS), Preliminary Certificate in Social Care (PCSC) or In-service Course in Social Care (ICSC).

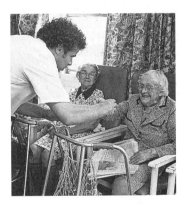

. THE ROLES OF HEALTH AND . CARE WORKERS

Health and care services are delivered by a wide range of both professional and voluntary workers.

Social care workers in the community

Social workers

Social workers, who are usually organised in teams, aim to provide a coordinated service to families and individuals with a range of social problems. Some social workers *specialise* in child care, others in working with people with mental illness. or with learning difficulties, a physical disability or with elders.

Many 'field' social workers (the name given to social workers who carry out their role in the community) hold the Certificate of Qualification in Social Work (CQSW) or alternatively the Diploma in Social Work (DipSW). Most field social workers are based in and work from Area Offices. One exception, however, is the hospital social worker.

Home care workers

Home care staff work in service users' homes, providing support in a number of ways which vary according to the individual needs of each service user. The home carer works with the full range of service users but is involved mainly with elders. Home carers can provide physical care, including helping with personal hygiene and every-day activities as well as offering companionship. Cooking, cleaning and shopping are also part of the role.

Home carers may be holders of NVQs in Care. The home carer may be the only contact an elder enjoys with the outside world. The role then, is of vital importance.

Task

Many elders enjoy talking about the past. Visit an elder and ask what life was like when they were young. Remembering about the past is called 'reminiscence' and requires mental effort. Talking about the past, then, stimulates mental activity, which is why reminiscence is used as a form of therapy.

Your visit will therefore be of benefit to the elder who will gain from being mentally stimulated, and you will learn something about the past and about communicating with others.

Health care workers in the community

General practitioners

General practitioners (GPs), or 'family doctors', work from their own premises or from health centres. The role of the GP is to provide consultation and physical examination as appropriate, in order to prevent, identify or treat illness, disease or injury. Providing immunisation and vaccination against infectious diseases such as measles, mumps, rubella (German measles) and polio, as well as more unusual diseases which can be contracted whilst travelling abroad, are also part of the role. When necessary, the GP refers patients to other service providers, including hospital consultants, social workers, community nurses and midwives, and to providers in the private and voluntary sectors.

Task

Visit your GP's surgery and find out what your doctor provides. Talk to the receptionist who might help you. Your GP's qualifications will probably also be displayed as a list of letters after the surname. Your GP probably provides a Practice Leaflet outlining the practice services. Ask for one.

Practice nurses

Practice nurses are employed by GPs to carry out a range of nursing functions, usually in the doctor's premises or 'practice'. Practice nurses give routine injections, screen elders to prevent or identify at the earliest stage those medical conditions that are treatable, and take part in health promotion.

Practice nurses are qualified Registered General Nurses (RGNs) or they may be Enrolled Nurses (ENs). Some practice nurses may have additional qualifications.

District nurses

District nurses, sometimes called 'community nurses', provide the full range of nursing care in service users' own homes. District Nursing Sisters are RGNs with an additional qualification, who may head a small team of ENs and health support care workers. The latter may have an NVQ in Care. Each member of the team is employed by the District Health Authority, but the team works with and is usually based at the GP's premises or health centre.

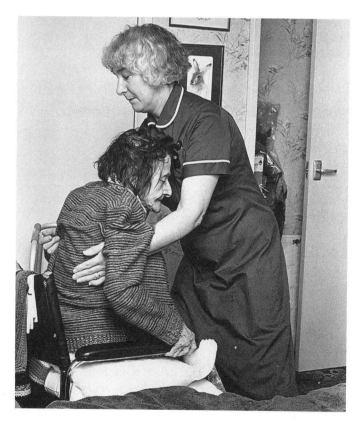

Think of the great variety of service users the district nursing team has contact with: people who have had an operation and need their stitches removing, and others who need long-term nursing care because of a medical condition or injury which cannot be cured.

Think it over

Compare the role of the practice nurse outlined previously with that of the District Nursing Sister. What are the differences?

Think it over

Imagine you are a service user who needs long-term care from the district nursing team. How might your own relationship with the members of the team develop over time?

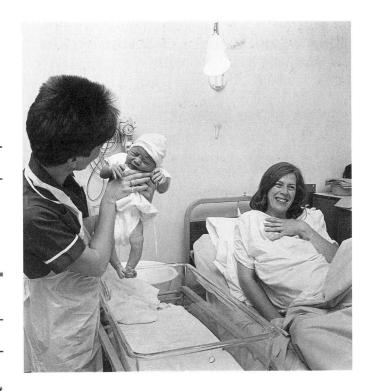

Midwives

Today most babies are born in a hospital. Community or domiciliary (which means home) midwives provide ante-natal and post-natal care as well as delivering babies. Community midwives, who work with GPs and hospital doctors, may be based in clinics, doctor's surgeries and health centres or they may work from home.

In some areas no distinction is made between hospital midwives and community midwives. In these cases the midwife works for a time in hospital followed by a period in the community, then returns to hospital and so on. In other areas, the hospital midwife operates within the hospital setting only.

All midwives, regardless of whether they work in the community or in a hospital, hold the same midwifery qualification of Registered Midwife (RM).

Task

Consider the advantages and disadvantages of hospital versus home confinement (giving birth). List your views under the four headings Safety, Social, Emotional and Cultural.

Health visitors

The health visitor has multiple qualifications: health visitors are RGNs, holders of an obstetric nurse's or midwifery qualification and a health visitor's certificate. Health visitors work from clinics or health centres mainly, and visit service users in their own homes.

The health visitor also teaches health education in schools and a variety of other settings. The role of the health visitor is to provide advice and guidance on health matters for all service users regardless of age, although the bulk of the work is related to children up to 5. The promotion of good health and the prevention of ill-health is the health visitor's main function.

Ask a friend, colleague or relative who has had a baby to explain what the health visitor did at his or her first visit. Make a note of any test or examination the health visitor might have carried out on the baby. Write down the main differences between the role of the health visitor and the midwife as seen by the mother.

Together, the GP, district nurse, community midwife, health visitor and social worker form the **primary care team**. The team is a sort of first-line defence against ill-health and potential or actual social problems. The team usually meets in the GP's premises or health centre on a regular basis in order to discuss clients' health and social problems.

Working together in this way provides an **'holistic'** approach to care. Holistic care means that each service user is seen as a whole person with different PISCES needs.

Community psychiatric nurses

Another important role is that of the community psychiatric nurse (CPN) whose main concern is enabling people with a mental illness to remain within the community or to return to the community following a period of hospitalisation.

The community psychiatric nurse works between the hospital and the community, visiting service users both in their own homes and in hospital. Close liaison or contact between the hospital consultant, GP, social worker, health visitor and other professional workers involved with service users and their care is an important aspect of the community psychiatric nurse's role.

At a practical level, the CPN may administer drugs by injection; or oversee clients' self-administration of oral drugs (pills, tablets and other forms of medication taken by mouth) which are an important part of the *control* of mental illness. The community psychiatric nurse is employed by the DHA and is always a qualified professional.

Chiropodists

Chiropodists are qualified professionals who specialise in foot care. Chiropodists provide a service for people of all ages and carry out their role in the full range of health care settings, including service users' homes. Some chiropodists are employed by the District Health Authority, others are self-employed and work from private practices.

Even a minor foot injury or condition, such as a corn, can lead to difficulty in walking. Think of the way you walk when your feet are hurting or if you have a small blister on your heel. For some service users, care from the chiropodist can mean the difference between being mobile and able to walk about or being immobile and housebound.

Ask friends and relatives if they have ever had treatment from a chiropodist. Find out what the treatment involved, and how they say their feet felt after the treatment.

Dentists

The role of the dentist is concerned with promoting dental health and hygiene as well as identifying and treating conditions of the teeth and gums. Dentists are contracted to the National Health Service through Family Health Service Authorities. Some dentist also provide their services on a private, fee-paying basis.

Consider carrying out a small survey amongst colleagues, friends and family to find out how much they know about the factors which lead to dental caries (bad teeth). Use your knowledge of nutrition and personal hygiene gained from Chapter 2 to do this.

Hospital workers

Consultants

Consultants are specialist doctors. Some (called 'surgeons') carry out operations. Others (called 'physicians') specialise in treatment using medicines. Consultants include the following:

a Paediatricians – specialists in the care of children
b Obstetricians – specialists in the care of women during and after pregnancy
c Gynaecologists – specialists concerned with the treatment of disorders affecting the female organs
d Dermatologists – specialists in the treatment of skin conditions.

Consultants are supported by a number of other professionals, including junior doctors.

Nurses

Nurses constitute the biggest workforce of professionals in a hospital. As a result of a new system of training for nurses, called Project 2000, learner nurses undertake most of their education and training in higher education (HE) establishments.

In a general hospital (one that does not specialise in a particular branch of medicine) ward sisters are usually Registered General Nurses (RGNs) and many have additional qualifications. Training for the Enrolled Nurse (EN) has gradually been phased out. A course for conversion from EN to RGN is available. Essential non-nursing care of service users, such as general hygiene and

helping elders with daily living skills, is now undertaken by health care assistants, many of whom will eventually hold NVQs.

Nurses who work in specialist hospitals or units normally hold a qualification relevant to the nursing area in which they practise.

An increasing number of nurses are qualified to degree level and the profession is now attracting many more men than it once did.

Physiotherapists

Physiotherapists help to prevent as well as treat disease or injury through the use of physical activity and exercise. The physiotherapist may be peripatetic (that is, working from house to house) or be based solely in hospital. Some physiotherapists work in private practice, others specialise, for example, in sports injuries.

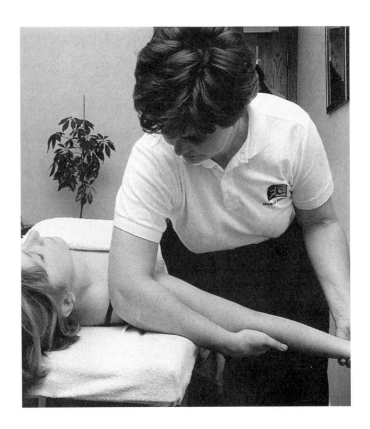

Think of all the situations, leisure activities, injuries, illnesses and diseases that the physiotherapist might see or be involved with and the scope and importance of the role becomes apparent.

Occupational therapists

Occupational therapists (OTs) use therapeutic activity in order to aid the recovery of people who suffer from either physical or mental illness or both. OTs may be based in hospitals, social service departments, voluntary organisations, or private establishments. They may work in domiciliary settings. The OT may treat people individually or in groups.

OTs works with people who have a disability, promoting independent living skills so that capabilities are maximised and disability minimised. The OT also uses craft work as a form of therapy.

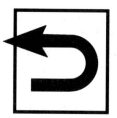

Think it over

Consider the ways in which you would be affected if you lost the use of one arm. How could the OT help you?

Try putting your coat on and off whilst keeping the arm you use most immobile (still). Later, try eating a meal with the same arm immobilised. How did you feel? Frustrated? How difficult was it? Now you have some idea of the affect of a disability and of the contribution of the OT to independent living, since the OT can show how to achieve these every-day activities in the most effective way. If you have a disability you will doubtless have overcome many such problems.

Health care support workers

Staff who support trained nurses and doctors in the hospital setting are called health care support workers. They were previously known as 'auxiliary' nurses. They carry out a range of non-specialist tasks such as bathing patients. They free the professionals to carry out tasks such as making health checks and dispensing medicines.

Paramedics

'Paramedic' is a collective term used for any health worker other than a doctor, nurse or dentist who supports the work of those professionals. Examples include physiotherapists, radiographers, laboratory assistants and ambulance workers.

Other personnel

Care assistants

Care assistants work in a range of settings but particularly in residential care. They carry out a range of personal care tasks. They can assist in all tasks which do not require specially trained staff.

Staff in early education

A range of staff work in early child education (e.g. in nursery and infant schools). The nursery or infant teacher will have a teaching qualification and will have trained to develop programmes for each individual child to enhance their development. They also teach the skills of reading and writing when the child is ready for them.

The nursery nurse or nursery assistant supports the work of the nursery teacher. They might usually have an NNEB or more recently an NVQ qualification where they have specialised in the development of young children. They are aware of stages of development and activities which encourage development. They are able to organise and supervise these activities but they do not have a teaching qualification.

ACCESS AND REFERRAL TO HEALTH AND CARE SERVICES

Access to health and care services can be achieved in one of three ways: through self-referral, by referral by a 'third party', or by being referred by a GP, health visitor, social worker or any other professional.

If you feel ill, for example, and your GP wants you to go to hospital, the GP will refer you for either special tests or to see a consultant. You cannot refer yourself to a consultant or for special tests. However, you can receive emergency treatment from the accident and emergency department at any hospital providing such a service, without being referred by anyone.

You can also approach social services directly for help and advice. Contacting a social worker, for example, counts as self-referral. A friend, neighbour or anyone concerned about your health and social well-being can refer you to social services or contact your GP. This is an example of a 'third party' referral.

According to the **Patients' Charter**, every citizen has the right to be registered with a GP. But, note that the GP also has the right not to accept a particular person, in which case the Family Health Service Authority will help in finding an alternative doctor. It is also necessary to register with a dentist before treatment can be made available – another form of self-referral.

Similarly, you can seek direct help from any voluntary organisation. Examples here include the Family Planning Association (FPA), MENCAP and MIND.

Self-help groups, and organisations concerned with specific medical disorders such as 'stroke clubs' and physically handicapped and able-bodied (PHAB) clubs are also in the self-referral category. The one voluntary organisation which is the exception for self-referral is the meals-on-wheels service that has been described earlier.

THE IMPORTANCE OF CLIENT RIGHTS

All of us are clients of the health and care services at some point in our lives. We are patients of our GP and our dentist, and as children we have been clients of the post-natal care facilities provided by our local health authority. Some people need more help from these services than we do, but whatever the level of need the word **client** describes anyone who uses the health and care services.

Health and care service clients come from all parts of the community and, as individuals, they differ in age, ethnic and cultural background, and gender. Some may have needs related to illness or disability, others may have needs of a different type. Whatever the personal characteristics and needs of people using the health and

caring services, all have the same rights as clients. Equality of care is a central value of the caring professions and is written into the codes of practice of health and care services, and in the government's Patients' Charter. There are also laws designed to protect vulnerable groups from discrimination and inequality of treatment in work, education, and in other areas of life, and we will examine them in more detail below. Client rights apply equally to all, and care workers need to be committed to promoting them.

Think about the types of health and care services that you know of. Make a list of all that you can think of and write your list as a column down one side of a sheet of paper. Your list could include special schools, residential homes and general practitioners (GPs) for example.

Now think about the people who use the facilities you have listed. Write down the types of people that the facilities are intended to serve next to the items on your list. You have now created a picture of the client groups that the health and care services are catering for.

Equality of treatment and the importance of client rights are **values** of the health and care services. This means that it is believed to be right to uphold these values and ensure that they are observed. The norms of behaviour expected of staff, and the structure of the services themselves, need to reflect these values. The idea of respect for clients as individuals is an important aspect of caring and helps to define clients' rights. As a carer it is important that you understand what these rights are and how you can help to promote them for all clients.

What are client rights?

Equality of treatment

Freedom from discrimination is a basic right in care situations, as it is elsewhere in life. We have seen how some people are discriminated against because of their

ethnic or racial background, their gender, their age or their disability. We have also looked at the different forms that this discrimination may take. It ranges from physical and verbal *abuse* to judgements made about people based on *stereotypes* with which they have been labelled.

Some people *are* discriminated against in their contacts with the health and caring services. They may be excluded from access to the help they need by being treated less well than other clients. The behaviour and attitude of a member of the caring staff may differ from client to client according to their own personal bias against the groups that the clients seem to belong to. Feelings of *hostility* can be projected in conversations with clients, which can put them off seeking the help they need and therefore exclude them from care. *Inadequate and misleading information* may be given, so that access to care is made more difficult for some people than for others.

Discrimination may also take the form of *rules* or *working practices* which make services less accessible for particular groups. For example, in a nursery the range of food provided for the children may not include items required by the religion and culture of some members of the community. Children from these families would not find their needs being met, and the nursery would be excluding some children from the facilities it provides. Managers need to make sure that all groups are equally well catered for in the way services are provided.

Dignity

Clients also have a right to **dignity** in the care they receive. This means that they are treated as being worthy of respect, and that their feelings are considered in the care they receive.

Some people are particularly vulnerable to loss of dignity because of the level of help they need from others. People such as infirm elders or disabled people may need assistance with many personal aspects of their care. It is important that the dignity of the client is respected when providing this care. Clients who feel that they are treated as though their feelings do not matter may find that their self-esteem is affected by their experience of care. Maintaining the dignity of a client in situations where they are very dependent on others is a skill that carers need to develop, and it is a right of clients to have their dignity respected.

Facilities provided must meet the needs of clients from all religious and cultural backgrounds to ensure discrimination does not occur.

Independence

Clients of the health and care services have a right to as much **independence** as possible during their care. People who need help may find that they lose their independence because of the care that is provided for them. For example, if a disabled person finds that their domestic tasks are always done for them, instead of being helped to do the work themselves, they may feel that their independence is threatened.

In a dependent care situation a client is vulnerable to loss of independence. It is up to care workers to make sure that clients' rights to independence are respected in care situations by ensuring that they are helped to do as many things as possible for themselves.

Choice

Linked to the right to independence is the right to **choice.** Clients who use the health and caring services may find that they have little choice in the care they are offered. They may be unaware of the alternatives available to them, and of the ways in which their care package was decided. Clients have a right to choice and it is important that carers involve them in decisions about their care as much as possible.

Confidentiality

Clients also have a right to **confidentiality** in their dealings with the health and caring services. They need to feel confident that information about themselves will not be repeated to others.

There are circumstances when care workers may wish to share information with other professionals to help clients to get the care that they need. In this case the clients need to feel that they have a choice in the matter, and carers must explain why they want to share the information with others.

Carers must *always* respect the principle of client confidentiality. The right to confidentiality ensures that clients continue to trust the carer and talk to them freely about their situation and their needs.

A healthy and safe environment

Clients also have a right to be cared for in a **healthy and safe environment**. This means that the practice of care, and the situations in which it takes place, must be monitored in terms of health and safety at all times.

Health and safety covers a wide area, including:

- cleanliness and sanitation in food preparation and in the general environment
- buildings and services that are well maintained and designed to ensure safety for users
- equipment that is safely used and stored
- working practices that promote health and safety for clients.

Clients coming into a care situation have a right to expect that they will be treated in a way which promotes their health and safety, not in one that threatens it.

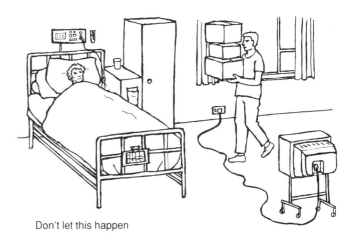

Don't let this happen

Task

Think about the client rights that we have looked at. Imagine that you had to explain to someone who was not a carer why these rights were important in the health and care field.

Write down your explanation of the importance of maintaining client rights in the form of a letter to a non-carer.

Legislation against discrimination

There are **legal safeguards** against discrimination which are designed to protect vulnerable groups. Laws have been passed in Parliament which seek to prevent discrimination on the basis of race, gender and disability. Also, bodies like the Equal Opportunities Commission and the Commission for Racial Equality have been set up to help make the law effective.

The **Race Relations Act** was passed in 1976 in an attempt to eradicate racial discrimination. The Act makes it illegal to discriminate against any individual on the grounds of race in employment, access to goods and services, education, and in many other situations. The Act deals with discrimination on racial grounds – that is, on the grounds of a person's colour, nationality or ethnic origin. If defines three ways in which discrimination can take place.

Direct discrimination means treating a person *less favourably* than others would be treated in the same circumstances. This includes refusing employment, or care, to a person because of his or her skin colour or ethnic background. It also includes deliberately giving a lower standard of care to certain people because of their race.

Secondly the Act prohibits **indirect discrimination**. This is where conditions are attached to applications for jobs and services which exclude certain groups of people and which cannot be justified on non-racial grounds. For example, to require a high standard of English from a labourer may break the law if it excludes people from a racial group who have limited English but could do the job perfectly well.

The third category of discrimination that the Act identifies is the **victimisation** of people who have made or supported complaints of discrimination. This is intended to support those who make complaints under the Act, and people who act as witnesses for them. It also makes it unlawful to victimise or discriminate against people who are thought to be about to make a complaint.

The Race Relations Act, then, is intended to *prevent* discrimination on the grounds of race or ethnicity, and to help people to report instances where it seems to be occurring. The Commission for Racial Equality was set up to help make the Act work. It offers advice and support to people who wish to report a complaint of discrimination on racial grounds, and has offices in several major cities.

Task

The Race Relations Act is intended to prevent discrimination on racial grounds and promote equality of opportunity. Think about the ways in which discrimination can take place that you have looked at in this and in an earlier chapter. List these ways on a sheet of paper.

Now think about the way that the Act deals with acts of discrimination. For each item on your list try to decide how the Act would deal with it. What do you think would be the biggest barrier to the Act being effective in preventing discrimination in each case?

The **Sex Discrimination Act** of 1986 makes it illegal to discriminate against people on the grounds of their gender. This Act has similarities with the Race Relations Act, and covers the same categories of discrimination.

Direct discrimination is again defined as treating a person less favourably than others, and the Act makes direct discrimination on the grounds of a persons' gender illegal. For example this means that it is illegal to refuse to employ a woman purely on the grounds of her gender; and in a care situation clients who have been treated less well than others because of their gender would be able to bring a complaint under the Act.

Indirect discrimination is also covered by the Sex Discrimination Act. Here it refers to setting conditions that exclude people from a particular gender group in employment, access to services, and in many other situations. While not directly excluded by their gender indirect discrimination has taken place if for example an upper age limit of 32 years on applicants has been set for a post making it more difficult for women to apply because many women under this age will have stopped work temporarily to raise young children. A condition like this which prevents women from applying for jobs that they could do perfectly well is indirect discrimination against them, and is illegal under the Act.

Victimisation of people who are making complaints under the Act, and victimisation of their supporters and witnesses, is also illegal under the Sex Discrimination Act.

The Equal Opportunities Commission was set up to help and advise people who feel that they have been discriminated against. It functions in a similar way to the Commission for Racial Equality.

There is also legislation designed to protect disabled people from discrimination. The **Disabled Persons Act** of 1986 was intended to protect disabled people from discrimination in the field of employment. It states that businesses employing more than 20 people must employ a proportion of disabled people. At least three per cent of the workforce in these firms must be registered disabled.

. MAINTAINING CLIENT RIGHTS . IN PRACTICE

Empowerment

Client rights can be supported and maintained both by the actions of individual carers and through the design of the delivery of health and care services. As a carer you need to be aware of how your own behaviour can affect clients' rights, and how the systems you work in can be developed to maintain them.

A basic concept in this process is that of **empowerment.** Empowerment means giving clients respect and control in their lives by the promotion of the client rights described above. The work that *you* do should aim to empower the

individual clients in the care process by ensuring that their rights are met.

Challenging discrimination

Discrimination on the basis of race or gender is against the law, but nevertheless in reality clients are sometimes discriminated against on these and on other grounds. As a carer you need to look at your own behaviour and that of other carers to see whether any groups are being treated less well than others in terms of the service they get and the way you communicate with them. *It is part of your role as a care worker to promote anti-discriminatory practice both in yourself and in others.*

You need to *recognise* when assumptions have been made about a person that are based on stereotypes. Check your own conversations with clients. Do you ever assume things about them because of their appearance? Are your non-verbal messages conveying warmth and interest? Remember that all clients are individuals and must be respected as such.

In your work place you should find out the local policy on dealing with acts of discrimination. This policy will have been designed to help you to promote anti-discriminatory practice. Anti-discriminatory and equal opportunities policies are only effective if they are put into practice.

Discrimination may, however, be built into the systems that the care services use or into their environment. The fictitious case given earlier, of a nursery which failed to provide a diet that allowed all children to attend, is an example of this. Failure to provide adequate access and facilities for disabled people is also a way in which discrimination can occur. Provision of service delivery should take account of the needs of potential clients in all aspects of planning, and failure to do so is a form of discrimination against those who are excluded.

Challenging discrimination is a difficult process, and there are no simple rules to guide you in all the situations you may face. A knowledge of the local policies may help you to decide what to do and you could begin by speaking to someone in authority whom you trust. If left unchallenged, discrimination is likely to continue and you should not let incidents pass.

Maintaining dignity

Clients whose needs include close personal care (such as toileting) need to be treated with respect to help maintain their dignity. It is easy to feel that you have lost your dignity if simple and personal tasks are being done for you, and clients may not be in a position to demand their rights. However, there are ways in which carers, and the systems they operate, can help to preserve the dignity of clients.

In personal contacts and conversations with a client it is important to remember that he or she is an individual with feelings and emotions. If a client has difficulty in communicating it is important to help with getting their message across, and not to show impatience or lack of interest. Try to conduct all conversations with clients on as normal a basis as possible so that they feel that they are being treated with the same respect as other people. Personal matters should always be discussed with clients in private, not in front of other staff or clients. Never talk to others about a client as though they were not there, and make sure that you give clients a chance to speak for themselves.

A client's dignity can be maintained during personal care functions. These should always be carried out in a way that the individual client feels happy with. Allow clients as much privacy as it is possible to give safely when performing functions such as bathing or toileting. Avoid conveying feelings of disapproval when carrying out tasks which you may find unpleasant, such as dealing with the effects of incontinence.

Clients should feel comfortable with the care that they receive and must not be made to feel that they are causing problems because of their needs.

Promoting independence

Clients' rights to independence can be maintained by helping them to be as involved as possible in their own care. People need to be empowered in the control of their own lives and encouraged to do as much as possible for themselves. Carers can help this to take place by the way in which they deal with clients and their needs.

Try not to do things for clients that they can do for themselves. This may not always be easy when a client is dependent on carers for many of his or her basic needs to be met. It may seem quicker and easier to do a task yourself rather than to take the time to show the client how to do it – but it is important that clients are given the chance to care for themselves. Allow clients time to learn how to help with their own care and involve them in decisions about how it is conducted. Try to discuss care issues with clients so that they are able to feel a part of the care that they receive. Involving clients in decisions about their own care helps to empower them and increases their independence.

Clients can be further empowered by ensuring that they have the necessary equipment and aids. They should be helped to make best use of the aids that are available to them so that their independence is improved.

Maximising client choice

It is important to maintain clients' right of choice in the care they receive. This means involving them as much as possible in the decisions made concerning their care. In many cases the needs of the clients will *dictate* the type of care that they receive, and so the amount of choice will be limited. However, if clients are made aware of this situation, and are told the alternatives that are possible, they will be able to contribute to the decision-making process.

The behaviour and working practices of staff should operate to maximise client choice and not prevent it. Try to spot where alternatives may be offered to a client in their daily care, rather than carrying on in a routine way. For instance, in residential care it may be possible to offer some choice in the arrangement of the environment, and clients should be encouraged to make their own decisions about this.

Some clients may have difficulties expressing their wishes, either because of a disability or because their past experience of care has discouraged them from doing so. Carers can help by assisting people to speak up for themselves – this is called **self-advocacy**. Helping people to understand their rights, and giving them the skills to express them, are the principles on which self-advocacy is based.

In practice, promoting self-advocacy is a process requiring sensitivity, skill and knowledge, and programmes aiming to promote it are sometimes integrated into the care that people receive. You will be contributing to the aim of maintaining clients' choice if you get people to express their feelings about the care they are receiving and their views on changes they would like to see.

For some people it is difficult or impossible to advocate for themselves. Then it is up to carers to ensure that their wishes are expressed. Advocacy for others also requires sensitivity and care – for one thing you must be sure that you are conveying the messages that the person intended. It is sometimes the people in close care situations who find that they have an understanding of a clients' wishes.

Confidentiality

Health and caring agencies obviously need to keep detailed records about clients. Information within these records is often vital to clients' care and well-being. However, only certain people need to have access to all this information. Service managers should therefore ensure that clients' records remain confidential and yet available to those who need them. Systems through which information about clients is handled need to balance these two aims.

As a carer you need to understand how client information is dealt with in the care setting you are in. You must respect the clients' right to confidentiality and realise that you will be given enough information about them to support their care. It is up to an individual client to decide whether or not he or she wishes to reveal to you other confidential information. In such a case it is important to keep it to yourself – to maintain the client's trust in you. Breaches of confidentiality are seen as serious failings in caring staff.

There may be a dilemma for you in some situations, such as when information is told to you in confidence which you feel needs to be passed on to others and acted upon. If you think that you are being told something that others should hear, it is vital to stop the client and let them know your feelings about what they are saying. If they do not want their comments to go further then their wishes must be respected.

Care should be conducted in an atmosphere which promotes respect for clients, and for their right to confidentiality. Staff should avoid gossiping with other carers about particular clients and their private affairs. Whilst it is natural to want to share your working experiences with your colleagues, it is important to remember that you are working with people and that some aspects of your job need to remain private between you and the client.

Task

Imagine that you are a manager in a health and care service setting and are writing a guide for new care staff.

Think about the ways in which rights to dignity, choice and independence can be promoted for clients. Write the part of the guide that helps new staff to ensure that these client rights are maintained. Try to explain the importance of these rights and give ways in which staff can support them.

Ensuring a safe environment

A carer has a major role to play in ensuring that clients have a safe environment. The day-to-day practices in care settings should have been developed with health and safety in mind. It is vital that you follow the ways of working that you are shown so that clients and other staff are not endangered. Some clients are particularly vulnerable if routines are not followed, and you need to be particularly careful where a client's safety may be affected.

Always use and store equipment as directed, and ensure that any cleaning is done thoroughly and in the ways directed. If equipment seems to be faulty or broken don't try to repair it yourself – report the fault. If you are in doubt about safety in any aspect of your work, seek immediate advice from senior staff. It is far better to check your actions than create dangers for yourself and others.

All care settings must by law have arrangements for certain aspects of health and safety. You must be aware of what these are in your place of work.

Find out, for instance, what the procedures are in case of fire. Make sure you know where the fire alarms and exits are, and where extinguishers are located. Check on the procedures for the evacuation of clients in an emergency. Also find out the procedure to be followed in case of accidents. Do you know which staff are qualified to administer first aid, and where the first aid box is located? There are procedures for the treatment and recording of accidents and you need to know what to do if you are in that situation.

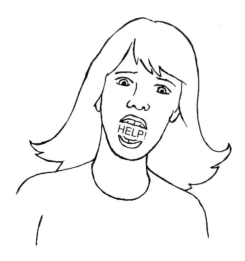

Clients have a right to receive care in a healthy and safe environment, and it is the responsibility of health and care services and their staff to ensure that this is available.

Self-assessment test

1 Which of the following services are free to all?
   a Prescription items.
   b An appointment with a GP.
   c Treatment by a dentist.
   d An eye-test.

2 Which of the following are included in a primary health care team?
   a GP, practice nurse and health visitor.
   b Dentist, optician and physiotherapist.
   c GP, social worker and Family Health Service Authority.
   d Practice nurse, GP and surgeon.

3 Which of the following is an example of preventative medicine offered by a doctor's surgery?
   a Prescriptions.
   b Well-woman and well-man clinics.
   c Pregnancy tests.

4 Explain briefly the difference between a nursing home and a rest home.

5 Which of the following describes a statutory service?
   a One which must be provided by law (statute).
   b One provided by volunteers.
   c One which makes money.
   d One that is provided once a week.

6 Which of the following describes a Trust Hospital?
   a One where the treatment is good.
   b A self-governing body which provides care and treatment.
   c One controlled by the District Health Authority.
   d A District General Hospital.

7 Which of the following is/are true of voluntary bodies?
   a They are controlled by Community Health Councils.
   b They provide health and care services often free of charge.
   c They run on a profit-making basis.

8 Which of the following is/are true of private health and care services?

a They form a part of the NHS.

b They are controlled by the Secretary of State for Health.

c They provide their services free of charge.

d They are paid for by the users themselves.

9 Which of the following is/are true of a GP fund-holding doctor?

a The GP controls his or her own budget.

b He/she collects money for charity.

c He/she can give money to clients in need of financial assistance.

d He/she works only in the private sector.

10 Answer the following true or false:

a Needs can be identified as general and specific.

b A need is always the same as a want.

c A good standard of care should meet the needs of the individual.

d The needs of all service users are the same.

e A field social worker is one who is based in the countryside.

f Social workers always know what is best for clients.

g Community care means that people will no longer be cared for in residential accommodation.

11 Who are the clients of the health and care services?

12 Name *six* rights that people have as clients of the health and care services.

13 What is indirect discrimination?

14 Explain what is meant by empowerment of clients.

15 Assumptions based on stereotypes can lead to discrimination against clients. What is a stereotype?

16 State two ways in which carers can promote dignity in clients.

17 Allowing clients to have a role in making decisions about their care is helping them to maintain their right to:

a independence   **c** choice

b dignity   **d** freedom from discrimination?

18 What is confidentiality?

19 Explain one way in which a client who has difficulty in communicating may be helped to express their wishes.

20 What does the term 'anti-discriminatory practice' mean?

Fast Facts

Advocacy Speaking for another person and representing their interests on their behalf.

Categorising Clients must be treated as individuals with their own specific needs and not viewed as a 'category'. Categorising is used to make explanation easier and no more than that.

Choice The right of clients to be able to make choices about the care that they receive.

Client/service user Children and their families, adolescents, people with a physical disability, people with learning difficulties and disability, people with mental illness and elders make up the main categories of those taking up services.

Client rights The rights of clients to a particular standard of treatment by the health and care services.

Commission for Racial Equality A body set up to help the **Race Relations Act** be effective. It helps with support and information for people making complaints.

Community Health Councils These monitor the services provided by District Health Authorities (DHAs) and represent the views of service users.

Confidentiality The right of clients to have private information about themselves kept secret.

Department of Health A central government body which administers health care. Regional Health Authorities and the **Family Health Services Authority** are influenced and controlled by Department of Health policy. Health services, hospitals and social services are controlled from the Department of Health.

Department of Social Security (DSS) A central government body which provides benefits such as income support, child benefit, and is responsible for general social security. The Benefits Agency covers one section of social security work. The agency is responsible to the DSS.

Dependency Reliance on others for your needs to be met.

Dignity Being worthy of respect and possessing pride and self-esteem.

Discrimination   To treat some people less well than others.

District Health Authorities   DHAs can be either providers of care or purchasers of care. Hospitals may be controlled by a DHA. Alternatively, hospitals with Trust status are outside the control of the DHA and are self-governing.

Empowerment   To give power to someone. The word is used to describe the results of maintaining client rights, so allowing people more freedom and control of their own lives.

Family Health Service Authorities (FHSAs)   Family Health Service Authorities employ the services of GPs, dentists, opticians and chemists. Family Health Service Authorities and District Authorities share the same geographical boundaries and there are links between the two organisations.

General and specific needs   Some **needs** are common to everyone and these are called general needs. Other needs are specific to the individual and stem from the individual's unique make-up, circumstances and experiences.

Independence   The right of clients to be free of control by others, and to be able to help attend to their own needs.

Local Authority social services   Local Authority social service departments are responsible for ensuring that clients' social care needs are met in the community.

National Health Service (NHS)   In England, the Secretary of State for Health has overall responsibility for the NHS. The organisation of the NHS in England involves the Department of Health, Regional Health Authorities and District Health Authorities. Organisation of the NHS in Northern Ireland, Scotland and Wales is different from that of England.

Need   A need is an essential requirement which must be satisfied in order to ensure that an individual reaches a state of health and social well-being.

PISCES   Needs can be described as physical, intellectual, social, cultural, emotional and sexual (PISCES). Needs cannot be separated because changes in one can affect each and all of the others.

Primary health care team   A local team of professional health workers including GPs, district nurses, health visitors, local practice nurses, and community psychiatric nurses.

Private services   Private services provide an alternative form of care for which there is a charge. Private organisations are run on business lines and are profit-making.

Provider   An organisation that sells services to a purchaser.

Purchaser   An organisation that buys in necessary services.

Race Relations Act   An Act of Parliament which made discrimination on the grounds of race illegal.

Self-advocacy   Speaking out for your own rights and putting your own case.

Sex Discrimination Act   An Act of Parliament which was designed to prevent discrimination on the grounds of gender.

Statutory organisations   Health and care services are provided by statutory, voluntary and private organisations. Statutory organisations are those which must be set up by law (statute) to provide a service or range of services. The NHS and Local Authority social service departments form the two main branches of the health and care industry.

Voluntary organisations   Voluntary organisations provide a vast network of services to bridge the gaps in statutory provision. Voluntary services are often provided free of charge.

5 COMMUNICATION

In this chapter you will learn about communication skills. Communication covers a whole range of verbal and non-verbal behaviour. It includes taking part in discussions, both with people you know and people you don't. It includes communicating in writing in a way that is accurate and easily understood. You will also need to know how to use images – that is, sketches, diagrams, photographs and tables – to illustrate points you are trying to make. As a care worker you will need to be able to read and understand information in order to keep accurate records and make sure the care your clients get is appropriate and safe.

You can see, then, that communication is an important skill for a care worker. It is not something which is separate from other parts of the course, but a part you will need to use alongside the other units. It is about understanding other people's meanings and views and making clear what you want them to understand.

In your work you will meet a great number of people who will have different ways of saying what they mean. It will be your job to listen carefully and sort out what they are trying to tell you.

If you are doing this face to face with the person you will have the advantage of being able to take in non-verbal clues (body language). If you are speaking with someone on the telephone, however, you will have to rely purely on what is said.

Communication is the sending and receiving of information. *It is a two-way process.* In order to be sure that the correct message has been received, the receiving person will often check this by sending feedback – that is, asking a question to check their understanding is correct. For example, a supervisor might remind a care worker to sweeten a resident's tea. The care worker might need to check the meaning of 'sweeten' by asking if that is with sugar or a sweetener. If the resident were diabetic, this information would be essential.

UNDERSTANDING AND CHECKING INFORMATION

Read the following short story. On a separate piece of paper write the numbers 1 to 12. When you have read the story read the questions below. Write 'True', 'False' or 'Don't know' in answer to the questions against the numbers on your sheet of paper.

An officer-in-charge had just turned off the lights in a community home when a man appeared and demanded drugs and hypodermic needles. The owner opened the drugs cupboard. The contents of the drugs cupboard were snatched up and the man dashed off. The police were informed of what had happened.

Questions

1 The man appeared after the owner had turned off the lights at the community home.
2 The robber was a man.
3 The man who appeared did not demand drugs.
4 The man who opened the drugs cupboard was the owner.

5 The home's owner snatched the contents of the drug cupboard and ran away.

6 Someone opened a drugs cupboard.

7 The robber demanded drugs of the owner.

8 The robber opened the drugs cupboard.

9 The robber did not take the drugs with him.

10 The robber did not demand drugs of the owner.

11 The owner opened a drugs cupboard.

12 Taking the contents of the drugs cupboard with him, the man ran out of the community home.

The full story ... The authorities in a particular area were worried about the use of low-quality drugs and sharing of dirty needles amongst addicts. They therefore offered drug users an amnesty. If they took their drugs and dirty needles to the local community home they would be entered on a list of Registered Addicts. This would mean they could get prescribed drugs. The home would be the centre for a Needle Exchange where addicts could be supplied with fresh hypodermics in an effort to prevent the spread of AIDS. The drugs were collected from the home and the police were involved in the routine collection of drugs for destruction.

Answers to the questions

1 *Don't know.* We don't know because we are only told the officer-in-charge had turned the lights off. We don't know if this was in fact the owner or another person.

2 *Don't know.* We have nothing to prove the man who demanded drugs and hypodermic needles was a robber.

3 *False.* The man who appeared did demand drugs.

4 *Don't know.* We know the owner opened the drugs cupboard, but we don't know if the owner was a man.

5 *Don't know.* We are not told who snatched the contents of the drugs cupboard.

6 *True.* We know someone opened the drugs cupboard.

7 *Don't know.* We don't know if the officer-in-charge and the owner were the same person.

8 *Don't know.* We don't know if the owner was the robber or if it was a different person.

9 *Don't know.* We can't tell who snatched the drugs.

10 *Don't know.* Again we don't know if the officer-in-charge was the owner, or if in fact the owner was the robber.

11 *True.*

12 *Don't know.* We don't know if the person who snatched the drugs was the robber or the owner or the officer-in-charge.

Comments

If you feel confused it is not surprising. When you first read the story it probably seemed quite straightforward! You almost certainly thought that a man had held up the owner of a community home and stolen the store of drugs. The point of the exercise was to show that in order to come to that conclusion *a lot of assumptions have to be made*. We often think we know the whole story but what we see and hear is often very superficial. We jump to conclusions without understanding the whole story.

It is particularly important to remember this when dealing with people. You are only seeing what is happening to them *now*. Before you met them they had many experiences of which you are not aware. These experiences have made them what they are now, and this is nearly always more complex than can be seen from the surface. It is therefore very important to ask the right kind of questions and to think around many possibilities before even trying to come to a conclusion.

The second point of the above exercise was to show how unwilling most people are to say they don't know something. Most of the correct answers to the questions were 'Don't know', but people often feel they *should* know, so they try to avoid admitting they don't.

When you were doing the exercise you probably found you had to constantly check back on the first simple story to see if you had understood the points made. As a care worker you will need to make sure you check your understanding often, both when reading and when speaking with colleagues and clients. The 'drug robbery' story shows how easy it is to assume you are thinking what someone else is thinking when in fact you aren't.

Think it over

Think back to what you read in Chapter 1 – the section on checking assumptions. Skilled care work depends on good questioning!

USING AN APPROPRIATE TONE OF VOICE

Consider this situation. A care worker is pushing a client in a wheelchair through a busy shopping centre. Sometimes people are courteous and politely hold open shop doors for the chair to be pushed through. Today, however, it seems as if the client and chair are invisible. No one is taking the time to help. Finally, after the swing door has almost squashed the client yet again, the care worker says loudly 'Thanks very much!'

It is easy to identify with that situation, and no one would be in any doubt that the care worker meant the very opposite of 'Thanks'. We all know it's not what you say, it's the way that you say it.

Think it over

Think back to Chapter 1 – the discussion on looking at the whole picture, and the different meanings that 'I really do care for you' might have!

It is important to use the **tone** and **manner** suited to the people you are talking with. This seems straightforward, but because a care worker will be working with people of all ages, backgrounds, intelligence and experience it is quite a skill to judge the right tone and manner.

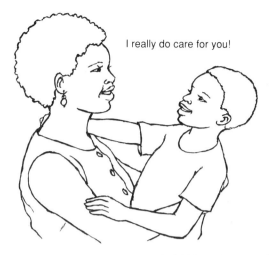

I really do care for you!

When people are talking with small children they tend to use short sentences, repeat what they say in different ways, and use a high-pitched voice. This is called 'mother-ese'. We speak in this way to small children to help them understand unfamiliar words. However, if you are working with an adult client with limited understanding – perhaps someone with learning difficulties or with a hearing disability – it would not be appropriate to speak to them as though they were a child. It would be **patronising**. The important thing to remember is that your tone and manner should be **appropriate**. This means it should be appropriate to the person's age as well as their understanding.

Think it over

Can you remember a time when someone spoke to you in what you felt to be a patronising way? How did you feel?

A skilful communicator is aware of the person being spoken to and the surroundings in which the conversation takes place. What is appropriate in one set of circumstances is inappropriate in another.

Consider the following situation. A group of people are sitting together quietly. 'Did you see that programme last night about Heavy Metal?' someone asks. A conversation starts among the group. Some people had enjoyed the programme, some had not. Was this an appropriate discussion?

The answer is that we cannot tell because we don't know where it took place. If it took place in the canteen at lunchtime it would have been appropriate and enjoyable. However, if it took place while the group was supposed to be revising for a test or while bathing an elderly client, it would have been inappropriate. What is acceptable in one situation is not in another.

If you only ate carrots like my
mum you would not take up so much room

To some extent learning to use the appropriate tone and manner is something we learn as we grow up. Children are famous for saying exactly what they are thinking, often to the embarrassment of their parents. As people mature they realise they have to make **judgements** about when to say what they are thinking and when it is advisable to keep quiet. This is because it is easy to be hurtful to others by saying tactless things. We all know of people who proudly state that they always say what they think, speak their mind. To do this, however, is to fail to consider the effect of what you say on other people.

• USING THE TELEPHONE •

Most people are familiar with using the telephone as a convenient means of keeping in touch with friends and family. When you know someone well it is easy to chat without being able to see them. You are familiar enough with the way they speak to be able to tell when they have finished talking and you can begin.

If you are talking on the telephone with someone you don't know, however, you do not have the advantage of non-verbal language to tell you when it is your turn to speak. When you are speaking face-to-face with someone

you can see their facial expression, you have eye-contact, you can see if their body is tense or relaxed and you will each be positioned in relation to the other. On the telephone you will have to make do with hearing the speed and tone of the person's voice to give you extra clues as to their meaning.

Making a call

Many people are afraid of making business telephone calls. One of the reasons they are worried is because they fear they may forget what they intended to say. If you feel like this it will help you to make a list of what you need to say before you dial the number. Then, if your mind goes blank with panic you can refer back to your list.

When you make a business call, the person at the other end will not recognise your voice as a friend would, *so you need first to say who you are and then who you would like to speak with*. You should have your list of what you want to say, and it is a good idea to make quick notes of the replies. *Always* have a pencil and paper with you beside the telephone.

Task

Here is an exercise to practise making telephone calls. Write down some notes of the points you would need answers for.

You are a care worker working with young adults with physical disabilities. All need to use wheelchairs. There is a rock concert in a local sports stadium and a group of residents wants to go. Before a decision is made it is necessary to find out if this will create access difficulties. Your officer-in-charge does not want to agree to the outing and then find the group cannot be accommodated and risk disappointing them. You are asked to ring the stadium to see if a visit by your clients would be possible. Don't forget to ask about toilet and refreshment facilities and any fire regulations. Make notes of what you would say.

Sample conversation

1 Ask to speak to the Concert Organiser.
2 Say where you are from; i.e. where you work and your own name.
3 Say you are ringing about the possibility of a group of people using wheelchairs attending the rock concert.
4 Ask if there is wheelchair access to:
   a the stadium
   b the toilets
   c the refreshment areas.
5 Ask if there are any fire restrictions regarding wheelchair usage.
6 Ask if there is a maximum number of wheelchairs that can be accommodated.
7 Thank the person for the information. Remember to stay polite if the answers were not what you would want them to be. The person you would speak to would probably not be responsible for making the rules, just for telling you what they are.

PS. You can award yourself extra points if you asked if there was a group discount!

It is a great deal easier to make telephone calls which need answers to several questions if you make a note of what you need to ask in advance and the answers as you get them.

Think it over

It is important to reflect before making telephone calls in the same way as reflecting before speaking to a group.

Answering the telephone

Taking notes of what someone tells you when you are answering the telephone is vital. If you are busy, or a nervous 'phone user, it is easy to forget exactly what the message was.

When you answer the telephone at work you should immediately say either the telephone number or the name of the establishment. You should then say '… speaking', using your own name.

The person calling will usually then say who they are. If they don't, you need to ask who is calling in order to give an accurate message about the call. An example might be:

'Good morning. "The Grange", Mary Knight speaking.'
'Good morning. This is Andrea Ahmed from Area Social Services. Could I speak to the officer-in-charge please?'

Below is a conversation between a care worker and a relative of a resident. The relative is in a pay phone-box and in a rush to leave a message.

Care worker: 'Hello. "The Grange", Mary Knight speaking.'
Relative: 'Hello. It's Emma Brown's daughter. I can't stay on long, I'm on a pay-phone. Tell her we'll have to cancel the hairdresser. I'm on the A27, broken down, think it's the fan-belt. Does she want to go tomorrow? I'm on afternoons so it would be after two and I'm going to the dentist at 4.30. It's up to her. Will you make the arrangements? Telephone me at home tonight. My money's running out, I'll have to go. Bye.'

In this situation your message could be something like this:

● Message for Emma Brown from her daughter.
● Daughter will not be coming this afternoon – her car has broken down.
● The appointment at the hairdressers needs cancelling.
● Does Mrs Brown want to go to the hairdresser tomorrow between 2 and 4.30?
● If she does a new appointment will have to be made.
● Mrs Brown should telephone her daughter at home this evening to let her know if she wants to go to the hairdresser tomorrow and if an appointment has been made.

Task

Compose a sample message you would write before making each of the two telephone calls outlined below.

1 You need to call the meals-on-wheels supervisor. Sam Kent has to go into hospital for two weeks (give the dates) and will not be needing his meals delivered. Give his address and say when he would like them restarted. He is having an operation for the removal of his gall-bladder and will need a special diet for a month after he leaves hospital. He would like meals on alternate days of the week beginning on Mondays. His family will provide the others and weekend meals.

2 *Kim Havel has been waiting for a shower with ramp and rails for six months. Until it is installed the district nurse is having to call every day to bath her. This is a waste of resources because she does not need medical care every day. You are her social work assistant and will need an exact date and time from the Area Housing Office so that the home help can be on hand to help move household effects for the workmen to do the alterations.*

· WRITING CORRECTLY ·

Why do we bother to use punctuation? The answer is that we use **punctuation marks** – such as capital letters, commas, full stops, apostrophes – to make what we write easy for others to understand.

A **sentence** will tell you something about someone or something. To be complete it must make sense. A sentence is a group of words which begins with a capital letter and ends with a full stop. It must have a subject and a verb.

Below are some of the main parts of a grammar:

> **SENTENCE SUBJECT VERB NOUN PRONOUN ADJECTIVE**

- **Sentence.** This is words put together to make complete sense. A sentence must have a verb and a subject.
- **Verb.** A verb is simply a word which describes an action. For example, 'We *danced* all night' or 'I *wore* my uniform'.
- **Subject.** This is the name given to the noun or pronoun (see below) about which a statement is being made. In the examples above, 'We' were the people who went dancing and 'I' was the person wearing the uniform. 'We' and 'I' were the subjects of the sentences.
- **Noun.** This is the name of an object or person or place: cup, Indira, Australia. If the noun is a **proper noun** –

that is, the name of a town, country or person – it begins with a capital letter.
- **Pronoun.** A pronoun is a word used instead of a name (e.g. him, her, it). We often use pronouns when we are writing so as not to keep repeating the same word: 'It was Lee Ping's birthday. We gave *her* a present'. If we were to write a few sentences about the same person or object it would get boring to keep saying the noun, so we use pronouns sometimes.
- **Adjective.** This is a word which tells us something more about a noun we have used. For example, 'The old lady was *frail*', 'The weather was *bad*'.

Punctuation

The passage below has no capital letters or full stops. In fact it has no punctuation at all. Try reading it!

what is the difference between a playgroup and a school nursery they are both for young children they both prepare children for school by getting them used to mixing with other children whether children attend a playgroup or nursery they will have to get used to leaving their home and parents for short periods the difference is that a nursery school will build definite educational aims into the activities the activities may appear to be unstructured and the children given choice but in the nursery the teacher will have developed activities to teach specific skills in the playgroup the children will be offered a range of similar activities but there will be more or less free choice and the outcome of the learning will not be formally defined children in a nursery school attached to a primary school will also have the opportunity to see the older children and get used to the idea of going to school full time when they are old enough they will become familiar with the building and the move from home to school will be easier

The same passage is repeated below with the capital letters and full stops in. It should be easier to understand:

What is the difference between a playgroup and a school nursery? They are both for young children. They both prepare children for school by getting them used to mixing with other children. Whether children attend a playgroup or nursery, they will have to get used to leaving their home and parents for short periods. The difference is that a nursery school will build definite educational aims into the activities. The activities may appear to be unstructured and the children given choice, but in the nursery the teacher will have developed activities to teach specific skills. In the playgroup the children will be offered a range of similar activities, but there will be more-or-less free choice and the outcome of the learning will not be formally defined. Children in a nursery school attached to a primary school will also have the opportunity to see the older children and get used to the idea of going to school full-time when they are old enough. They will become familiar with the building, and the move from home to school will be easier.

As you can see, it is much easier to understand when it is written in sentences and with the help of a few commas and question marks.

A **comma** is used to show a pause and to separate items in a list. It is also used to separate different parts or descriptions within a sentence – for example, 'The bride's wedding gown, which was a family heirloom, was made from silk and antique lace'. The sentence would still have made sense without the 'which was a family heirloom'. This part was giving more information within the sentence, but putting it between commas made the sentence easier to understand.

A **question mark** is used *instead* of a full stop when a question has been asked. It only comes at the end of a sentence, in place of the full stop, not in the middle.

Remember:

Punctuation is to make writing easier to understand.

When we are speaking with each other we do not need to be as grammatically correct, because we use other ways of showing our meaning. For example, we use our facial expressions, actions, body language and tone of voice. On the other hand, when you are writing something, the reader can only tell what you mean from the marks on the page, and so you have to be much more careful about making meanings clear. Do not risk being misunderstood!

The apostrophe

Another device which we use to give clues about our meaning is the **apostrophe**. This little mark ' is used in two *different* ways.

Firstly, the apostrophe shows that a letter or letters have been **missed out** of a word. When we use the apostrophe in this way we put it where the missing letters would have been. For example, we sometimes shorten 'is not' to 'isn't', and in this case the apostrophe in 'isn't' goes where the 'o' would be in 'is not' if the full words had been written. In the same way, the apostrophe in 'I'm' goes where the 'a' in 'am' would be. Sometimes people put the apostrophe in the wrong place (or omit it all together) because they have not learnt this rule. Have you ever seen 'is'nt' or 'Im'?

The second use of the apostrophe is to show that something **belongs** to something else. For example: 'The care worker's wages have not been paid'. In this example the apostrophe is there to show that the wages belong to the care worker.

Note that if we were referring to the wages of more than one care worker, the apostrophe would be in a different place: 'The care workers' wages have not been paid'. The wages still belong to the care workers, but putting the apostrophe after the 's' shows that there is more than one care worker owed wages.

Think it over

Can you see that if this was written in a message from the Wages Department it would be important to the care workers to get the apostrophe in the right place?

Task

Write out the two passages below, putting in possessive apostrophes.

1 *Ten minutes walk from the towns centre, on ones way to the technical college, is Park Nursery. The Education Departments plan for this, the towns main nursery, is that it should be privatised and used for both visitors and students children. The fees charged would be according to the parents income.*

2 *(Taken from Stan Barstow's book A Kind of Loving) Hes lucky he could go to bed. Ive spent the night on the front room sofa and the last four or five hours trying to get in the bathroom. By the time I do manage to get in there Im feeling a bit sour at having all these people barging about the place, and forget to shoot the bolt behind me. It doesnt improve my temper when young Dorothy and Angela catch me without pants. This amuses them no end and I wonder if I cant arrange to fall downstairs and break a leg and give them a real laugh. A couple of proper horrors, Dorothy and Angela, twins, belonging to Auntie Agnes, one of my mothers sisters. I know the Old Lady cant abide them and she only had Chris ask them to be bridesmaids because she didnt want to get across Auntie Agnes whos one of them sensitive types who go through life looking for any offence left lying about for the taking.*

Remember:

- *Apostrophes show possession or omission.*
- *If in doubt, leave them out – you should never use them simply because you think an 's' looks lonely!*

· WRITING LETTERS AND MEMOS ·

You will often need to write letters as part of your work. A business letter needs to be written in a more formal way than a letter to a friend. If a business letter is not set out correctly, it may be delayed in getting to the correct person, or the reply you expect may be delayed. Figure 5.1 shows a sample layout.

Task

Practise letter writing by writing a letter to your local Social Services Department. Write on behalf of an elderly gentleman saying you are his son or daughter. You have been asking the Social Services Department to arrange for a wheelchair ramp to be put outside your father's front door. Until this work is done, getting his chair in and out is impossible without someone to lift it. Ask for a definite appointment for someone to come and assess what is needed. Quote the reference on the sample letter.

```
                                    23 Ramsey Street
                                    Erinsburgh
                                    Cheshire 1CV 6SJ
Your Ref: AS/md324
23 April 199–
Social Services Department
Town Hall
Summerbay
Cheshire 1FF 3AG



Dear Sir/Madam

Application for Ramp

Main part of letter . . .




Yours faithfully

[signature]

M. Green
```

Figure 5.1 *A typical layout of a formal letter*

Sometimes messages within a department or company are written in the form of a memo (which is short for memorandum). This is a written message, like a letter, but because it is internal to the department or company it does not need to have addresses. Figure 5.2 shows an example.

Task

Practise writing memos by writing one back to T Burnley from yourself saying you are on leave next week but have made an appointment for …(state the date). You can use both the letter and the memo as evidence of correspondence for your portfolio.

MEMORANDUM

To: T Burnley

From: S Dontineni

Date: 3 April 9–

Subject: Wheelchair access

I attach a copy of a letter regarding arranging a ramp for this client. Please make an appointment to visit within the next week.

SD

Figure 5.2 *Sample memorandum*

• FILLING IN FORMS •

From the very minute we are born details about us need to be recorded. Whether a baby is born at home with a midwife in attendance, or in hospital, details of its weight, length, head circumference and family name are recorded immediately. Within a few days details of the time and place of birth and its parent/s names are recorded on a birth certificate. This makes the child a citizen of the country in which it was born.

Think it over

You have probably filled in forms such as an application for a provisional driving licence, a family allowance form or maybe the back of a doctor's prescription to get your medication. Think for a moment about whether you had problems doing this.

Care workers will often be called upon to help clients fill in forms. For example, when someone goes into care the establishment needs to record that person's details in an organised way on a form called an Admission Form (see Figure 5.3). Below are details of a lady talking with a care worker. See if you can work out from what she says what details would need to go on the Admission Form.

ADMISSION FORM

Surname: Date of birth:

Forenames: Religion:

Home address:

Next of kin: Relationship:

Address of kin:

Telephone number:

General practitioner:

GP's address:

GP's telephone number:

Medication:

Diet preferences:

Wears dentures: yes/no

Wears spectacles: yes/no/for reading only

Aids used:

Figure 5.3 *How an Admission Form might look*

I came into the world on 19 June 1919. I was the youngest of six. I had two brothers and three sisters. Emma Webster I was born and Emma Webster I have stayed. I never had any children, I was always too busy helping with my nieces and nephews.

There's only me and our Alice now. My two brothers were killed in a mining accident and our Marjorie went to Australia to be with her son. We 'phone each other every day, me and our Alice – Alice Dixon as she is now. I had her number on my telephone memory button, Horbury 270509. Funny I can remember things that happened years ago but I can't always remember things now, so I put her number on my 'phone memory just in case.

I had a lovely flat you know, in Water Lane, Horbury, number 10 it was. It had views of the river and everything, but it got that I couldn't manage the stairs with my Zimmer frame and the lift didn't work always. Our Alice lives just round the corner on The Wharf, 37, but her's is a ground floor flat.

Dr Smith, lovely man, you know, Grove Surgery in Horbury, wanted me to have a hip replacement, but I said no, not at my age. I've never had anything, you know, except my teeth out. Apart from that it's only been visits to the optician. Funny, I can see things far away, but I can't see to read the paper or do my knitting. I have to have them when I go to church too, or I can't see the hymn book. I go to St Austin's Catholic you know.

We couldn't afford the doctor when I was young. We had to keep ourselves healthy eating the right food. We had none of this fast food. There wasn't much meat, but we had plenty of veg' that we grew on the allotments. I don't believe in them laxatives or tablets, make you dopey half the time. No, I keep my system healthy eating the right food. The only tablets I take are those for my arthritis and I only have one of those before bed so I'm not kept awake by the pain.

Task

Now you have read Emma's account, try to put the details on the Admission Form. You can use it as evidence for your portfolio of completing a preset form.

WRITING YOUR CURRICULUM VITAE (CV)

One document which you will almost certainly need to prepare is a **curriculum vitae**. This is a Latin name for a document which people send to potential employers when applying for a job. It gives all their personal details and information about their qualifications and experience. Figure 5.4 shows an example of how a curriculum vitae may be set out.

Task

Prepare your own CV using a word-processor. You can use it as evidence for your portfolio, both for completing outline forms and your word-processing skills (IT).

CURRICULUM VITAE

Surname: Singh

Forenames: Parvees

Address: 69 Cumbrian Way, Summerbay

Date of birth: 4.3.76

Education:
  1987–1992: Summerbay High School
  1992 to date: Summerbay College

Qualifications:

GCSE	Grade
English	C
Combined Science	C
Mathematics	D
Childcare	D
French	E

Work experience:
I have worked for one year on a toffee stall in the market. I have to control stock, serve customers and handle cash. I am entirely responsible for the stall. I also baby-sit once a week for a child of three.

Interests:
I am taking the Silver Stage of the Duke of Edinburgh Award Scheme. I have undertaken an expedition which meant a group of us had to live for three days and two nights in the countryside. We had to cook our own food and walk each day. This taught me to co-operate and take responsibility for both myself and others.
For the Community part of the Award, I have been helping a family with a child who has learning difficulties. I have found it very rewarding to see the progress he has made. When I first began he could not speak, but now he will point to pictures and say small words. I also enjoy swimming and playing badminton.

Figure 5.4 *A curriculum vitae*

USING IMAGES TO ILLUSTRATE POINTS

A care worker often has to help people who have difficulty understanding spoken words. Their difficulties can be caused by many factors. They may not hear well, they may have a learning difficulty and not understand the meaning of some words, they may have had damage to the

part of their brain which deals with language following a stroke or an accident.

Whatever the cause of their difficulty, you can help by using as many means, besides words, as possible to get meanings across. This is called 'total communication'.

Think it over

Make a list of as many different ways of communicating as you can think of.

You have probably thought of using hand-signing, body language, sketches, diagrams, still photographs, graphs and maybe more ways of communicating.

Written language is a fairly complex system of 'talking' to someone. In our society it is essential but has obvious limitations. For example, most of us can only communicate well in writing in our own language. If we need to communicate with someone who speaks another language things may be more difficult. Before written language as we know it now was invented, people used to leave messages for each other by drawing what they had to say. We know this because some of the 'conversations' still exist in caves today. This is a very useful way of extending language where people speak different languages, or where there is difficulty in understanding.

Task

Below is an explanation, written for teenagers with learning difficulties, to let them know what a key worker is and how they can be helped by their key worker. The first two examples have a small drawing beside them to help the person understand and remember what the written part said.
Read through the information and draw symbols to show how you would illustrate the six sentences which are shown without a drawing.

While you are at school your key worker will help you:
in your learning both in class and in the group

to make friends and learn to be a member of a group

... to keep in contact with your family and friends at home
... by listening to what you say and knowing how you feel
... by helping you to decide what you need for your life
... to arrange special times in your life like birthdays, holidays, Christmas and your free time
... to look after yourself and your clothes
... to look after your money and possessions.

These are the sort of diagrams you might have produced:

to keep in contact with your family and friends at home (The telephone and envelope show the person that these are means of 'talking' with family and friends when they are living far away from them.)

by listening to what you say and knowing how you feel (The picture of an ear tells the client that the key worker is always – within reason – ready to listen to them and try to understand their feelings.)

by helping you to decide what you need for your life (The picture of someone apparently 'balancing' with their hands is meant to indicate choices, decisions which the key worker would help the client to talk through.)

arranging special times in your life like birthdays, holidays, Christmas, and free time (This diagram reminds the client that on special occasions we don't always follow the same routine and the key worker will help them plan for different times in their life.)

to look after yourself and your clothes (A picture of neat clothes reminds the client they will need to take responsibility for some aspects of looking after themselves and their key worker will help them with the necessary skills.)

to look after your money and possessions (A picture of money and a person keeping something to the body reminds the client not to leave valuables around.

Below is an explanation of a group meeting. Make a small drawing for each statement to help someone who has difficulty reading and remembering to understand the meaning of what is written.

- *We have a meeting in each cottage each week.*
- *Everyone living or working in the cottage can attend the meeting if they wish.* ● *We have meetings so that everyone is able to share in making decisions about the cottage.* ● *As a member of the group, you will be able to put your ideas to the people at the meeting. You will be helped to put these ideas on a list called an 'agenda' by your key worker.* ● *Each week a different member is encouraged to lead the meeting. Someone will also take notes so that we can remember what has been agreed. The notes will be pinned up on the noticeboard and you will be given help to read them if you need it.*
- *We make a cassette of our meetings so if you would rather listen than read, you can borrow the cassette.*
- *If you feel that your ideas have not been fairly heard, you can complain to your key worker who will help you deal with your claim.* ● *We look forward to seeing you at our next cottage meeting.*

When you have made your drawings to illustrate this information, you can use them as evidence in your portfolio of sketches produced to meet a specific need.

Take a skill you might teach a client – perhaps something like frying an egg or making potato chips. Write down the basic steps, and then use diagrams to explain what needs to be done.

There are times when it is helpful for anyone to have something to refer to in the form of a sketch or diagram to remind them of what they need to do. Can you remember asking someone how to get to somewhere and them giving you verbal instructions?

When we give people verbal instructions on how to get somewhere we are 'reading' a 'mind map' which is in our heads but not theirs. It seems perfectly simple to the person giving the instructions because they are familiar with the place, but to someone who isn't familiar it is very hard to follow if nothing is written, either in words or better still in the form of a diagram.

Below is a conversation between Sharon, a student on placement at a community health centre, and a mother, new to the area, asking where the local hospital was so that she could take her child to an appointment.

Read through Sharon's directions and draw a map to direct the mother to hospital. You can use this map for your portfolio as evidence of drawing diagrams to illustrate points.

It's easy to get to the hospital. You just go down Drake Street, to the corner shop – what's its name – the dress shop? Lynn, what's that dress shop called? You know the one where you got that yellow dress in the sale last summer. Cor, did it? I bet you felt embarrassed. Did you take it back? Well I would have. I mean, sale or no sale you don't expect it to split first time on do you? Well, what's it called, then? Oh, yes, 'Inspirations'. Yes, that's it. Well you turn right at 'Inspirations' and then left again into another road. That's Green Street. I mean the road you get into after you turn left is. You turn left again in Green Street you see. The hospital is right at the end on the left. It's a big new building. Well, that's the front of it. You won't be allowed in there. That's only for emergencies. Outpatients have to go through the side entrance. That's in Greek Street. Come to think of it, Greek Street comes out on to Drake Street further down just past Boots. You'd do better really to go down Drake Street to Boots and turn right just past it. Oh, you don't know Drake Street? I thought you'd have known that well, you know where the No 3 buses go down? Oh, you don't know how to get there from here? Well you go out through the front door and turn right outside. Well, not exactly right because that goes into the swimming baths, but sort of crooked way right. Past the Bingo, well, when you come on to the road there's two roads come together opposite you. You take the right hand one – right hand if you got your back to the Bingo I mean, of course, and follow it down to Drake Street. You'll recognise Drake Street because of the traffic lights. You turn left in Drake Street and that dress shop I was telling you about is about a hundred yards down on the right and the hospital is just past it.

It's a good thing it wasn't an emergency hospital visit! One of the main reasons people don't give clear directions is that they assume others know what they know. This is often not the case. If it were, the person asking would not need directions!

· USING TABLES AND CHARTS ·

Sometimes information is displayed in columns arranged in a certain order. These columns (or tables) of information are useful for making comparisons. The information is easier to understand than it would be if it were all written out in sentences.

A care worker may use tables in many ways. An example might be of comparing how nutritious different foods are, or how to make up a bottle for a baby of a certain weight.

Task

1 *While Sharon Lee was on placement at the community centre she often had to help people read tables and charts. Below is part of a table on the back of a packet of dried baby milk.*

FEEDING TABLE

Approx. age	1–3 weeks	6 weeks	3 months	4 months
Approx. weight — kg	3.5	4.5	5.5	6.5
Approx. weight — lb	8	10	12	14
Number of feeds per 24 hours	5	5	5	5
Number of scoops per feed	4	5	6	7
Water per feed — oz	4	5	6	7
Water per feed — ml	115	140	170	200

a *How much milk should Sharon advise a mother to give a baby who weighed 4.5kg or 10lb?*

b *How many feeds a day would the baby need?*

2 *Another client, Mr Nicholaus, has been referred to the clinic by his doctor who has told him he is overweight. He is 1.75 metres tall and 40 years old. How much would Mr Nicholaus be advised he should weigh according to the table shown here?*

WEIGHT CHART FOR MEN (in stones and pounds)				
Height without shoes (m)	25 yrs+	23–24 yrs	21–22 yrs	19–20 yrs
1.52	9.12–8.3	9.11–8.2	9.9–8.0	9.7–7.12
1.55	10.1–8.6	10.0–8.5	9.12–8.3	9.10–8.1
1.57	10.4–8.9	10.2–8.8	10.0–8.6	9.13–8.4
1.60	10.8–8.12	10.7–8.11	10.5–8.9	10.3–8.7
1.63	10.12–9.1	10.11–9.0	10.9–8.12	10.7–8.10
1.65	11.2–9.4	11.1–9.3	10.13–9.1	10.11–8.13
1.68	11.7–9.8	11.6–9.7	11.4–9.5	11.2–9.3
1.70	11.12–9.12	11.11–9.10	11.9–9.8	11.7–9.7
1.73	12.2–10.2	12.1–10.0	11.13–9.12	11.11–9.10
1.75	12.6–10.6	12.5–10.4	12.3–10.2	12.1–10.1
1.78	12.11–10.10	12.10–10.8	12.7–10.6	12.5–10.4
1.80	13.2–11.0	13.1–10.12	12.13–10.10	12.11–10.8
1.83	13.7–11.4	13.6–11.2	13.4–11.0·	13.2–10.12

3 *Convert a sample of these measures to kilograms as part of your Number evidence.*

4 *In order to lose weight, Mr Nicholaus will need to be aware of how many calories he is eating in different foods. He has been told to cut down on fat but is not clear about what energy value different foods have. He likes cakes and biscuits. He needs to know what he can eat of different foods to keep him at the correct calorie intake.*

Below is a list of different foods and their calorie values. Make a simple chart of different food types and their calories for Mr Nicholaus so he will know when he is being naughty! You can use this as evidence of 'Responding to written material' for your portfolio.

Caramel wafer, 54 each
Baked beans per oz, 26
Tomato soup per oz, 10.8
Toast and butter, 119
Mars bar, 284

Weetabix per oz, 100
Prawns per oz, 29.5
Orange, 10
Cheddar cheese per oz, 120
Melon per oz, 6

Mayonnaise per oz, 105
Sausage roll, 112
Frozen peas per oz, 18.5
Medium pork sausages, 72 each
Choc ice, 145 each
White bread per oz, 69
Apple, 46 each
Packet of peanuts (small), 160
Crumpet per oz, 54
Banana, 119
Cod in batter, 210 per portion
Raspberries per oz, 22

Cola per oz, 12
Brown ale per 10 oz, 80
Steak and kidney pie per oz, 87
Ovaltine per oz, 109
Pork chop (grilled) per oz, 129
Butter per oz, 226
Clear mints per oz, 100
Corn flakes per oz, 102
Whisky per pub measure, 60
Fish fingers per oz, 54
Chips per oz, 68

5 *Convert ounces to grams as evidence for gathering and processing (Application of Number core skill).*

· USING PHOTOGRAPHS ·

Another way of communicating with images is to use photographs. Photographs can record images with almost total accuracy. When used over a lifetime they can become a personal pictorial history.

It is very important to particular client groups to have photographs of themselves to help them form a clearer

A photograph is a valuable visual reminder of people, events and places past.

picture of where they came from, what their experiences have been and who they are now.

Photographs can be used to help elders to remember their lives. Photographs can help people with learning difficulties to remember what they did and where they went. They can be especially useful to help people come to terms with loss. If a person no longer has a loved one, or if a child is no longer living with birth parents, having a photograph is very valuable. A photograph is a permanent visual reminder of people, events and places past.

Task

If you are on work placement you may notice clients' pictures around, and they may like to talk to you about them.

Keep a record of your conversations to provide evidence of using images.

· DEVELOPING WRITTEN SKILLS – IDENTIFYING IMPORTANT POINTS ·

Every day, in both our working and personal lives, we take in a great deal of information. We cannot possibly remember word for word all of what is said to us or all we read. What happens is that we listen to what is said or read and *pick out the important points*. This is sometimes called **précising**. Can you remember the last time you did this?

It is almost impossible not to précis all the time. You have probably told a friend about what happened in a television programme that you saw and he missed. You could not repeat all that was said, but what you could do was to pick out the important parts of the storyline and update the other person. If you have been out for an evening you can tell a friend about the conversations you had without going through them word for word.

Once you realise that you are already very skilled at précising, it is easy to précis written words too.

Task

Read the sentences below, which are rather long-winded, and write out shortened versions that quickly get to the point.

'I am extremely pessimistic, at the moment, about the possibility of our team gaining victory'.

'Anyone who owns, or has ever owned, a dog will know that a dog prefers a bone to any other form of nourishment'.

'To discover in detail what the life of man or woman on earth was like a hundred, a thousand, ten thousand years ago is a tremendous achievement – just as great an achievement, in fact, as to make ships sail under the sea or through the air'.

If you have practised shortening sentences, you could try a longer passage (taken perhaps from a magazine article). The same principles apply:

- Look for the important point in each sentence or group of sentences.
- Try to find a single word or phrase which will replace a group of words or a longer phrase.
- Find a general term instead of listing examples.
- It is often better to completely rephrase something rather than try to chop out words and end up with a 'jerky' sentence.

Task

Revision work

Earlier in the chapter (page 160) there was an exercise about checking to see if people using wheelchairs could be accommodated at a stadium for a rock concert. If the access at the concert had been all right the next step for a care worker would be to plan the actual outing.

The outline map shown here is of the city where the rock concert would take place. You need to plan for a group of five wheelchair users and five helpers to spend the day in the city before going to the concert.

Like most groups, this one has people who want to do different things. Some people want to look at museums, some at churches, some at shops and some want to take a trip on the river.

Look at the map to see where the museums, churches, river and shops are. Look to see where the minivan you will travel in could be parked. You will have time for two activities in the morning and two in the afternoon. You will also need to go to a cafe for something to eat before going to the concert, and will need to identify where the toilets are for use during your tour.

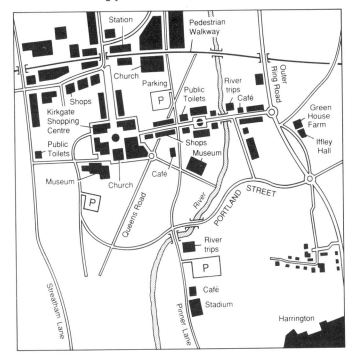

Write out a plan showing:

1 *where you will park for each activity*
2 *where you will visit in the morning and in the afternoon*
3 *where you will have a meal*
4 *where you will have opportunities to use toilets.*

Remember that the wheelchair pushers will not be supermen/women, so take distances into account.

You can use this as evidence in your portfolio of using diagrams produced to meet a specific need. If you discuss and tape-record the reasons for your decisions with another person, you could use the tape as evidence of taking part in discussions.

Fast Facts

Adjective   A word which says something about a noun.

Agenda   A list of items for discussion at a meeting.

Apostrophe   A punctuation mark used either (i) to show something belongs, or (ii) that something has been omitted. If the person or thing to which the object belongs is plural, the apostrophe goes after the 's'. When a letter or letters are missing the apostrophe is put where they would have been.

Assumption   You make an assumption when you think you know something without checking it first.

Capital letter   This is used at the beginning of a sentence, and for names of people or places.

Comma   This is used to separate items in a list, or different parts within a sentence.

Communication   An activity that can be verbal or non-verbal (or both). It can involve using sketches, diagrams, photographs, tables or graphs to make meanings clearer.

Curriculum vitae (CV)   A form used when applying for a job. It gives all the necessary details about the applicant, such as name, address, date of birth, qualifications and experience.

Key worker   A care worker who has special responsibility for certain clients. A key worker helps the client with all aspects of their daily life, gets to know them well and helps them plan their lives. Key workers will help plan leisure activities, holidays, birthdays and help the client keep in touch with friends and family.

Memorandum (memo)   A message between workers of the same organisation. It will not have an address in the heading.

'Mother-ese'   The way we might speak with a child, using short sentences and repeating the meaning in different ways. Sometimes a higher pitched voice is used.

Non-verbal communication   Using our face, body or voice tone to convey meaning (see Chapter 1).

Noun   The name of a person, place or object.

Précis   Picking out the important points from information in order to make a shorter version.

Pronoun   A word used instead of a noun (e.g. him, her, it).

Sentence   A group of words put together to make complete sense. It must have a subject and a verb.

Subject   The name given to the noun or pronoun about which a statement is being made.

Total communication   Using words, body language and signs, often together, to help get meaning across.

Verb   A word describing an action (e.g. 'I *walked* to college').

6 APPLICATION OF NUMBER

chapter

This chapter is designed to help you achieve your core skills in the Application of Number. It will also show you how often number skills are used in everyday life and in the field of health and social care to work things out. Examples are working out by how much to increase the quantities in a recipe that serves four to serve twenty in a residential setting, and calculating how many staff are needed for effective care of a particular number of clients.

Number skills are also used to collect *data*, to put it into a suitable form for *analysis*, and then to draw *conclusions* from the results. This can help to show patterns that might, for example, be used for forward planning of services.

Throughout this book evidence tasks have asked you to use number skills (e.g. in surveys and questionnaires). This chapter supports those tasks and gives you further opportunities to achieve your core skills in the Application of Number.

· WHOLE-NUMBER CALCULATIONS ·

Most readers of this book will already be able to carry out whole-number calculations using $+$ $-$ $\times$ and $\div$. If these are totally new to you, you will need to refer to a textbook of basic mathematics, to practise the techniques and gain a thorough understanding of methods. This part of the chapter will provide a brief revision for other readers who have previously mastered the techniques but who are a little out of practice. If you are confident of your ability to use the four rules of number $(+ - \times \div)$ you might prefer to move straight on to 'Other signs and symbols' on page 177.

There are two ways of working out calculations. You may choose to do them on paper and carry out the workings by hand, or you may choose to use a *calculator* which will do the calculations quickly at the touch of a button.

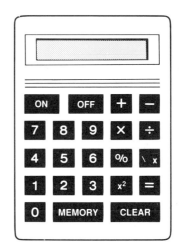

Figure 6.1 *A typical hand-held calculator*

Calculators vary in the layout of their buttons (or keys), but they will all be able to carry out most of the calculations discussed in the rest of this chapter.

This chapter presents calculations worked out using 'pen and paper' arithmetic. This method shows how the calculations work. You may choose to follow the working with a calculator, so you can see better how the calculations work. You will need to be sure of your method whichever option you choose to use.

Addition

The symbol for addition is +, which means 'plus' or 'add'. It is placed between two numbers that are to be added together. Numbers can be added together in rows or in columns, although columns are always used if there are a lot of numbers to be added or if they are large.

First the *units* are added. If the units add up to more than ten, the right-hand part (the unit) is put down and the left-hand part is carried to the next column to the left. This 'carry over' can be written in tiny figures below the total lines. There may be no 'carry over'.

Next the tens column is added up, not forgetting any carried over from the units column. Once again, if double figures are reached, the left is carried over to the next column, and the right is written down in the total. Carry on with this same procedure until all the columns of figures are dealt with. An example is shown below. *Always remember to line up the columns correctly!*

Example: Add together 72, 578 and 2319

$$
\begin{array}{r}
72 \\
578 \\
+\ 2319 \\
\hline
2969 \\
\end{array}
$$
$_{1\ 1}$ ← Numbers carried over

Subtraction

The symbol for subtraction is −, which means 'minus' or 'less'. It is placed between two numbers when the second is to be taken away from the first. As with addition, we may do the sum in rows or in columns but must be careful to line up the units under one another, then the tens and so on.

When we take the second number away from the first, which is bigger, that poses no problem (e.g. $9 - 7 = 2$). However, if the first number in the units column is smaller, we will have to 'borrow' from the tens column of the first number. You have to be careful to note that the figure in the tens column of the first number is now one less.

Example: In a mixed school of 1836 pupils, 789 are girls. How many pupils are boys?

$$
\begin{array}{r}
{}^{7\ 12\ 1} \\
1836 \\
-\ \ 789 \\
\hline
1047 \\
\end{array}
$$

Multiplication

The symbol for multiplication is ×, which means 'times'.

Imagine that 8 hospital patients each needed 3 units of blood to be transfused. How much blood would have been used in total? To find this we could add:

$$8 + 8 + 8 = 24$$
$$\text{or } 3 + 3 + 3 + 3 + 3 + 3 + 3 + 3 = 24$$

but it is easier to say:

$$8 \times 3 = 24$$

If calculations are done without using a calculator multiplication tables can be memorised. This can shorten the time taken to do calculations by hand.

When multiplying involves double or more figures a simple technique solves the problem.

Example: A hospital has 350 beds and the manager has allowed for 3 sheets per bed each week. It costs 58 pence to launder each sheet. Calculate the weekly cost of laundry.

```
      350    beds
  ×     3    sheets
     ─────
     1050    sheets

     1 050   sheets
  ×    58    pence
     ─────
     8 400
  + 52 500
    ──────
    60 900   pence
```

In the second calculation, multiply first by the 8, then by the 5. You only have to multiply by 5 (instead of 50, which it really is) because putting a 0 under the left-hand figure converts multiplying by 5 into multiplying by 50. This works in exactly the same way if you are multiplying by 253 or by 1937 – merely add an extra 0 every time you move to the next left figure.

> **Remember:**
>
> *You must make sure the columns line up under one another.*

Example: In the section on addition, the health visitor had travelled 27 km. Now calculate her expenses claim if the Health Authority paid 44 pence per kilometre.

```
        27     kilometre
  ×     44     pence
      ─────
       108
      1080
      ─────
      1188     pence (=£11.88)
```

Task

1 A candidate had an assignment to do for her GNVQ qualification and her tutor said 2500 words would be acceptable. She decided to word-process her work and found that she could get on average 12 words to a line. The candidate had written 8 sides of A4 paper, which had 24 lines to each page. Was what she had written too much, too little or approximately correct? You could try this calculation 'by hand' and check your answer using a calculator.

2 At his work placement, a candidate found that one of the elderly residents was going to have a 100th birthday party in three weeks' time. The officer-in-charge was trying to fit the organisation of the party in with a busy schedule, and asked the candidate for some help. The cook thought that each guest would eat 4 small sandwiches and 2 cakes. From 2 slices of bread, they

would make 4 sandwiches and each loaf contained 22 slices, including crusts (which they were not using). The officer-in-charge estimated that 50 guests from outside, 24 other residents and 10 staff would be present. How many loaves and cakes did the candidate have to order?

Check your answers: (1) The candidate had probably written 2304 words, so this was approximately correct. (2) A loaf of 20 slices of bread (excluding crusts) makes 40 sandwiches, which feeds 10 people. There were 84 people likely to come. He needs to order 9 loaves and 172 small cakes.

Division

The symbol for division is either ÷ or a line —, both of which mean 'divided by'.

Division is a process involving sharing. The first number is to be shared between the second number of groups. For example, $15 \div 5 = 3$ means that 15 is to be divided into 5 groups, and there will be 3 in each group.

There are two methods of dividing without using a calculator. These two methods depend on the size of the figure you are dividing by (sometimes called the *divisor*).

The first method uses figures less than 12. This is because many people know their multiplication tables up to ×12. It is called **short division**.

Example: Divide 8896 by 4

$$4 \overline{)8896} \quad \frac{2224}{}$$

The thought processes in carrying out this division could be as follows:

- 4 into 8 goes 2, none left over. Write down 2.
- 4 into 8 goes 2, none left over. Write down 2.
- 4 into 9 goes 2, but 1 left over. Write down 2 and carry 1 to next column to the right.
- 4 into 16 goes 4, none left over. Write down 4 and the sum is finished.

If the sum does not divide exactly as in that example, you will have some left over.

Example: Divide 397 by 5

$$5 \overline{)397} \quad \frac{79}{} \quad \leftarrow \text{with 2 left over}$$

In this case there are 2 left over. Sometimes it would be fitting to say *79 remainder 2*, but modern techniques are more likely to ask you to put this as a fraction or a decimal. There will be more to say of this later.

The second method of dividing is known as **long division** and is used mainly when the sharing figure is over 12 (for the reason already given).

Example: Divide 7395 by 35

$$
\begin{array}{r}
211 \\
35 \overline{)7395} \\
-70 \\
\hline
39 \\
-35 \\
\hline
45 \\
-35 \\
\hline
10 \quad \leftarrow \text{remainder}
\end{array}
$$

Now the thought process is like this:

- 35 into 7, won't go.
- 35 into *73* goes 2. Write down 2 immediately above the 3 (*not* above the 7!). Now do a multiplication (35 times 2 = 70) and put 70 below the 73. Subtract it, leaving 3.
- Bring down the next figure to the side of this 3. In this sum, *39*. Now 35 will go into 39 once, so write 1 next to the 2 on the top row, carry out a multiplication (1 × 35 = 35) and subtract 35 from 39. This leaves 4.
- Bring down the next and last figure, which is 5, to give *45*. Again 35 will go once into 45, so write the 1 up at the top and do a multiplication (1 × 35 = 35). Subtract 35 from 45.
- This leaves 10 as a *remainder*.

This is the type of whole-number arithmetic many people have forgotten or never learned, because it is much easier to use a calculator. To explore how the arithmetic works, however, try working out these sums. Cover up the workings on the right – they are there so that you can check your answers.

a Divide 240 by 15

$$
\begin{array}{r}
16 \\
15\overline{)240} \\
15 \\
\hline
90 \\
90 \\
\hline
00
\end{array}
$$

b Divide 268 006 by 33

$$
\begin{array}{r}
8121 \\
33\overline{)268006} \\
264 \\
\hline
40 \\
33 \\
\hline
70 \\
66 \\
\hline
46 \\
33 \\
\hline
\end{array}
$$

remainder → 13

I wish I had learned to do divisions properly

area is mostly rural, there are very few petrol stations around and her clients are expecting her to turn up. Work out how many litres of petrol will enable the health visitor to see all her clients.

Check your answers: (1) 10 rows used, so 40 rows blocked off. Therefore 80 notices needed. Total capacity of hall is 1450. (2) 3 litres of petrol needed.

A word about brackets

Brackets are used with more than one number, when those numbers are to be treated as a single number. For example:

$$4 \times (6-2) = 4 \times 4 = 16.$$

The sums inside the brackets are always worked out first, as in the above. When more than one pair of brackets appears in a sum, the *innermost* ones are always worked out first, and then the next, and so on. For example:

$$20 - (4 \times (6 - 3))$$
$$= 20 - (4 \times 3)$$
$$= 20 - 12 = 8.$$

Other signs and symbols

Greater than or less than

This symbol is a vee laid on its side, like this: $>$ or $<$. The number against the point is the smaller number, so it goes like this:

Task

1 You have been asked to organise seating for a lecture on NVQ training at your workplace. The supervisor tells you that they expect about 270 people to attend. When you investigate the lecture hall you find it is already laid out in rows with 29 seats in a row. You do not want some people in the front rows nor others right at the back, so you decide to limit the number of rows to be used and mark the rest: 'Not to be occupied'. Work out how many rows you need. If there are 50 rows in total, how many need to be closed off? If the outside chairs of each row only will carry the closed notice, how many notices do you need to make? How many people could be seated in the hall if necessary?

2 A health visitor finds that she has almost no fuel left in her car's petrol tank. She is going on holiday by train tomorrow and she reckons on travelling by car to see four clients today. They are 16 km, 12 km, 8 km and 13 km apart. The health visitor is anxious not to leave excess fuel in her car while she is away. She estimates that her car can travel 19 km on 1 litre of petrol. She certainly cannot risk running out of petrol because her

6 < 9 means 6 is less than 9

9 > 6 means 9 is greater than 6.

Squares and square-root signs

When a number is multiplied once by *itself*, the result is known as the **square** of that number. It is represented by a small number 2 after and to the top of that number:

4^2 is the same as 4×4

25^2 is the same as 25×25

The **square-root** is denoted by a $\sqrt{\ }$. This symbol means that a number can be made from the multiplication of another number times itself (squared). For example, $4 \times 4 = 16$, so the square-root of 16 is 4. The square-root of 625 is 25, because 25×25 makes 625. These can be written:

$$\sqrt{16} = 4 \text{ and } \sqrt{625} = 25.$$

Percentages

Percentages mean exactly what the name tells us. 'Per' stands for 'for each' and 'cent' stands for 'one hundred'. So 'per cent' means 'for each hundred'. We can use the symbol % to represent a percentage.

Ratios

A **ratio** is a comparison of two figures. We can either write the two figures like a fraction, or more commonly with the symbol : in between. For example, if one care worker earns £10 per hour and another earns £5, their earnings are in the ratio of 10:5, which is the same as 2:1. Note that in ratios the units for the quantities *must* be the same. You can multiply ratios up or down to simplify the figures *as long as you do the same to both sides* (as we did above). It is better to get one of the sides down to 1 as this gives you an idea of the relationship very quickly.

π and r

These symbols are to do with circles. *r* represents the **radius** of a circle, which is the measurement from its centre to its outside.

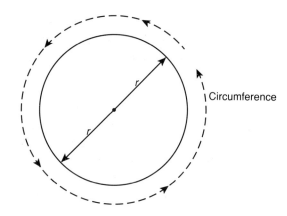

π represents the *ratio* (see above) between the *circumference* of a circle and its *diameter* (which is twice the radius, or 2*r*). It is a Greek letter pronounced 'pie'. It *always* has the same value – as a decimal it is about 3.142 as a fraction it is $\frac{22}{7}$. So:

circumference ÷ diameter = π

circumference = $\pi \times$ diameter.

These are simple formulae expressed in words. They are important in calculating circumferences and areas of circles as we see later.

These are just a few of the symbols and signs in number work. You may meet others.

A word about the use of calculators

Calculators are important tools in today's society. They shorten the tedious business of long and complicated calculations and of repeating the same type of sum over and over again. Yes, of course, you should use a calculator in your GNVQ work, but a word of warning: *they cannot get the sum correct for you if you do not enter the correct data or use the right method.* It is therefore sensible to make sure you know what you are doing with the figures first.

People sometimes use a calculator to perform a long division sum and quote their answer to 6 or 7 decimal figures. They may be surprised or upset if tutors cross out all but the first decimal place or two! The fact is that those last figures are nonsense, because the data entered into the calculator may only have been gathered to an accuracy of one decimal place!

It says that there are 2.4892134005632 children in the average European family

If you take a ruler and measure the page width of this book, you will have good eyesight to be accurate in measuring to half of a millimetre, and you certainly could not be accurate to a 1000th of a millimetre. So it is usually nonsense to quote an answer to that degree of accuracy in health and care situations. A calculator has not got common sense and will go on dividing as long as it has spaces to do so.

· DECIMALS ·

A decimal number is one that includes a decimal point (e.g. 0.681, 12.833, 143.99). The figures to the *left* of the decimal point count as a whole number. The place values of figures on the *right* of the decimal point are tenths, hundredths, thousandths, tens of thousandths etc. For example, in the number 6.983 there are 6 whole numbers, 9 tenths, 8 hundredths and 3 thousandths.

Think it over

If you get the places and decimal points in numbers muddled, make a table like the one shown here and insert the following numbers into the table:

100.5	*0.35*	*40.69*
14.008	*0.99*	*1.10*
0.1	*10.95*	*10.10*

Hundreds	Tens	Units	●	Tenths	Hundredths	Thousandths
		6		9	8	3

The number 6.983 is said to have three decimal places. So has 0.003, but 142.89 only has two decimal places. The **numbers of decimal places** is simply the number of figures on the right of the decimal point.

Adding decimals

This is no more difficult than adding together whole numbers. All you have to remember is to keep the columns of tenths together, then the hundredths and so on.

Example: 2.4 litres of saline, 0.65 litres of dextrose and 0.005 litres of penicillin solution have to be added to a patient's intravenous drip. Calculate the extra volume.

$$\begin{array}{r} 2.4 \\ 0.65 \\ \underline{0.005} \\ 3.055 \end{array}$$

Notice how carefully all the figures and points line up vertically. If you wish to make it easier to line them up, you *can* add 0's (zeros) at the end of a decimal figure or at the beginning *without altering the value*. But you cannot add them anywhere else. For example, 2.400 is the same as 2.4, 02.4 or 2.40, but 20.4 and 2.04 are not the same. In the latter two cases you have altered the values.

It is usual to put a 0 before a decimal point when there is no other figure on the left. For example, put 0.656, not just .656. This helps to reduce mistakes.

Subtracting decimals

Follow exactly the same procedures for subtraction as for adding. Lining up correctly is just as important.

Example: Subtract 12.993 from 103.004

$$
\begin{array}{r}
103.004 \\
\underline{12.993} \\
90.011
\end{array}
$$

If you line the sum correctly you can place the decimal point in easily as you come to it.

Multiplying decimals

Multiplying (or dividing) by 10, 100, 1000 etc. is very easy with decimals – follow this foolproof method. Count the number of zeros in your multiplying figure (e.g. 100 has two), and then move the decimal point in the other figure that number of places to the *right* (in division, to the *left*). Some people say that they can't remember which way to move the decimal point, but this should not be a problem. If you are multiplying then the answer *must get bigger*, so 0.12×10 must become 1.2 (you did not have a whole one before but you have now!). If you are dividing or sharing then the answer *must get smaller*, so $0.12 \div 10$ becomes 0.012 (before you had one-tenth but now this has become a hundredth because it is two places from the decimal point).

Multiplying a decimal number by a whole number

Again a simple method works if you learn it well. We can illustrate it best by an example.

Example: 234.991×6

$$
\begin{array}{r}
234.991 \\
\times \qquad 6 \\
\hline
1409.946
\end{array}
$$

←3 figures after point

←3 figures after point

Starting from the right, count the number of figures up to the decimal point (i.e. three). Then put the point back after the sum is done, counting in the *same* number of places from the right. Whatever you do, *don't guess!*

Multiplying a decimal number by another decimal

When doing this without a calculator the trick is to carry out a long multiplication and ignore the decimal points to start with. Then, when you have this answer, count the number of decimal places from the right until the point is reached *in both original figures*. Add these two numbers together and count this number of places in from the right in the answer. Put the decimal point there.

Example: 2.3771×35.8

$$
\begin{array}{r}
2.3771 \\
\underline{35.8} \\
190168 \\
1188550 \\
\underline{7131300} \\
85.10018
\end{array}
$$

← 4 places

← 1 place

← 5 places

Dividing a decimal number by a whole number

Short division is essentially the same as ordinary division. Put the decimal point in the answer *directly above* its place in the original figure.

Example: $6.566 \div 4$

$$
\begin{array}{r}
1.6415 \\
4\overline{)6.5660}
\end{array}
$$

Note that a zero has been added at the end in order to finish the sum (remember, this does not change its value).

Dividing a decimal number by another decimal

When doing this without a calculator the trick is to move the decimal point in each figure by an equal number of places until the *divisor* becomes a whole number. When *both* decimal points are moved in this way the answer is not affected.

Example: 6.566 ÷ 0.44

$$6.566 \xrightarrow{\times 100} 656.6$$
$$0.44 \xrightarrow{\times 100} 44$$

The sum becomes:

$$
\begin{array}{r}
14.92 \\
44\overline{)656.60} \\
\underline{44} \\
216 \\
\underline{176} \\
406 \\
\underline{396} \\
100 \\
\underline{88}
\end{array}
$$

Again remember to put the decimal point in the answer *directly above* the one in the sum.

> **Remember:**
>
> *It is so very important with decimals to lay out your calculations neatly and orderly. Most mistakes can be avoided if care is taken.*

▪ FRACTIONS ▪

A part or section expressed in relation to the whole is known as a **fraction**. For instance, a birthday cake is to be cut into 12 portions, so one piece is one-twelfth share of the cake. This is usually written:

$$\frac{1}{12}$$

The top figure is known as the **numerator** and the bottom figure is the **denominator**. The bar between the two figures means 'divide' (it replaces ÷), so the above fraction is literally 1 divided by 12.

If a person is lucky enough to receive two portions of cake, then they have:

$$\frac{1}{12} + \frac{1}{12} = \frac{2}{12}$$

This is the same quantity of cake they would have received if the cake had been divided into six parts and they had received one-sixth. So:

$$\frac{2}{12} = \frac{1}{6}$$

We can see that numerator and denominator could both be divided by 2 to reach one-sixth. If top and bottom of a fraction are divided by the same number, we are said to be **simplifying the fraction**. When it cannot be simplified any more it is the **lowest form** of the fraction. For example:

$$\frac{60}{300} \rightarrow \frac{15}{75} \rightarrow \frac{3}{15} \rightarrow \frac{1}{5} \quad \text{(lowest form)}$$

Adding and subtracting fractions

The principle is the same for both types of calculation. First *get the denominators of the fractions to be the same*.

Example: $\frac{1}{2} + \frac{3}{4}$

$$\frac{1}{2} \text{ becomes } \frac{2}{4}$$

So $\frac{1}{2} + \frac{3}{4}$

$$= \frac{2}{4} + \frac{3}{4} = \frac{5}{4}$$

Example: $\frac{7}{32} + \frac{5}{8}$

$$\frac{5}{8} \text{ becomes } \frac{20}{32}$$

So $\frac{7}{32} + \frac{5}{8} = \frac{7}{32} + \frac{20}{32} = \frac{27}{32}$

Example: $\frac{3}{7} - \frac{2}{11}$

$$\frac{3}{7} \text{ becomes } \frac{33}{77}$$

$$\frac{2}{11} \text{ becomes } \frac{14}{77}$$

So $\frac{3}{7} - \frac{2}{11} = \frac{33}{77} - \frac{14}{77} = \frac{19}{77}$

A whole number and a fraction together is known as a **mixed number**. When dealing with mixed numbers it may or may not be necessary to convert them first into fractions only.

Example: $5\frac{23}{25} - 3\frac{4}{25}$

Here it is obvious that the fractions have a common denominator, which is 25. So, deal with the whole numbers first, which gives $5 - 3 = 2$. Then:

$$\frac{23}{25} - \frac{4}{25} = \frac{19}{25}$$

So the answer is $2\frac{19}{25}$

Example: $5\frac{3}{5} - 3\frac{2}{3}$

In this case, first find the common denominator of the fractions. It is $3 \times 5 = 15$. Then proceed as follows:

$5\frac{3}{5}$ becomes $\frac{28}{5} = \frac{84}{15}$

$3\frac{2}{3}$ becomes $\frac{11}{3} = \frac{55}{15}$

So $5\frac{3}{5} - 3\frac{2}{3}$

$= \frac{84}{15} - \frac{55}{15}$

$= \frac{29}{15} = 1\frac{14}{15}$

This method works for both addition and subtraction.

Multiplying fractions

First convert any mixed numbers into fractions and then just multiply across the tops and bottoms.

Example: $4\frac{7}{8} \times 3\frac{1}{3}$

$4\frac{7}{8}$ becomes $\frac{39}{8}$

$3\frac{1}{3}$ becomes $\frac{10}{3}$

So $4\frac{7}{8} \times 3\frac{1}{3}$

$= \frac{39}{8} \times \frac{10}{3}$

$= \frac{390}{24}$

$= 16\frac{6}{24}$

$= 16\frac{1}{4}$

Dividing fractions

To divide a whole number by 6, for example, we multiply the number by one-sixth.

Example: $16 \div 6$

$$16 \times \frac{1}{6}$$

$$= \frac{16}{6} = 2\frac{4}{6}$$

$$= 2\frac{2}{3}$$

To divide one fraction by another, the second one is turned upside down and multiplied!

Example: $\frac{5}{7} \div \frac{7}{8}$

$$\frac{5}{7} \times \frac{8}{7} = \frac{40}{49}$$

Task

1 A hospital ward 33 was very short of sheets, so nurse Troy asked ward 36 for 20 sheets from their stock. A nurse learner on the ward looked worried and explained that 20 sheets was one-third of their stock. She said this was too much, but nurse Troy could have a quarter of their stock. Nurse Troy thought the learner was hopeless at mathematics because $\frac{1}{4}$ was larger than $\frac{1}{3}$. Returning with the borrowed sheets, she met a staff nurse from ward 35, on her way to ward 33 to borrow 4 sheets! Nurse Troy gave her 4 of the sheets she had been given.

a How many sheets had ward 36 to start with?
b How many sheets did nurse Troy take away?
c Who was right: which is the larger, $\frac{1}{3}$ or $\frac{1}{4}$?
d What fraction of ward 36's stock went to ward 35?
e What fraction of ward 36's stock eventually went to ward 33?
f What fraction of nurse Troy's borrowed sheets went to ward 35?

2 Mrs Biggs had a large 70th birthday cake given to her by her sons and she insisted on cutting it in half first. She intended one half to be cut into pieces for the residents and staff in the nursing home where she stayed, and the other half was to be cut up into pieces and put into small boxes for posting to all her relatives. There were 10 residents and 5 staff at work on the birthday. Mrs Biggs had 4 sons, 3 of whom were married, and 6 grandchildren.

a What fraction of the cake did each resident receive?
b What did each relative receive?
c Who got the largest pieces of cake?

(NB: Mrs Biggs was counted in with the residents)

I was expecting fractionally more!

Check your answers: (1) (a) Ward 36 had 60 sheets in stock. (b) Nurse Troy collected 15 sheets. (c) The learner was correct ($\frac{1}{3}>\frac{1}{4}$). (d) Ward 35 had $\frac{4}{60}=\frac{1}{15}$ of ward 36's stock. (e) Nurse Troy had 11 sheets remaining, or $\frac{11}{60}$ of ward 36's stock. (f) $\frac{4}{15}$ went to ward 35.

(2) (a) A resident received $\frac{1}{15}\times\frac{1}{2}=\frac{1}{30}$ of cake.
(b) Each relative (13 total) received $\frac{1}{13}\times\frac{1}{2}=\frac{1}{26}$ of cake.
(c) The relatives' pieces were the larger ($\frac{1}{26}>\frac{1}{30}$).

· PERCENTAGES ·

You have already come across the symbol and meaning of per cent (%) and have reviewed fractions. Percentages are really fractions which always have the denominator of 100. Fractions and percentages are therefore easily interchanged.

Fraction into percentage

Simply multiply the fraction by 100 to convert it into a percentage. For example:

$$\frac{6}{20}\times 100 = 30\%$$

Example: Out of 396 people surveyed, 132 still smoked. Express this as a percentage

$$\frac{132}{396}\times 100 = 33\frac{1}{3}\%$$

Percentage into fraction

Divide the percentage by 100 and simplify the fraction if possible. For example:

$$55\% = \frac{55}{100} = \frac{11}{20}$$

In a nursing home with 40 residents, 15% of the patients had suffered a stroke in the last twelve months. How many patients did not have a stroke in that period?

Check your answer: Either (i) work out 15% of 40 and subtract the figure from 40, or (ii) work out (100 − 15)% of 40:

(i) $\qquad 40\times\frac{15}{100}=6$, and $40-6=34$

(ii) $\qquad 40\times\frac{85}{100}=34$

· RATIOS ·

The symbol (:) and meaning of a ratio has been mentioned earlier, and now we can look at some examples.

Mr and Mrs Winston have discussed with the elder Mrs Winston whether it is the right time for her to stop living on her own and get expert care in a nursing home close by. They all decide to look further into the costs. There are two nursing homes nearby. The first costs £110 per week and the second costs £500 per 4-week month. Find out the ratio of the cost of the first home to that of the second.

First the costs must all be expressed in the same units, so it is important to bring the second home's costs to a weekly figure (or the first's to a 4-week month figure). So divide £500 by 4 to make £125 per week. Then:

$$\frac{\text{cost of first home}}{\text{cost of second home}} = \frac{110}{125} = \frac{22}{25}$$

The ratio is 22:25 in lowest terms.

Further example: Nurse Osborne works 37 hours each week on ward 33. Find the ratio of her working hours to non-working hours.

Time working = 37 hours
Time in week = 24 × 7 = 168 hours
Time not working = 168 − 37 = 131 hours

$$\text{Ratio} = \frac{37}{131} \text{ or } 37{:}131$$

Task

1 *Mr Biggs received a very pretty card signed by all the residents of the nursing home to celebrate his 100th birthday. He is so attached to the card that everyone decides to pay a share so that the card can be framed to ensure it will last for a long time. You decide it would be much better to enlarge the card at the colour copy centre in the next street and frame it so that Mr Biggs still has the original to look at and touch. The card measures 12 cm by 8 cm with a border 3 cm wide. It is increased so that the length becomes 27 cm.*
   a *What does its width become (it is increased in the same ratio)?*
   b *Find the ratio by which the area has increased.*

2 *The costs of three similar drugs for treating migraine are £3, £2.50 and £2 for 100 tablets, and the numbers of*

pharmacists who buy these drugs are in the ratios of 3:4:5.
   a *Find the number of drugs bought in a locality if the total amount spent is £1914.*
   b *What fraction of pharmacists buy the cheapest drugs?*

Check your answers: (1) (a) 18 cm. (b) Original area = 12 × 8 = 96 cm² and new area = 27 × 18 = 486 cm². So ratio of increase 96:486, which is the same as 1:6.

(2) (a) 79 200 tablets. (b) $\frac{5}{12}$.

· ESTIMATION ·

This means an **approximate judgement**. You certainly want to get your number applications correct, so it is very useful to have a rough idea of what your answer should be so that you know when you have made a mistake. Many people don't use estimation and common sense in their arithmetic, and then they complain about the number of sums they get wrong.

For instance, many people don't realise that when two fractions are multiplied together the answer is *smaller*. Take two simple fractions you are familiar with, $\frac{1}{2}$ and $\frac{1}{2}$. Multiply them together and you get $\frac{1}{4}$. This may seem puzzling because you are used to thinking that $\frac{1}{2} + \frac{1}{2} = 1$, and indeed it does. But when multiplying these fractions together you are in fact saying a half of a half – and when you reflect on that the answer *is* a quarter.

Another estimating tip useful with both fractions and decimals is to look at the whole-number parts. For example, if adding together 16.956 and 2.305 look at the whole numbers 16 and 2 (added together = 18). Next look at the decimals – the first shows 9 in the tenths position and the second shows 3, so when added together these are going to make at least another whole one. Hence your answer is going to be 19 point 'something not very big'.

Also try to get into the habit of 'rounding' in your estimates. Take for example 3.75 × 5.02. This sum is 'nearly 4' multiplied by 'just over 5', so your answer must be in the region of 4 × 5, which is 20.

Think it over

Do you remember how to multiply the sum above using the 'pen and paper' method described earlier in this chapter? How many figures will there be after the decimal point in the answer? Do the sum to check that the answer is in the region of 20.

Remember:

Practise estimation in your work – it only takes a few seconds, but pays off in accuracy.

Another useful tip is to get used to the mental images of lengths, areas, volumes, weights etc. so you have a better understanding of them. For instance:

- The average weight of an adult man is 70 kg, but it is not unknown for a care worker to write someone's weight as 7000 kg! Clearly the unit has no clear meaning for such a person.
- A litre is approximately $1\frac{3}{4}$ pints – we are all familiar with a pint milk bottle, so a pint is roughly $\frac{1}{2}$ a litre (just over in fact).
- Most people know the feel and size of a 2 pound bag of sugar, but many have not noticed that sugar comes now in 1 kilogram bags (= 2.2 pounds). They did not notice that it had changed because the weight is so similar. So, try to remember that a pound is roughly $\frac{1}{2}$ a kilogram, or 500 grams (just under in fact).
- Fabric used to be measured by the yard, and a popular way of 'measuring' in the UK was to hold the length

of fabric between your nose and fingers of an outstretched arm – this was approximately a yard. Now, a metre is only about 3 inches longer than a yard, and this is about the length of a nose – so if the head is turned away from the outstretched fingers, one can still use the old-fashioned way to measure a metre!

- An excellent way of estimating some lengths or heights is to use your own body. Get to know your own height in metres and in centimetres (or millimetres). The average height for a woman is 1.60 metres, and her fully stretched handspan (from little finger tip to thumb tip) is about 20 centimetres. Measure yours to check.
- Measure your biggest stride and you will always be able to pace out a distance.

When you get a feel for measurements, estimating will be that much easier for you.

· CONVERSION TABLES ·

It is useful to have conversion tables (or scales) to help you transfer measurements from one system to another. It is often necessary where different sets of scales are regularly used (e.g. metric and imperial in weights and heights, miles and kilometres for distance). Figures 6.2 – 6.4 show some examples. You should note that these tables give *approximate* conversions for convenience.

imperial (fl oz)	metric (ml)	imperial (fl oz)	metric (ml)
1	30	8	230
2	60	9	260
3	85	10 ($\frac{1}{2}$ pint)	280
4	110	15 ($\frac{3}{4}$ pint)	425
5 ($\frac{1}{4}$ pint)	140	20 (1 pint)	570
6	170	40 (1 quart)	1140
7	200	160 (1 gallon)	4500

Figure 6.2 *Approximate imperial to metric conversion table for volumes*

To use the tables, find the figure on the reading you have taken and read directly across to the adjacent figure. That is the equivalent in the other scale.

You can also convert by doing simple calculations. To convert TO metric you MULTIPLY by the figure shown. To convert FROM metric you DIVIDE by the figure shown.

miles/kilometres	1.61
feet/metres	0.30
inches/centimetres	2.54
pints/litres	0.56

metric (g)	imperial (oz)	metric (g)	imperial (oz)
10	$\frac{1}{3}$	100	3
20	$\frac{2}{3}$	120	4
30	1	150	5
40	$1\frac{1}{2}$	200	7
50	$1\frac{3}{4}$	250	9
60	2	300	$10\frac{1}{2}$
70	$2\frac{1}{2}$	400	14
80	3	450	16
90	3	500	$17\frac{1}{2}$

Figure 6.3 *Approximate imperial to metric conversion table for weight*

pounds/kilograms	0.45
ounces/grams	28.34
stones/kilograms	6.35

For example, to convert 12 stones to kilograms:

$$12 \times 6.35 = 76.2 \text{ kg}$$

To convert 400 grams to ounces:

$$400 \div 28.34 = 14.1 \text{ oz.}$$

For convenience, these figures are sometimes rounded to the nearest whole number – so 400 grams would be 14 ounces. You can use these conversion figures to make *estimates* of the approximate answer before you complete the calculation. This can help you to judge if your final answer is likely to be correct.

For example, if converting 4 inches into centimetres, a rough estimate of the result would be $4 \times 2.5 = 10$ cm (2.5 is used because it is close to the actual figure and easy to multiply).

Remember:
- *You can check your result by converting the answer back to the original figure (e.g. 10cm ÷ 2.5 = 4 inches).*
- *You can use estimates and checks like this for many kinds of calculations.*

Gas Regulo ⟶ Centigrade ⟶ Fahrenheit			Gas Regulo ⟶ Centigrade ⟶ Fahrenheit		
	°C	°F		°C	°F
	70	150	4	180	350 (normal hot frying)
	80	175	5	190	375 (upper limit for frying)
	100	212 (boiling point of water)	6	200	400
$\frac{1}{4}$	120	225	7	220	425 ('hot' oven)
$\frac{1}{2}$	130	250	8	230	450
1	140	275	9	240	475 ('very hot' oven)
2	150	300	10	250	500
	160	310 (normal gentle frying)		270	525
3	170	325		290	550

Figure 6.4 *Cooking temperatures*

A district nurse has to travel the following distances in a day to visit clients:

- *from home to client 1: 4 miles*
- *from client 1 to client 2: 3 miles*
- *from client 2 to client 3: 6 miles*
- *from client 3 to client 4: 6 miles*
- *from client 4 to client 5: 3 miles*
- *from client 5 to surgery: 4 miles*
- *from surgery to home: 8 miles*

1 If the nurse followed this pattern each day for a six-day rota, how many miles would be covered?

2 On the mileage record, the nurse has to record the distance in kilometres. What is the figure to the nearest whole kilometre:
a per day
b per week (6 days)?

Check your answers: (1) 34 miles. (2) (a) 55 km per day. (b) 328 km per week.

· COLLECTING DATA ·

Questionnaires

Applying a questionnaire is a cheap, effective way to find out about people's activities, thoughts and opinions on various topics. It can be used to collect information about why people choose to do things. It can be short or long, but to get effective results it has to be very well thought out and planned. There are several things you need to do before you start to write questions for a questionnaire:

a Research and read around the topic area. This will give you some ideas about the questions to ask.

b Decide on the aim/focus of the questionnaire. This helps to keep the questions relevant. For example, in a questionnaire on people's attitude to smoke-free areas it would not be relevant to ask how much a packet of cigarettes costs.

c Decide who you intend to ask. Is it focused on one group (e.g. adolescents) or should there be a cross-section of ages.

d Plan what type and how many questions you are going to ask. It is often useful to trial these on a small number of people first to ensure they are clear and draw out the information you want.

e Think about how you are going to record your results. This can be affected by the type of question you ask.

You should also consider the people who you hope are going to answer your questionnaire. Its style and size can encourage a person to complete or not complete a questionnaire. Bear the following points in mind:

1 *The length of the questionnaire.* Don't make it too long as this puts people off. Don't make it so short that it's ineffective.

2 *Format of the questions.* People are less likely to answer a questionnaire if they have to do a lot of writing. Use a mixture of questions where they can tick boxes and write short answers.

3 *Who you give the questionnaire to.* If the person knows you, they are more likely to reply.

4 *An introductory letter.* This is useful if you are not giving out the questionnaire face-to-face. The letter would explain the purpose and importance of the questionnaire and encourage people to fill it in.

If you wish people to return the questionnaire, a stamped addressed envelope provided by you will get a better response.

To obtain the most unbiased, honest answers, a questionnaire that the respondent can complete alone is sometimes best. If you ask the respondent to complete it in front of you, you may be likely to get the accepted 'norm' of attitudes and feelings. If you suggest that the respondent answers the questionnaire alone, you may also get more thoughtful and detailed answers – they have more time to think and consider their replies.

Types of questions

Once you have planned the approach to the questionnaire, you need to write the questions. The type of question used is the key to obtaining relevant data. There are two types of question: those which seek **facts** and those which record **attitudes and opinions**.

Factual questions gain *objective* information – that which is not so open to individual interpretation. For example:

What annual income bracket do you fall into:

Up to £5000 ☐

£5001 – £10 000 ☐

£10 001 – £15 000 ☐

Other areas often covered by factual questions include sex, age, marital status, number of children, level of education etc.

Attitude or opinion questions aim to collect *subjective* information – that which is the thoughts or opinions of the individual. For example:

Do you think young people today are brought up:
☐ too strictly?
☐ not strictly enough?

Questions to gain thought or opinions can be open or closed. Open questions allow the respondent to answer more fully than 'yes' or 'no'. An example would be: 'What do you feel makes a caring environment?'

Closed questions limit the replies the respondents can give. They *can* require just a 'yes/no' answer (e.g. 'Do you feel a carpet is necessary for a caring environment?'). Alternatively they can allow a number of restricted choices. The following is an example of the latter type:

A carpet is essential for a caring environment.

Strongly agree ☐

Agree ☐

Neither agree nor disagree ☐

Disagree ☐

Strongly disagree ☐

Please tick the box which reflects your thoughts closest.

You should avoid asking questions which cover more than one aspect. The question 'Do you think that old people should be encouraged to live in residential care and to be as independent as possible?' asks two separate things – the risk is that you will only get one answer!

Trialling

Once you have written your questionnaire, you should trial it on at least five people to check that the questions are clear and are gaining the information you need. Adjustments may need to be made before you use the questionnaire with larger numbers of people.

Sampling

When collecting data, it is important to get a balanced view of the group you have chosen to study. For example, if you were doing research into people's thoughts on banning smoking in public places, you would not get a fair picture if you asked only smokers. You need to select your respondents at random (e.g. every sixth person who goes by). This would give you fairer results. However, if you were trying to find out smokers' views on this then using only smokers is appropriate.

Observation

Another way to find out how people behave is to **observe** them. You could do this by *participant observation*, where you become part of the situation you are observing. For example, in watching children play you could play with them as you observe – this makes you less obvious as a researcher and you can get fairer results as those being observed do not start 'acting'. However, it can be difficult to be involved and get detailed observations.

Alternately, you could use *non-participant observation*, where you are more likely to sit back and observe from a distance. You are likely to see a lot of detail using this method, but sometimes those being observed feel uncomfortable and do not act naturally.

With the observation method you do not always know *why* people are behaving the way they do.

If you wish to use observation as a way of collecting data, you should do the following:

a Decide what you want to observe (e.g. discussion at a mealtime at a residential home).

b Compile an **observation sheet** using headings to cover what you want to observe (e.g. situation, people involved, seating arrangements, topics of conversation). This will help you to focus your observations and help you note relevant points. However, as observation is active, it is impossible to predict all that will happen and a sheet should not stop you noting the unexpected or unusual.

Surveys

A survey is another way to collect data. To carry out a survey you may talk to people to gain opinions or you may just record what you see. A survey is sometimes shorter than a questionnaire and may have less detail than an observation sheet. It can be a quick way to gain information. Before you carry out a survey, you need to be clear about:

a what you wish to survey
b where you are going to carry out the survey
c if you need to sample the participants in any way (e.g. talk to every sixth person).

You also need to construct your recording sheet *before* going to do your survey.

The recording sheet needs to reflect the possible answers/results you may get. It should allow the results to be recorded easily. For example, if you were going to survey the age ranges of the people who visited care workers at the local health centre on a particular morning, the sheet might look like Figure 6.5. Ticks are inserted for each consultation. This would give you a view of both age range and who visitors were seeing. A variety of conclusions could then be drawn from the data.

Age range	Nurse	Doctor	Health visitor	Other
5 yrs	✓	✓✓	✓✓	✓
5–10 yrs	✓	✓	✓	
11–19 yrs	✓✓✓	✓✓✓✓	✓	✓
20–30 yrs	✓✓	✓✓✓✓		
31–50 yrs		✓✓✓✓	✓✓	
51–70 yrs	✓✓	✓✓✓✓	✓✓	
70 yrs		✓	✓✓	✓✓

Figure 6.5 *A simple survey recording sheet*

There is a range of different ways to present data you have collected. Graphs are often used to show *changes* in data over a certain period of time. Graphs, bar charts, pie charts and tables can be used to illustrate text, and doing this will help you gain core skills in Communication.

When collecting data, however you choose to do it, *always be well prepared*. Make sure your notes are clear and legible, so that when you come back to use them at a later date you can still understand them.

Whatever method you choose to present your data, you should always label the presentation clearly. The work should be neat (and coloured if appropriate).

If you are using figures to work out an answer, *always* show your workings. Core skills credit the methods used and the process followed, as well as getting the right answer!

Bar charts

One common type of data presentation is a bar chart. An example is shown in Figure 6.6. (Also see Chapter 7.)

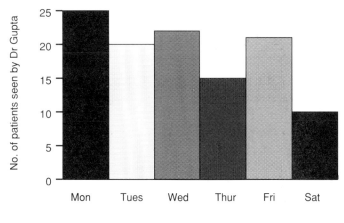

Week beginning 3 August

Figure 6.6 *Bar chart*

Line graphs

A line graph can be used to show clearly how values have changed over a period. It can also show cumulative information. An example of each is shown in Figure 6.7.

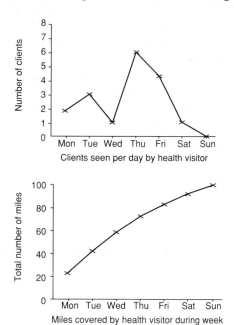

Figure 6.7 *Line graphs*

Pie charts

A pie chart presents the total picture of the data collected. To compile a pie chart you first have to convert your results into percentages. To do this you divide the component number by the total number and then multiply by 100.

For example, imagine you are looking at the number of students whose holiday jobs were in areas of care, and your results were as follows:

Care assistants with elders: 20
Baby-sitting: 10
Care assistant with special needs: 5
Nursery work: 5
Total: 40

To work out the percentage of those with jobs with elders, you would do the following:

$$\frac{\text{Those working with elders}}{\text{Total}} = \frac{20}{40} = 0.5$$

$$0.5 \times 100 = 50\%$$

The other percentages come out as 25%, 12.5% and 12.5%. Figure 6.8 shows how these can be presented as a pie chart.

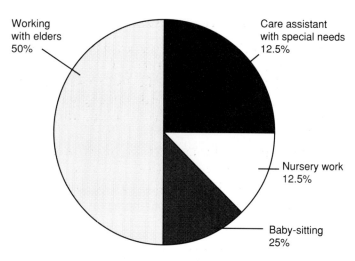

Figure 6.8 *Pie chart*

Tables

A table can be used to present a range of information in a neat way. It is particularly useful if you want to compare data.

For example, the table in Figure 6.9 shows the formal qualifications of staff in a nursery at two different times since it opened.

Qualification changes of staff				
	1985	%	1991	%
NNEB	2	20	5	50
BTEC Nursery Nursing	0	0	2	20
Teaching	1	10	1	10
PPA	3	30	2	20
None	4	40	0	0
Total	10	100	10	100

Figure 6.9 *Tabulated data*

Statistical averages

When you have collected a mass of data it will be in a suitable form for analysis until it is arranged in a chart or graph format.

Another way of making data easier to understand is to try to find one value to represent several values in your data. This single value is called an **average**.

There are three kinds of average known as:

a The (arithmetic) **mean** which is equal to the total of all the values divided by the number of values.

b The **median** is the value which lies half-way along your values arranged in ascending or descending order of size. If there is an even number of values take the mean of the two values.

c The **mode** of a set of values is the one which occurs most often. Should everything occur the same number of times there may be no mode, or conversely more than one mode may occur.

CALCULATIONS INVOLVING SHAPES

Plane shapes

A plane shape is one that is flat (i.e. not curved or round).

Rectangles and squares

A rectangle (or *oblong* as it is sometimes known) is a plane shape that has opposite sides equal in length and parallel to each other. If all the sides of the rectangle are equal, we call it a **square**, so that is also a plane shape.

To calculate the **area** of a square or a rectangle is a simple matter of multiplying together the lengths of two adjacent sides, provided they are already in the same units. The answer is then expressed in 'square' units and may be written with a small 2 raised after the unit name.

For example, the area of a rectangle whose sides are 6 cm and 4 cm is:

$$6 \times 4 = 24 \text{ cm}^2$$

and the area of a square whose sides are 1 metre is:

$$1 \times 1 = 1 \text{ m}^2$$

We can construct a simple formula for calculating area:

> Area = Length × Width

The **perimeter** of a rectangle is the distance around the edge. It will therefore be twice the length and twice the width added together. For the rectangle mentioned above

this is $6 + 4 + 6 + 4 = 20$ cm. (Note that as we are simply adding up lengths there is no 'square-ing' involved.) The square mentioned above has a perimeter of 4 metres. We can construct a simple formula for working out perimeters:

> Perimeter = 2 × (Length + Width)

he two boxed examples above represent word equations to which you may wish to refer to produce core skills evidence.

Triangles

To calculate the area of a **triangle** you need to multiply the base by the height and divide by 2.

Think it over

Can you say why you have to divide by 2?
Think of a rectangle cut in half diagonally.

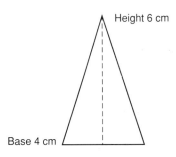

To find the area of the triangle shown here, multiply 4 cm by 6 cm and divide by 2. Note that we are 'square-ing' again, so the answer will be in 'square' units. It is:

$$\tfrac{1}{2} \times (6 \times 4) = 12 \text{ cm}^2$$

Complex plane shapes

Many shapes are *combinations* of rectangles, squares and triangles, and appropriate dividing lines can be drawn if the areas or perimeter needs to be calculated.

Task

A group of students held a fund-raising activity to carpet a newly opened day centre for elders in their neighbourhood. They chose a carpet priced at £25 per square metre and decided to make a plan of the area to find out how much money they needed. Their plan is given here.

Work out how much money they needed to raise.

☐ Area to be carpeted

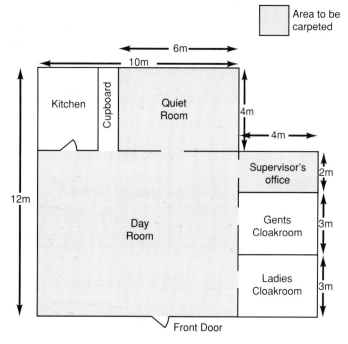

Check your answer: Area of day room = (12 − 4) × 10 = 80 m². Area of quiet room = 6 × 4 = 24 m². Area of supervisor's office = 4 × 2 = 8 m². Total area to be carpeted = 80 + 24 + 8 = 112 m². Cost of carpet = 25 × 112 = £2800.

Irregular shapes

Occasionally you may be required to measure the area of something which cannot be divided into rectangles and triangles and where you want more accuracy than rough estimation, an example might be the hand!

A reasonably accurate method is to draw around the shape on to a piece of squared paper such as graph

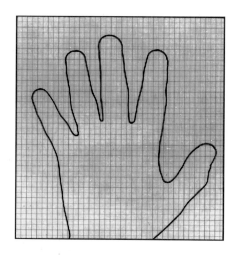

paper. With larger objects you might need to make your own squared paper in bigger units. Having done that, count the *number of squares* the shape occupies.

Have a system for counting parts of squares. For example, if half or more than half a certain square is included in the shape outline then count it as a whole one, but if less than half ignore it. Finally, multiply the number of squares you have counted by the area of a single square. A surface calculation for the hand would be doubled as there are two surfaces, the palm and the back of the hand. Remember that your answer is in 'square' units (for area).

Volume of a simple solid

The **volume** of something is the amount of space it occupies. For a symmetrical shape it can be worked out by multiplying the length, width and height together. Note that this time we are dealing with three dimensions, so the answer is in 'cubed' units. This is shown by a small raised 3 after the units.

For regular shapes such as cubes or rectangular blocks, the lengths of the sides are multiplied together. For example, the volume of a block with sides measuring 5 cm, 3 cm and 4 cm is:

$$5 \times 3 \times 4 = 60 \, \text{cm}^3$$

We can construct another formula for this:

Volume of solid = Length × Width × Height

Different units may be used depending on the shape of the object, but always remember to make all the units the same before multiplying (e.g. all in millimetres, or all in inches).

Volume of a cylinder

The volume of a cylinder is found by multiplying the area of its cross-section (a circle) by the length.

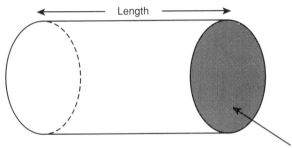

You now need to know that the area of a circle is calculated from πr^2. Pie and r have already been explained on page 178. The units will again be 'square' as *all* areas are measured in such units. When the area of the circle is multiplied by the length of the cylinder, the units become 'cubed'.

For example, a cylinder with a radius of 2.5 cm and length 10 cm has a volume of:

$$3.142 \text{ (pie)} \times 2.5 \times 2.5 \times 10$$
$$= 196 \text{ cm}^3$$

Task

A baby's feeding bottle has a diameter of 6 cm and it is 15 cm long. What is its capacity when full? Give your answer in cubic centimetres. Also try converting the capacity to fluid ounces (fl oz) and pints, making use of the table in Figure 6.2. One millilitre (ml) is the same as 1 cm³.

Check your answer: Volume = 424 cm³. Did you remember to take half the diameter to get the radius before doing your calculation?

Some other two- and three-dimensional shapes

A parallelogram

This is a four-sided shape with its opposite sides parallel to each other. None of the angles is a right-angle (90°).

A trapezium

This is best described as a four-sided shape with only *one pair* of opposite sides parallel.

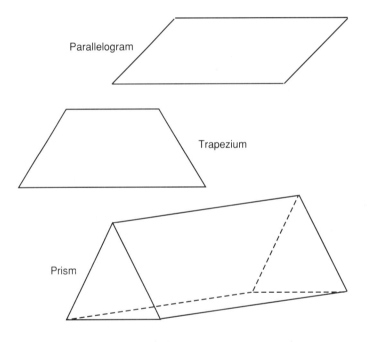

A prism

Any solid object with a *uniform* (i.e. unchanging) cross-section can be called a prism. It can have any shape for the cross-section. The most common cross-sections are triangles (like some well-known triangular chocolate bars) or squares. If the section is a circle or an oval, the solid is known as a cylinder.

A SIMPLE APPRECIATION OF PROBABILITY

If a coin is tossed it has an equal chance of coming down heads or tails. In this case we often say there is a 50/50 chance (or an even chance) that it will show heads (or tails). In number work we give a value to the likelihood of a particular outcome.

For instance, the likelihood of heads turning up with a tossed coin is 1 out of 2 (= $\frac{1}{2}$ or 0.5). The probability of a particular score on a die (singular of dice) is 1 out of 6 (= $\frac{1}{6}$), as there are 6 possible numbers. Similarly, the probability of producing the Queen of Hearts from a pack of cards is 1 out of 52.

Example

Suppose now we have two dice, one with numbers and one with colours. What is the probability of a red and a 6 turning up? What is the probability of blue and an odd number being thrown together?

The table below will help us to work this out.

Colours	Numbers					
	1	2	3	4	5	6
Yellow	×	×	×	×	×	×
Green	×	×	×	×	×	×
Blue	**×**	×	**×**	×	**×**	×
Brown	×	×	×	×	×	×
Red	×	×	×	×	×	**×**
Black	×	×	×	×	×	×

All the equally likely outcomes are shown with a cross, and we can see that there are 36 possibilities (= 6 × 6). The favourable ones we are seeking are shown in bolder type. From this we can see that 'red + 6' can only happen in one way, so that the probability of this happening is 1 out of 36, or $\frac{1}{36}$ (= 0.028). On the other hand, 'blue + any odd number' can happen in three ways, so the probability of this happening is 3 out of 36, or $\frac{3}{36}$ (=0.083).

Task

1 Find a client group that you can access in a group setting.
2 Choose an aspect of their physical development which can be measured and recorded accurately (e.g. height, age, mass, feet size).
3 Collect the appropriate data from the clients, and collate it in a pictorial form.
4 Calculate the mean from your sample (show your workings). See page 191.
5 Draw conclusions from your findings and justify why you have drawn those conclusions.

Task

Study the chart below and answer the questions, showing your workings.

1 What trend can you identify from the data?
2 What reasons can you give for this trend?
3 What was the increase in places between 1970 and 1990?

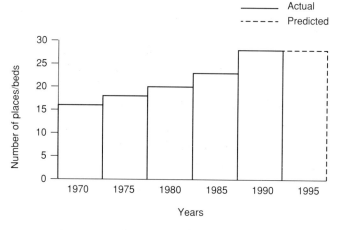

——— Actual
- - - - - Predicted

4 The ratio of nursing staff to clients is 1:4. How many nurses were needed in 1970, 1980 and 1990?
5 If a nurse was paid £120 for a 30-hour week in 1990, what would the salary bill have been for one week in the ward?
6 There is also one sister who works on the ward who is paid £200 per week. What ratio is this to the nurse's pay?
7 A pay rise of £6 per week is awarded for 1991 for the nurses. What percentage of their salary is this?
8 The sister was given the same percentage rise. How much increase in salary per week will she receive?
9 How much extra pay per week would the hospital need to find in total for this ward following the pay rise?
10 If the ward was asked to make a 5% cut in its staffing budget, how much would this be? How many nurses' hours would they have cut to cover this cost?

Task

Designing a child's toy

A task such as this will provide you with the opportunity to describe shapes, make two-dimensional representations (plans) of a three-dimensional object, calculate areas and volumes, set out calculations properly, scale-up drawings or plans to the real thing using ratios, use the simple formulae we have reviewed, practise estimation, tackle problems and carry out activities to appropriate precision.

With careful thought and planning, remembering to log all of this for your grading, you can achieve many, if not most, of your Application of Number skills on this assignment.

You can probably think of many ideas for toy construction. If you cannot, what about a ball and cup toy, or a numbered dice decorated with pictures, a kaleidoscope or diabolo? If you have not heard of any of these, ask someone or use the library (or maybe the museum). You might have great fun finding out and using your research skills.

*Do remember, don't choose the easiest you can think of. Find out which number core skills you need to show **and design this work to achieve it**.*

Fast Facts

Area The space covered by a shape. It can be a regular shape (e.g. square) or irregular.

Area of a circle Pie (π) multiplied by the radius squared.

Area of a rectangle Length multiplied by the width.

Area of a triangle Half the base length times the height.

Calculator A device for calculating quickly. Beware of quoting answers to large numbers of decimal places – rounding to two is usually enough (for example: 6.3486 would be 6.35).

Circumference of a circle Pie (π) times the diameter.

Closed questions Questions with closed types of answers (e.g. yes/no).

Conversion Changing one unit into another (e.g. pounds to ounces or ounces to grams). If you are using any of the four rules of number, *always* check that all figures are in the same unit.

Decimal number A number which includes a decimal point. Remember during calculation, moving the point to the left makes the figure smaller; moving the point to the right makes the figure larger.

Estimation Making a close guess or approximate judgement as to the value of your answer. This helps to check that no serious mistakes have been made.

Four rules of number Plus, minus, divide and multiply. (Remember always to line your units under one another if not using a calculator.)

Fractions Expressing a part in relation to the whole. The upper number is the numerator, the lower figure is a demoninator. Remember when using the four rules of number with fractions, you must work out a common denominator.

Generalisation Picking out the pattern or trend shown by a set of figures or chart.

Justification Reasons or proof used to back up statements made.

Mean The average of a set of values. The total amount of a set of values divided by the number of values.
e.g. 1, 3, 3, 3, 4, 6, 9, 15, 19 mean = 63 ÷ 9 = 7

Median The half-way value of a series of values.
e.g. 1, 3, 3, 3, 4, 6, 9, 15, 19 median = 4

Mode The most common value in a set of values.
e.g. 1, 3, 3, 3, 4, 6, 9, 15, 19 mode = 3

Observation Collecting data by watching a set of activities for a certain period.

Open questions Questions with no fixed answer.

Percentage Rate or proportion per hundred (per cent). A fraction can be converted to a percentage by multiplying by 100. The symbol is %.

Perimeter The distance around the outside of any shape. The perimeter of a circle is the same as its circumference.

Prediction   Using figures or data to guess what might happen in the future.

Precision   This is the same as accuracy. Measurements made with precision are therefore accurate rather than estimates.

Probability   The likelihood of an event happening.

Questionnaire   A written set of questions used to obtain data about a particular topic.

Ratios   Ratios are a way of comparing two or more quantities.

Recording   This is the noting down of information.

Respondents   People who answer questions put to them.

Sample   A name given to a group of your choosing to represent the whole set.

Sequence   Doing a calculation in the correct order (e.g. BODMAS – this gives you the correct order for calculating Brackets Of (usually means multiplying) Division Multiplication Addition Subtraction.

Survey   A collection and examination of information on an area – perhaps to draw conclusions.

Three-dimensional object   One with depth as well as area. Everything in the world is really 3-dimensional. A piece of paper is 3-dimensional because it does have some depth (its thickness).

Two-dimensional object   A shape that is flat on the page and which is therefore reckoned to have an area but not a volume.

Trialling   Using a new questionnaire with a sample of respondents before applying it to the whole set of a chosen group of people.

Volume   The volume of a container is the same as its capacity. It is the amount of space inside the shape.

Volume of a rectangular block   Length times width times height.

Volume of a cylinder   Pie (π) times radius squared times length (i.e. πr^2). The radius is half the diameter.

chapter 7 INFORMATION TECHNOLOGY

This chapter is designed to help you to get the most out of the information technology (IT) resources that are available to you during your health and social care studies. We look at:

- background information about the use of computers
- planning the use of IT resources in your work
- how three popular computer programs can help you with your course work.

The aim is to help you to become more familiar with IT and to show how the computers that you now have access to can be applied to your work as a health and care student.

INFORMATION TECHNOLOGY – A CORE SKILL

You will have already have encountered IT in your daily life, perhaps as a computer-generated telephone bill or bank statement, or a mass mail letter with your name and address neatly printed on it.

When you shop at the supermarket your purchases are recorded by a computerised till, and your daily newspaper is produced with the help of the new technologies. In many ways IT has become an important feature of the society in which we live and there is good reason for this. IT is a very powerful tool that can help us to store, work on, and present many different types of information. IT is so versatile that organisations, businesses and individuals in many different areas now see IT as a basic tool in their work.

As a student of health and social care you have the opportunity to discover how IT can help you in your work. You will find out how to store, organise, work on, and present the different types of information that you will be dealing with; and you will have gained skills that you can apply in your further studies, in your career and in your own areas of interest

IT is a GNVQ core skill, along with Communication and Application of Number, because it is so widely used . This means that a certain level of skill and knowledge in the use of IT is expected of everyone who is awarded an Intermediate GNVQ qualification, whatever subject it is in. The IT core skills unit sets standards that you have to meet, just as other units do.

You will find that most of the evidence you need to pass the IT unit will be there amongst the work that you do in the course of your health and care studies. This chapter will help you to use IT effectively by showing you how it can be applied to things that you will be doing as a health and care student, and it will help you to identify work which may count as evidence towards the IT unit. The computer screen icon appears occasionally to emphasise important points.

Watch this space

You may have used IT before, or you may be a complete beginner, but the chapter should be useful to you whatever your level of experience. If you have never used IT before, the best thing is to read it all carefully, and be sure to do all the tasks that are set. The chapter has been written with no prior knowledge expected and you should find that it all begins to make sense when you put IT into action. If you *have* used IT before you will still be able to benefit from this chapter as it shows you how to apply IT to the study of health and caring, and may contain some techniques and ideas you haven't met.

The most important thing you need to do is actually use the equipment that is available to you. You need to become familiar with the machines that you will be using, and with the tutors who can help you to use them. This book can indicate what you are able to do – it is up to you to put it into action for yourself.

· JUST WHAT ARE WE TALKING · ABOUT?

What do we mean when we speak about information technology? Obviously it refers to the use of new technologies to deal with information, but there are a number of terms used where the meaning is not so obvious. So let's start with some basic explanations.

Hardware

Hardware simply means the physical equipment used in IT. This includes the computer itself, the monitor screen, the keyboard and the printer (Figure 7.1).

Figure 7.1 *Hardware*

There are other useful devices that fall into the description of hardware and you may have access to some of them, but the key point is that the term means the physical equipment that is used in IT.

Software

Software is the term used for the set of instructions which the computer follows when performing a task. You may also have heard this referred to as a **program**, or as an **application**. This can seem confusing, but remember that they are just different words for the same thing.

There are different types of software designed to perform different types of task. One important type are programs known as operating systems, which are used to start the computer running and to control its activities. Operating systems *manage* the entry, flow and display of information and software between different parts of the computer, and so the operating system must be running before you can run other types of software.

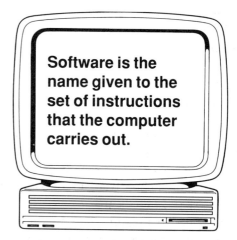

Software is the name given to the set of instructions that the computer carries out.

There is also software which is designed for you to use to do particular jobs, like writing letters, doing calculations or even playing a game. The software applications that you will be using have been produced commercially and are intended to be easy to use. You certainly don't need to know anything about programming a computer to use it effectively, any more than you have to understand mechanics in order to drive a car.

You will be making use of some of the most widely used and most useful types of application available. Firstly, one of the most common uses of IT is **word processing.** This may be thought of as a very sophisticated typewriter, and it allows the non-typist to produce well-presented documents very easily. Word-processors are capable of a lot more than an ordinary typewriter though, and you will discover how easy it is to create, edit and print professional-looking documents.

The second type of application that we will look at is **the database**. Databases are a way of storing information in the form of lists, so your address book is a form of database. They resemble a file card record system such as you may have seen in libraries or offices, but they are much easier to use and can do more useful things than simply record data. Databases are an ideal way of storing any repetitive form of information, such as names and addresses, or types and prices of equipment.

A third application is the **spreadsheet** which is designed to handle numerical information. It can help you to arrange numbers in columns and rows, perform calculations on them, and present the results as a chart or graph. Spreadsheets are used for scientific work, in finance, and in any activity where calculation of numbers occurs. As you will see, spreadsheets can help you to handle the numerical information you will deal with during your studies.

All three applications are powerful tools for handling information, and each has a wide range of uses which fall beyond the scope of this chapter. This power is considerably increased when applications are used in conjunction with each other. A word-processor, used together with a database of names and addresses, can produce a mass 'mail-shot' for you. The graph or chart from your spreadsheet can be sent to the word-processor and incorporated into your report. The ability of software applications to share information like this creates many opportunities to make your work easier, better presented, and more effective. We will be looking in detail at some of these techniques later.

Memory

The computer's memory is known as **RAM**, which stands for Random Access Memory. The RAM holds the information and instructions that are being used by the computer during your work sessions. However, RAM is not a permanent storage place for your work as everything

is deleted from it when you turn off the computer. We will soon be looking at how you can *save* your work.

Computer memory is measured in **bytes**. A byte is a single piece of information and any single keypress such as a letter, a number or a space is one byte of information. You are more likely to hear memory size described in terms of **kilobytes** and **megabytes**. One kilobyte (K) equals 1024 bytes and one megabyte (Mb) equals 1024 kilobytes (or 1048456 bytes).

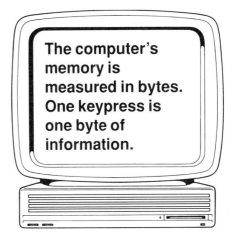

The computer's memory is measured in bytes. One keypress is one byte of information.

Compatibility

Compatibility is a term used in conjunction with both hardware and software. It means the ability of computers and applications to work with other computers and applications. To see why this is an important issue we will look briefly at the recent history of IT.

Over the last twenty years the rapid development of the IT industry has allowed the growth and success of many computer hardware companies. Several different types of computer have been produced during this time, and many of these were designed to work in their own particular way and run their own type of software. This meant that work begun on one machine could not be taken away and completed on another.

Eventually a small number of operating systems became widely used, and this popularity led new manufacturers to produce hardware that was compatible with these big-selling types of computer. One of the most popular is a type of computer known as the 'IBM compatible' or Personal Computer (PC). PCs are made by many different companies but are all compatible with each other, so software applications that are run on one PC should generally run quite happily on another provided it is powerful enough (i.e. has enough memory space). The computers that you have access to may be PCs, or of another popular type, or there may be a mixture of both available.

Compatibility between software applications is another issue, and here the word refers to the ability of applications to share information with each other. There are a number of versions of the popular applications (word-processors, spreadsheets and databases) available for use on the PC. Some of these are compatible with each other, others are not. The applications that you will be using will need to be compatible so that information can be shared and transferred between them.

Now it's time to get into action. The task below is the first of a series that will appear in this chapter and it would be best to attempt each one as you come to it. This first task might seem an obvious one, but some later tasks might appear harder to fulfil. Please get advice if you are not sure what to do about a particular task. You need to do your best to complete them in order to get the most from this chapter, and from the IT resources that are available to you.

Task

You need to find out:
- *what equipment you will be working with during your studies*
- *which machines are compatible with each other*
- *which machines are running compatible software applications of the type you need*
- *what access you can get to the machines you wish to use*
- *what tutor support is available to help you to use the software applications.*

Your first step might be to talk to your tutor or an IT specialist. Find out about the equipment and its compatibility, and make sure that you have identified times when you have access, and times when someone might be there to help you. Remember that if you plan to work on more than one computer you must ensure that you use

machines which are compatible with each other, and are running compatible software applications.

▪ USING COMPUTERS SAFELY ▪

The equipment that you are using has been designed to be as safe to use as possible. The computer itself and peripheral equipment like printers are powered from the mains electricity supply, like other domestic electrical appliances. They are insulated and earthed to protect users from electrical hazard but they must be treated with care to prevent accidents.

Cables connecting items of equipment to the electrical supply, or to each other, must be arranged so that they don't endanger health and safety. Cables must be protected from damage, and must not be allowed to loop around work areas so that they form a hazard in themselves. If you connect up items of equipment like printers, be sure to arrange the cables safely.

The arrangement of your work surface is also important. The computer keyboard is light and mobile, which means that you can arrange its position to suit your own preferred way of working. It also means that you can clutter up your work surface with paper notes, pens and other equipment. Try to avoid doing this as a crowded work surface increases the chance of accidents, and is not likely to make your work any more efficient!

Don't let this happen

Never eat or drink around IT equipment! Liquids are particularly dangerous and a spilled drink can cause a serious electrical hazard, as well as causing considerable damage to equipment. Try to make sure that this rule is enforced, both for your own safety and that of others.

Computer equipment is designed to be adjustable so that it can be set to the individual requirements of the user and the environment. The keyboard has small pull-out feet at the back edge to increase its angle of incline, which some people prefer, and it is easily moved into the most comfortable position for typing. The monitor may be swivelled left and right, and tilted up and down. This allows you to orientate the screen to a position where it is facing you directly, so that you are not forced to sit in an awkward or uncomfortable position to see it clearly.

The screen is also adjustable for brightness and contrast and you need to set these so that you can see your work clearly. It is also important, however, not to work with the screen turned up too brightly. Prolonged use of a bright screen at close quarters can strain eyes and should be avoided. The lighting in the room can affect the visibility of monitor screens. The screen will need to be turned up much more brightly to be seen in a well-lit room, particularly if lights are reflected directly on to it. Sunlight creates the same problem, and a screen facing a sunny window can be very difficult to see. Try to make sure that you adjust the lighting conditions so that you do not need to have your screen excessively bright to be able to work.

Another important feature of the environment is the seating used with the computer equipment. Most institutions provide adjustable typist's chairs for IT users. They are designed to be adjusted to a variety of positions to suit the height and build of the user, and it *is* important to set yours to your own requirements. Set the seat height so that your feet are comfortably on the floor, and the back rest so your back is adequately supported. Working at a keyboard in a badly adjusted chair can lead to backache and discomfort in quite a short time, so always take the trouble to adjust the chair to your needs.

Apart from protecting yourself and the computer hardware from damage, it is also important to look after your stored data. Though floppy disks are quite hard really and durable enough when used and stored correctly, they must be protected from physical damage. Keep them in a dry secure place as you would a CD or cassette tape.

Remember also that information is stored electrically on floppy disks, and that this can be damaged or erased if the disk is exposed to strong magnetic or electrical fields. Many domestic appliances produce electrical fields so the best rule is to keep disks away from other electrical apparatus.

• SAVING YOUR WORK •

As we have seen, the work that you do on the computer is temporarily stored in the memory, and when the computer is switched off the work is lost unless you save it first. And where do you save your work? The answer is on disks. There are two types that you are likely to encounter, hard disks and floppy disks.

Hard disks

Most computers that you meet will have a hard disk installed in them. The hard disk is permanently fixed inside the computer's case and cannot be removed from it.

The disk cannot be removed from the computer.

It can be used to store large amounts of information and can be heard clicking away to itself when you switch the computer on (known as 'booting up'), and when you use some software applications. This is because some of the information the computer needs to set itself up for use is permanently stored on the hard disk inside it, and because some applications are themselves stored on the hard disk. It is possible to save your work on the hard disk, but this practice is extremely unwise and will probably be against the local IT users' rules. It is unwise because any work saved on the hard disk can be called up later by any other user, which could result in tampering or even accidental but complete erasure of your work! This dreadful prospect can be avoided easily by saving your work on your own floppy disk.

Floppy disks

Floppy disks are a compact, cheap and secure way to save your work. You can buy a disk for well under £1 and most will store the equivalent of over 200 pages of text, which is very good value for money! Physically they come in two sizes, $3\frac{1}{2}$-inch and $5\frac{1}{4}$-inch, and your machine may take either or both.

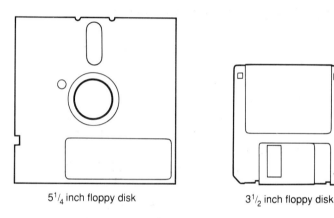

Figure 7.2 *Two sizes of floppy disks*

In fact the smaller $3\frac{1}{2}$-inch disks can store more information than $5\frac{1}{4}$-inch disks and they are the type you are most likely to be using.

Floppy disks are the best way of keeping your work secure. You can insert your own personal disk into the computer and save your work on it. When you correctly shut down the computer the only copy of your work that remains is on your floppy disk. Remove your disk and you will have all your work safely in your own possession, which is the safest way to keep it.

Formatting a floppy disk

Floppy disks are similar in one respect to a cassette tape, in that you can 'record' and 'playback' information on them. However, the way they store your work may seem

more like a CD or LP record as the surface of the floppy disk is divided into tracks and sectors. These invisible storage blocks are created by the computer in a process called **formatting**, and you need to format a new floppy disk before you can save your work on it. It is very easy to format a disk: simply put it into the disk slot and tell the computer to format it! Beware when reformatting a used disk though, because formatting permanently removes any work that was previously stored on it and you could lose something you didn't mean to! You can avoid loss of work by closing the read/write gate on your floppy disk if you want to prevent the contents being erased. When the tab is closed you can still read the information on the disk but not alter or delete it. This is very secure but of course prevents you saving any new files on the disk.

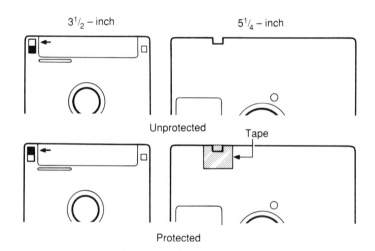

Figure 7.3 *Using tape to protect your work on the disk*

Disk capacity

The storage capacity of a floppy disk is measured in **bytes**, like the computer's memory size. This becomes important when you need to buy and format a $3\frac{1}{2}$-inch floppy disk because they come in two common sizes, 720K and 1.4Mb. The only difference between them is that a 1.4Mb disk can hold twice as much information. You can use either type to store your work, but you need to format your disk according to its storage capacity.

Now you need to find out the details of how to format a disk on your local equipment.

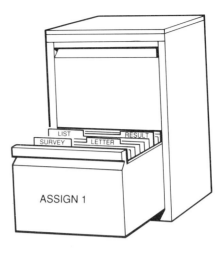

ORGANISING YOUR WORK USING FILES AND DIRECTORIES

Each separate piece of work that you create and save on the computer is known as a **file**. Files are linked to the applications that they were created in, so that a word-processed letter is saved as a word-processor file and a database that lists books you have read is saved as a database file.

The computer will ask you to give your files a name as you save them, and it will add its own bit of code at the end to remind you what application the file belongs to. The problem is that you are restricted to a maximum name length of only eight characters when you save, and as you add files to your floppy disk it can soon contain a confusing list of meaningless initials, *unless you organise it.*

Directories

There is an easy way to avoid having to deal with a bewildering list of file names, and that is to organise your files into *groups*. The computer can set up your floppy disks so that files that you want to keep together are stored in the same place, in a **directory**.

It may be helpful to think of all the files you save as though they were paper files and were to be stored in a filing cabinet. You would probably want to put all the work you were doing for a particular assignment together in the same drawer, but you may want to divide that up further so that you can easily find work intended for a particular part of the assignment. So you could label the drawer ASSIGN1, and

label the sections inside SURVEY, LETTER, LIST, RESULTS – and so on as your needs dictate.

The computer can create a similar arrangement for the files that you save on your floppy disk. Suppose that you are beginning work on a new assignment on safety – perhaps the third assignment you have tackled – and plan to use IT to help you with parts of the work and to write the final report. You can tell the computer to create a directory on your floppy disk called ASS3SAFE, and then save all the files you create for the assignment in the ASS3SAFE directory.

The directory can be used to save any type of file, so you can save a word-processed letter together with a spreadsheet in the same place. If it is a large assignment and you expect to be using IT for different parts of it, then you can create further divisions within your directory, known as *sub-directories*. You can think of this arrangement as a branching tree, with one route to the tip of a particular branch (Figure 7.4).

Figure 7.4 *Splitting one directory into several sub-directories*

Suppose your safety assignment involved you in looking at safety in the *college*, safety and the *law*, and safety in a *care est*ablishment. You may decide to save the IT work that you do for the assignment in three separate sub-directories called, say, COLLEGE, LAW and CAREEST (Figure 7.5).

Figure 7.5 *Giving names to the sub-directories*

When you want to save a piece of work in a particular sub-directory you need to tell the computer the path to follow to that sub-directory. Suppose you have written a survey form to help assess students' awareness of safety in college, and you wish to save it with the name SURVEY, in the COLLEGE sub-directory of the ASS3SAFE directory. Then you specify the path: ASS3SAFE/COLLEGE/SURVEY, and your file is then saved where you want it.

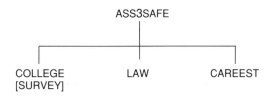

Figure 7.6 *Giving a file a unique address in a sub-directory*

This path provides a unique *address* for your file, which you can subsequently use to reload it for editing or printing.

You can easily keep track of your work by thoughtful use of directories and sub-directories. The computer can quickly *show you* the layout and contents of your floppy disk, so there is no need to remember the paths to all your files.

USING INFORMATION TECHNOLOGY IN YOUR WORK

All the work you do during your studies has to be planned. When you begin a new assignment you will first need to decide on a plan of action to carry out the work, and this is the time to consider how IT can be used to help you. Of course, to be able to do this you first need to know the kind of things that IT can do for you and how to

put them into practice. We will follow the progress of a group of three GNVQ Intermediate Health and Social Care students as they use IT in their work for an assignment, from the early planning stages to the completion of a finished report.

Action planning

Sharon, Aysha and Jason are studying GNVQ Intermediate Health and Social Care. They have been looking at unit 2 – Social influences on health and well-being – and are working as a group to complete an assignment on Health and Lifestyle. They are particularly concerned with cigarette smoking as a hazard to health and decide to examine attitudes to smoking amongst the public and in the business community.

They begin by sitting down together to decide in detail what they need to do, and to formulate an action plan to help them organise the work. The discussion results in the decision to carry out a *questionnaire* of smoking habits and attitudes amongst their fellow students, and to carry out a postal *survey* to discover the policy on smoking in local cinemas and restaurants. They hope to be able to compare the results of their research and find out how aware businesses and the public are of the health risks of smoking.

Sharon, Aysha and Jason have been using the local IT facilities and plan to use them to help with this assignment. They have designed and created their own action planning forms using the computer and have printed the result. They can then alter their form if they wish to, and print copies whenever they are needed. Figure 7.7 shows a copy of Aysha's first action plan for the smoking research project. They will be writing further action plans later to help them to deal with the results of their research.

Aysha's action planning form shows the steps that the group intend to take in their research, and the deadlines they have set themselves. Sharon, Aysha and Jason have planned their use of IT resources and have predicted where there will be opportunities to collect evidence. They know that their work will provide evidence towards an element of unit 2, but they also know that their planned use of IT will allow them to collect evidence towards information technology core skill units at the same time.

GNVQ Action Plan			Date:			Aysha	
Aim	Activity	Knowledge needs	Sources of information	Dates for completion	Reflection opportunities	Evidence opportunities	Elements
To conduct a survey of students' views on smoking	Write questionnaire form with Sharon and Jason. Sharon to design and print out form on word processor. All to carry out questionnaire in canteen at lunchtime.	How to write questionnaire questions. Word processor techniques to help with layout. Issues involved in carrying out a questionnaire.	Speak to tutors about questions. See I.T. tutor for WP layout tips. Check library for books on questionnaires.	Questionnaire form to be produced by 17 Nov. Questionnaire to be completed by 21 Nov.	Meet with Sharon and Jason to discuss survey wording and layout. Meet with Sharon and Jason to decide how we do questionnaire.	Towards I.T. Core Skill Unit: Creation of form, saving, editing and printing.	
To conduct a survey of smoking rules in local cinemas and restaurants	All to write letter to cinema and restaurant managers. Type into WP for mail merge. Create a database of names and addresses. Send letters.	How to create a letter for merging with a database of names and addresses. How to set up a database. Where to find addresses.	Talk to I.T. tutor for help on mail merge. Talk to I.T. tutor for help on databases. Check library for addresses.	Letter to be produced by 17 Nov. Database to be completed by 17 Nov. Letters to be sent by 19 Nov.		Towards I.T. Core Skills Unit: Creation of database, creation of form letter, transfer of information between applications.	

Figure 7.7   *Aysha's action plan*

We have seen that Aysha has identified on her action plan some possible evidence collection opportunities towards the IT units. She prefers to identify evidence collection opportunities towards other units on separate copies of her action plan. In this case she has filled in another action plan to indicate evidence collection opportunities towards the mandatory unit 'Social influences on health and well-being'. As we are concerned here with collecting evidence towards IT units we don't need to see the other action plans. Now that we have seen how Aysha laid out her own action plan you can begin to do this for yourself.

Task

You can plan the headings and layout of your own action planning form, ready to create it on the computer. Look at the action plans in this book and at those you have met during your studies. You may have had a format suggested to you by your tutor, and probably already have ideas of your own.

Think about the way you approach planning your work and design a form that fits your own style. Discuss your ideas with your tutors: they will be helping you to use the action plan forms.

Your action plan form can be created later using the computer . The design you have done can provide evidence of planning in the use of IT.

An important aspect of the action plan is the identification of *knowledge needs*. Aysha realises that she needs to find out more about word-processing to carry out the work in her action plan, and now we also will look at word-processors in more detail.

· USING THE WORD-PROCESSOR ·

Using a word-processor can seem very similar to using a type-writer. The computer keyboard on which you type your text is arranged in the same layout as a typewriter keyboard, and the word-processor can certainly produce the sort of high-quality

documents that professional typists produce. But the word-processor lets you create these documents without needing the skills of a professional typist.

With a word-processor you can:

- enter any text you wish
- make corrections, revisions and even major changes easily and without a lot of retyping
- create special styles for headings and important points
- alter the layout to suit your requirements
- add headers and page numbers
- import information from other applications such as a spreadsheet or database, and incorporate into your document
- print your work when you are satisfied with it
- save your file on floppy disk so that you can reload it later and make further changes, and copies, if you wish.

As you can see, the word-processor is a powerful tool for dealing with text-based information. How can you put it to use with your work?

Task

Look through the course work you are doing at the moment and select a piece of writing that you could word-process. It could be a letter, a short report, or even a questionnaire form like Sharon, Aysha and Jason will use. The important thing is to choose something that will be presented as part of your portfolio or assignment work, and can be used to show evidence of planning the use of IT in your work.

Starting a new document

To begin with you need to switch on the computer and start up the word-processor. In this, as with other functions of IT described here, your local equipment will have particular ways of doing things and you need to find out the details from your IT tutor. The next step in creating your document is to start a new word-processor file and you will then see the screen in which you will be working.

Towards the top left of the screen is a flashing cursor which indicates where your typing will appear (the insertion point), and above this there is usually a ruler.

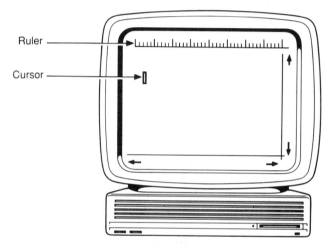

Figure 7.8 *What the screen may look like initially*

There are marks on the ruler to show the margins set for your text, and your **cursor** should be below the left-hand margin mark, ready for you to begin typing.

Entering text

As you type, the cursor moves to the right ahead of the text. As you approach the right-hand margin there is no need to press the return/enter key, as you would on a normal typewriter, because the word-processor automatically starts a new line without breaking up a word – you simply keep on typing. This is known as 'word-wrap'.

In fact it is very *unwise* to use the return key unless you want to start a new line. This is because the word-processor remembers *every* key push, including return and space, and unnecessary 'returns' can produce some very

New lines are started automatically. Don't press return unless you need to start a new line.

odd results if you change the layout of your document later.

You enter text just as you would on a typewriter, pressing return *twice* to create a blank line between paragraphs. If you make a mistake you can press the *backspace* key and the cursor moves to the left, deleting the incorrect text. You can also delete spaces and returns in the same way. When your lines of text increase so that the whole document can't be displayed at once, you will see that the document slips up the screen so that the insertion point is always visible. This is called **scrolling**.

Figure 7.9 *Imagine scrolling like this*

If you want to look at the earlier part of a document that has scrolled partly out of view, you can do this by moving the cursor with the *direction arrow* keys on your keyboard. These keys move the cursor left and right, and up and down, and as you move the cursor up your document the earlier parts scroll back into view. (Remember, though,

that you can't move the cursor down below the end of a document.)

The arrow keys allow you to position the cursor anywhere in the document. This is an extremely useful facility. You can move the cursor to a particular point and type in new text, and you can also delete using the backspace key. When you type new text within a document you will find that all the text below moves along to make room for it. This is called 'insert mode' and you can change it if you wish so that your typing overwrites the original text.

With this basic knowledge of how to enter text and make corrections you can begin to use your own word-processor.

The three students we have been studying have also been using the word-processor. Sharon, Aysha and Jason began their work by agreeing a list of questions to be asked. As they will be conducting their questionnaire in a crowded canteen, they wanted to keep each interview short, and so decided to use a small number of brief 'closed' questions which need only a yes or no answer.

Sharon has entered their questions into the word-processor and saved the file as SURVEY1 in a directory called SMOKE on her floppy disk.

```
Smoking Awareness Research
Project Survey

1. Do you think smoking can
harm other people's health?
2. Would you go out with
someone who smoked
cigarettes?
3. Do you smoke cigarettes?
4. If so, why do you smoke
cigarettes?
5. Do you think that smoking
is bad for your health?
6. Do you think that smoking
should be allowed in
enclosed public places like
cinemas and restaurants?
```

Figure 7.10 *The first printout of Aysha's questionnaire*

She has printed a copy of her file, which is shown in Figure 7.10.

Sharon, Aysha and Jason meet to check the questionnaire form and decide that they need to make some changes.

- They feel that question 4 should be left out as it is an open question which could lead to long answers that are difficult to assess numerically.
- They also feel think that the question order could be improved and decide to begin with question 5, followed by question 1, then question 6, with question 3 next and question 4 at the end.
- They also want to allow room for the other answers, and so decide to put more space between the questions and to indicate places for the answers to be filled in.
- They want to add a question to find out whether the respondent is male or female, and decide to put this near the bottom.
- Finally, they feel that the look of the form would be improved with better headings and with the question numbers hanging out to the left of the question text.

This sounds like a lot of work but in fact it can all be done in a few minutes, when you know how.

Task

Look at the printout of the document that you created for the last task, or of another document that you have created using the word-processor. You need to:

- *decide on improvements to the content, including: moving, adding, deleting and copying text*
- *decide on improvements to the layout, including headings and spacing.*

Indicate the changes you decide to make on your copy using pencil. This can be used as evidence towards the IT core skill unit.

Editing text

You have already met text editing in the form of the use of the backspace key to delete text you have just typed. As you now know how to move the cursor to any part of the document, you can delete and insert text wherever you wish. But suppose that you want to move a large piece of text to another part of the document. The method above would involve the slow (character by character) deletion of the existing text, and the even slower process of typing it back in another location. And what if you then changed your mind?

There is an easier way to manipulate text, whether you want to move, copy or delete it. It is made possible by the ability of the word processor to 'select' text. You can select a character, a word, a line, a sentence, a paragraph, even an entire document. Once you have selected the text it is easy to move, copy or delete it. In fact the backspace key can be used to delete selected text, and this is a much quicker method than working backwards character by character if you need to delete more than a few words.

Select text that you want to delete, copy or move.

The process of selecting and moving or copying text is also known as **cut and paste**, and this describes what you do quite well. First you select the text you want to move or copy. Then you tell the word-processor to 'cut' if you want to move the text , or 'copy' if you want to leave the original text unaltered. You then move the cursor to the place you want to insert the text and tell the word-processor to paste. Your text will then appear, and of course the text below moves down to make room for it.

You should now easily be able to rearrange your text to your satisfaction. Ask for help from an IT specialist if you have any difficulties. We now look at how to improve headings and layout.

Formatting characters

Changing the way your document looks is called **formatting**, and formatting characters refers to the effects that can be added to your text to alter its appearance. You can use **bold**, or *italic*, or underline, or CAPITAL LETTERS, or even ***ALL FOUR***, to make parts of your text stand out. The method of first selecting text and then changing it can be used to format headings with these highlights, which can be used in any combination.

As well as applying these effects you can also make changes to the size and shape of your chosen text. The text that is printed out by the computer has a consistent shape and style, whether it includes letters or numbers, and the term for a full set of characters in a particular style is *character set* or *font*. Most typewriters use a font called Courier `which looks like this` and this book is set in a font called Times. Text size is measured in *points*. Normal text is usually formatted at 10 point or 12 point , 6 point is getting too small to read and 24 point is too large for normal text.

You can change the font and size of selected text and greatly alter its appearance. Careful selection of fonts and sizes can much improve the look of the whole document, as any available fonts can be applied to any part of the text. You can add even greater emphasis to headings, and can create good-looking title pages, but beware! It is all too easy to ruin a perfectly good-looking document by going wild with a range of fonts and effects. The golden rule is to keep your character formatting simple and neat for the best presentation. You will be limited in the range of fonts and sizes available to you by the equipment you are using, but some word-processors and printers can produce a large number for you to choose from.

Remember that all the different character formats mentioned above either can be applied to text you have already entered by selecting it, or chosen before you begin so that everything you type comes out in the style you require.

Formatting paragraphs

Formatting can also be applied to paragraph layout, and you are able to control the alignment of the paragraph and the line spacing.

Printed text is aligned between the margins of the page in one of four ways, as illustrated in Figure 7.12.

This is 6 point

This is 10 point

This is 12 point

This is 24 point

Figure 7.11 *Text size is measured in points*

Left aligned text is arranged so that lines are even on the left hand side but the right-hand side is ragged.

Right aligned text is similar to the above except that it is lined up on the right.

Justified text is adjusted by the computer so that the lines are of an even length, though it can lead to a lot of extra spaces being added. Newspapers are printed with justified text.

Centred text is centred.

Figure 7.12 *Variations on alignment of text*

Line spacing can also be adjusted if you wish. The standard spacing is one line, but you can increase this in half space steps. You can choose a format and spacing before you type, or select and change as with other editing features we have looked at.

Alignment of paragraphs takes place between the margins, as was mentioned above, and you can change the position of these margins for particular paragraphs or for the whole document.

One of the changes that Sharon, Aysha and Jason want to make to their questionnaire is to have the question numbers hanging out to the left of the text. This can be achieved by selecting the question paragraphs, and then setting the left margin in a short way, but setting the first line of each paragraph back over to the left. This produces what is called a *hanging indent* (Figure 7.13). Although it may sound complicated it is a common procedure, so your word-processor will be designed to make it easy for you to do.

This is an example of a hanging indent. The 1st line protrudes on the left.

Figure 7.13 *Your word-processor can do hanging indents*

Sharon, Aysha and Jason have used some of these methods on their questionnaire form.

- They began by selecting and deleting question 4, then rearranged the order of the remaining questions by selecting and moving the text, and lastly renumbered them.

- Next they inserted a blank line between each question by moving the cursor to the question numbers and pressing return.
- Using the *tab* key they moved the cursor a short way over to the right along the blank line below each question and inserted a few dots. Using the tab key helps to line up the answer spaces correctly and it is easier and quicker to use than the *spacebar*.
- The students then selected the question paragraphs and set a left margin with a hanging indent so that the numbers stand out to the left.
- It had been decided to ask the sex of respondents, and Sharon, Aysha and Jason want to put this in a little below the other questions. They can't move the cursor directly to the spot because their document ends at the last question, so they add blank lines at the bottom by pressing return. They use the tab key again to space the check boxes along the line.
- They decide to add a 'thank you' line. This is done in the same way.
- Finally they tackle the headings. Both headings are centred and made bold, with 'survey' changed to 'Questionnaire' and put in capital letters. They decide to leave the size and font as they are for this document.

Smoking Awareness Research Project

QUESTIONNAIRE

1. Do you think smoking is bad for your health?
   . . . .

2. Do you think that smoking can harm other people's health?

3. Do you think that smoking should be allowed in enclosed public places like cinemas and restaurants?
   . . . .

4. Do you smoke cigarettes?

5. Would you go out with someone who smoked cigarettes?

Please tick the correct answer

   Male . . . . . .   Female . . . .

Thank you for your help with our survey

Figure 7.14 *The students' revamped survey document*

When they have completed these changes they save and print the file. The document now looks like Figure 7.14. This is much clearer to read than the original draft, and the students' survey form now looks like a well presented document.

You can now improve your document by applying some of the techniques we have discussed.

Task

You may have made some decisions about the changes you would like to make to your own document and now you could carry them out. You need to find out how to:

- *select text on your word-processor, and how to use the cut and paste method to move and copy selected text*
- *add effects to characters including bold, italic, capitals and underline*
- *align paragraphs to the left, to the right, justified or centred*
- *change margin markers to alter the width of paragraphs and create a hanging indent on the first line*
- *change the font and size of characters in your document.*

You might see your IT tutor for help with using your local word-processor to carry out these editing operations, and practise them on your document. Obtain a printout of one or two versions to give yourself an idea of how the changes you are making will affect the final appearance.

Try out all the editing features that have been described even if you don't intend using them for the final version of your document. You will get practice in using the equipment, and will be well prepared to use the techniques later with other documents.

Remember that you can make changes to your document, and print copies of your changed versions, without altering the original file saved on your floppy disk – provided that you don't save a changed version using the same name as the original. If you like an altered version but want to keep the original as well, you can save the new version with its own new name, thus keeping both files stored on your disk.

A printout showing editing changes to your document can be used as evidence towards the IT core skills unit.

· USING A DATABASE ·

For the next stage of their research Sharon, Aysha and Jason need to contact a range of cinemas and restaurants. They have decided to send out 20 letters and to use the local directories in the library to build a list of contact addresses.

They intend to create a database on the computer to store their contact list so that they can use the information in a variety of ways later.

What is a database?

A database is a list of information. We have already given examples, such as address books and library catalogue systems.

Computers are very good at handling lists and the software application that is used for this is called a *database manager*, though it is usually referred to simply as a database.

The sorts of things you can do with a computerised database include:

- locate particular information instantly
- add extra information
- update and alter information
- rearrange the order of the list
- make smaller sub-lists from your information
- share information with other software applications.

Setting up a database

To begin setting up a database you first need to decide what information you want to record.

Suppose that you want to keep track of books that you have read or referred to during an assignment. For each book you would want to note the title, author (first name and surname), publisher and date of publication. Each of these categories of information is known as a field, and you can enter data into these **fields** for each of the books you wish to list. The information held for a particular book is called a record, and in our example each record will contain the title, author, publisher and data fields.

To set up a new database you must tell the computer what fields you need. The information you are storing will be of different types – some will be numbers and some will be words (or perhaps words and numbers together). Data consisting of numbers, such as a price or a quantity, is known as *numeric data*, and data that is text, or a combination of text and numbers, is called *alphanumeric data*. Names, titles of books and telephone numbers are all alphanumeric data. Telephone numbers are not used to do calculations with, so it is easier to treat them as alphanumeric data. You need to decide what type of fields you need to create for your data, and in our example we would need only alphanumeric fields as no numbers are being stored.

Numeric fields store numbers, alphanumeric fields store text and text mixed with numbers.

You also need to decide on the *length* of your fields, which is specified by a number of characters. Let us allow 80 characters for the title, 20 characters for the author's surname, 20 characters for the author's first name, 25 characters for the publisher.

When you have set up your fields you will have a blank record looking something like this:

Title:
Author's surname:
Author's first name:
Publisher:
Publication date:

All you need to do now is enter the details of the first book into the fields. When you have finished you go on to the next record and fill in the data for the next book, and you carry on creating new records until all your data are stored. *When you have finished this process you have created a database.*

Sharon, Aysha and Jason have created a database of their local cinemas and restaurants and have included the following fields for each record:

Name:
Type:
Title:
Managers_surname:
Managers_firstname:
Address_1:
Address_2:
Address_3:
Postcode:

They are now able to look at the entries they have made in a variety of ways. Looking at records is known as *browsing* and you have a lot of control over how you arrange them.

When you browse records they are displayed in *rows* with the field names written as *column* titles at the top, like this:

Name	Type	Title	Managers-surname
Antoines	Restaurant	Mr	Destang
Beefhouse	Restaurant	Mr	Phillips
Blue Bay	Restaurant	Ms	Williams
Calcutta	Restaurant	Mrs	Shah
Clarion	Cinema	Mr	Collins
Decathlon	Restaurant	Mr	Platos

You can see that not all the field columns are displayed on the screen at once. They have not disappeared but simply cannot be fitted on the screen. You can think of the screen as a window that can only show part of the scene at once. You can move the window around to view other areas using the cursor keys. Just as you can scroll down a document with the word-processor, so you can move across the database to view the contents of the other fields.

In the student's case the records above have been displayed alphabetically using the name field as the index. The records could be displayed sorted by the manager's name, or by the address, or by using any of the fields.

The students have found that the Beefhouse Restaurant has recently changed hands and that it is now called the Vegibyte Restaurant. They don't know the new manager's name, but they decide to edit the record.

Records can be sorted by using any field as the index.

You can ask the computer to search for a particular record, or group of records, in a database and then edit the data they contain. You need to specify the text or numbers that you are looking for and all the records that contain it will be displayed. In this case the students search for the word 'Beefhouse' in theName field and the following record is displayed:

Name:Beefhouse
Type:Restaurant
Title: Mr
Managers_surname:Phillips
Managers_firstname:John
Address_1:High Street
Address_2:Upton
Address_3:Noneton
Postcode:NO1 2BE

The students amend the record by moving the cursor to the data they want to change and entering the new information. The record now looks like this:

Name:Vegibyte
Type:Restaurant
Title:Sir
Managers_surname:
Managers_firstname:
Address_1:High Street
Address_2:Upton
Address_3:Noneton
Postcode:NO1 2BE

They have left the manager's name fields *blank* but have included the word 'Sir' in the title field. The reason for this will become clearer later when we look at merging database information with a word-processed standard letter.

Jason has been told that the cinema in Station Road has closed down but none of the group can remember its name. This time all they know is that they are looking for a cinema in Station Road, so they decide to *search the database*. To make the search you need to specify which fields you are interested in and the data that you are looking for in these fields. So Jason specifies the data entry 'Cinema' in the Type field, and the data entry 'Station Road' in the Address_1 field. As there is only one cinema in Station Road the following record is displayed:

Name:Roxy
Type:Cinema
Title:Mr
Managers_surname:Rank
Managers_firstname:Arthur
Address_1:Station Road
Address_2:Downton
Address_3:Noneton
Postcode:NO2 8IT

Jason then deletes the entire record from the database.

Searching the database for a particular record is very useful, but what if you want to look at group of records that have something in common? Sharon, Aysha and Jason want to check how many cinemas they have included in their database, so they decide to *query the database*. A query is made by specifying the fields to be queried, and the information to be searched for . The records which fit the requirements are displayed as a list and you can work on this list using all the database management tools that we have described.

Query the database to list records with similar contents in certain fields

The students' query displays the following list of records:

Name	Type	Title	Managers_surname
Albion	Cinema	Mr	Grimes
Clarion	Cinema	Mr	Collins
Commodore	Cinema	Mrs	Plowright
Empire	Cinema	Mr	Attenbrough
Realto	Cinema	Ms	Taylor
Regal	Cinema	Mr	Hardy

Remember that these records have *not* been taken away from the main database but that they have simply been chosen for display, leaving the records on restaurants hidden. The students are satisfied that they have included enough cinemas and save their complete database file on a floppy disk.

Task

You can set up your own database containing information that you need to organise. Firstly you need to decide what information to store in your database. Remember that you can store any information that is in the form of a list. You then need to decide on the field titles and lengths that you will require. When you have decided on your data you need to find out how to:

- *set up a new database with the fields that you want on your local equipment*
- *search the database for particular records*
- *add, delete and edit records*
- *query the database for a list of records containing certain information in common.*

If necessary talk to your IT tutor to find out how to perform these tasks on your equipment. Practise using the database management tools that have been described and when you are satisfied save your file on floppy disk.

The work that you do can be used as evidence towards the IT core skill unit.

SHARING INFORMATION BETWEEN APPLICATIONS

The next stage of Sharon, Aysha and Jason's action plan involves sending letters to all the addresses on their database. They intend to use the word-processor to create a letter and to link it with their database of cinemas and restaurants. We will now see how this is done.

Creating a form letter

The document that you create on the word-processor for a mail-merge is known as a **form letter**. Form letters are typed in like an ordinary letter except that you indicate the places where information from the database is to appear. The students want to ask the same questions on smoking to each of the managers, but will need to have a different name and address on each copy of their letter.

Sharon, Aysha and Jason meet to decide on the wording of their letter. Jason has agreed to use his home as the sender's address so he will be sent all the responses. The group plan the letter leaving spaces where information from the database will be included. Figure 7.15 shows the text of their letter, with boxes to indicate where they want to put database information.

Now that they are happy with the *content*, Sharon, Aysha and Jason go to the word-processor to create their form letter. They intend to number their questions and use hanging indents to make the numbers stand out, and they need to use the tab key to create accurately positioned answer spaces.

They also need to indicate where *database information* is to be included so that the right things appear in the right places. This is done by typing the name of a database field into the letter, positioned where one wants the data contained in that field to appear. It has to be made clear to the computer that you have typed a field name and not just another word, and the word-processor you are using will have a way of indicating this. These specially marked field names are called *merge fields* and they instruct the computer to bring information from a database file into a word-processor file when it is printed.

It is important to realise that merging only takes place *when the document is printed.* You do *not* see the details of

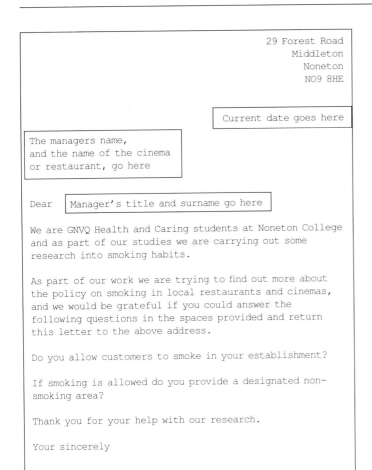

```
                                    29 Forest Road
                                        Middleton
                                         Noneton
                                         NO9 8HE

                            ┌─────────────────────────┐
                            │ Current date goes here   │
                            └─────────────────────────┘
┌────────────────────────────┐
│ The managers name,         │
│ and the name of the cinema │
│ or restaurant, go here     │
└────────────────────────────┘

         ┌──────────────────────────────────┐
Dear     │ Manager's title and surname go here │
         └──────────────────────────────────┘

We are GNVQ Health and Caring students at Noneton College
and as part of our studies we are carrying out some
research into smoking habits.

As part of our work we are trying to find out more about
the policy on smoking in local restaurants and cinemas,
and we would be grateful if you could answer the
following questions in the spaces provided and return
this letter to the above address.

Do you allow customers to smoke in your establishment?

If smoking is allowed do you provide a designated non-
smoking area?

Thank you for your help with our research.

Your sincerely
```

Figure 7.15   *The first draft of the students' letter*

particular records displayed in the letter on the screen, only the field names of the database which the records are stored in.

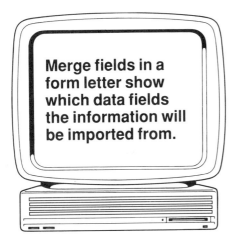

Merge fields in a form letter show which data fields the information will be imported from.

Sharon, Aysha and Jason have created a form letter on the word-processor, and have included merge fields where they want database information to appear. They have also

included a special field for the *current date* to be inserted when the letters are printed. They have been careful to type the field names *exactly* as they are written in their database file so that the computer can recognise them, and have enclosed them in angled brackets *which their particular word-processor uses to define a merge field.* Figure 7.16 shows their letter as it appears on the computer monitor screen. In this example the merge fields are shown in bold type so that they stand out, but on the computer screen this would not be the case.

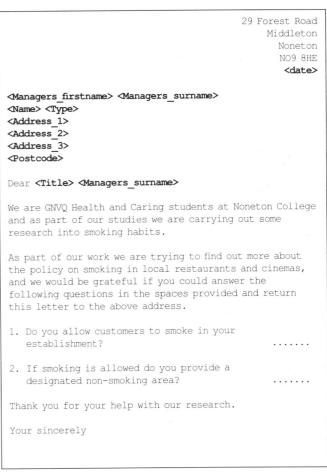

```
                                    29 Forest Road
                                        Middleton
                                         Noneton
                                         NO9 8HE
                                         <date>

<Managers_firstname> <Managers_surname>
<Name> <Type>
<Address_1>
<Address_2>
<Address_3>
<Postcode>

Dear <Title> <Managers_surname>

We are GNVQ Health and Caring students at Noneton College
and as part of our studies we are carrying out some
research into smoking habits.

As part of our work we are trying to find out more about
the policy on smoking in local restaurants and cinemas,
and we would be grateful if you could answer the
following questions in the spaces provided and return
this letter to the above address.

1. Do you allow customers to smoke in your
   establishment?                              .......

2. If smoking is allowed do you provide a
   designated non-smoking area?                .......

Thank you for your help with our research.

Your sincerely
```

Figure 7.16   *The students' letter with field names included*

The merge fields have been placed carefully so that the printed letter will have database information in the right places. The manager's surname and first name appear in the right order, and the address is laid out neatly beneath.

You may remember the Vegibyte Restaurant where the manager's name was unknown. For this record the students left the manager's name fields empty and typed Sir in the Title field. This means that the letter to the Vegibyte Restaurant will begin Dear Sir, as they require.

Now you can use the word-processor to create a form letter and link the merge fields to a database file that you have created.

Firstly, you need to decide on the content and layout of your merge document, and where you want the information from the database to appear. When you have planned your merge document, you need to find out how to indicate merge fields on your local word processor (does it use angled brackets?).

Now create your document. Take care to enter the field names accurately and in the correct positions, and be sure to indicate the merge fields so that your computer will recognise them. Finally save your document on a floppy disk when you are satisfied with it.

The planning that you do for your merge document may be used as evidence towards the IT core skill unit.

Carrying out a print merge

Sharon, Aysha and Jason are now ready to print their letters. To begin with they run the word-processor and *load* the file containing their merge letter. They then tell the computer to perform a *print merge*, which is one of the print options available. The students take care to specify the path to their database file, and its name, so that the computer can find it.

Mailing labels can be printed from a database.

Finally they tell it to print and the computer produces a personalised letter for each record on the database.

The students now need to print *labels* for the envelopes. This they will do also from the database. They run the database program and load their mailing list file. The database has address labels included in its printing options. They simply specify the fields to print and the position they are to appear on the label. When they instruct the computer to print it produces a label for each record in the database.

There may be occasions when it is necessary to print a letter for only a few records on the database. This can be done when printing the merge document with the word-processor. As well as specifying the name of the database you can identify *particular* records that you want to use by using a method similar to querying the database.

Sharon, Aysha and Jason could have used this method to print letters to all the cinemas on their list. With their merge letter loaded into the word-processor they would need to select 'print merge' and then specify not only the database name and path, but also the particular field contents to look for. In this case they would specify the entry Cinema in the Type field. The computer will then produce letters to all the cinema managers on the database.

Now you might wish to print a merged document. Run the word-processor and load the merge document you created earlier.

You probably don't want to produce a document for every record on your database, so you will need to decide what records you do want to include, and how to specify them by the contents of particular fields. When you have done this you need to find out how to:

- *select the print merge option on your word processor*
- *specify the records you want to merge with your document.*

Finally tell the computer to print out your merged document. The work that you do in performing a print merge can be used as evidence towards the IT core skill unit.

• USING A SPREADSHEET •

Sharon, Aysha and Jason have now sent out their letters and carried out their student survey. Whilst they wait for the postal responses to arrive they decide to begin work on the results they have so far.

They have asked 30 students to fill in questionnaire forms and now intend to use the **spreadsheet** to record and work on the results. We will now look at the sorts of things a spreadsheet can do for you.

What is a spreadsheet?

A spreadsheet is designed for working on numerical information. This information is organised into columns and rows, and you can see this arrangement on the screen when running the spreadsheet. Figure 7.17 shows part of a typical spreadsheet screen.

	A	B	C	D	E	F
1						
2						
3						
4						
5						
6						
7						
8						
9						
10						
11						
12						
13						
14						

Figure 7.17 *Part of a spreadsheet display*

As you can see, the spreadsheet is composed of **cells** which make up the columns and rows. Each row and column is labelled and in this spreadsheet example letters are used to label the columns and numbers are used to label the rows, which is the system found on most spreadsheets.

This labelling system means that each cell has a *unique address*, known as the **cell reference**, which is written using the column letter and the row number. The cell in the top left corner is highlighted and its cell reference is A1, as it is in the column labelled A and in the row labelled 1. You can move the highlight from cell to cell using the cursor arrow keys and highlight any cell in the spreadsheet.

The highlighted cell is called the *active cell*. Information that you type in is entered into the active cell, and to enter information in a particular cell you need to highlight it as the active cell first.

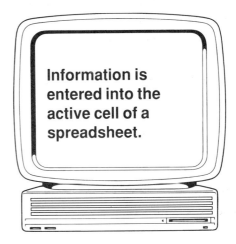

Information is entered into the active cell of a spreadsheet.

The computer screen can display only a part of the spreadsheet at any one time, as happens with the other software applications that we have looked at. You actually have a large number of rows and columns available to you, but these are off the screen. As you move the active cell highlight across, or up and down your spreadsheet, other parts will come into view.

You can enter text or numbers into the cells of a spreadsheet. Text is often used to label columns and rows, and to create titles. The principle job of a spreadsheet is to work with numbers though, and there is a range of facilities with which to do this.

What can a spreadsheet do?

With a spreadsheet you can perform calculations easily. To illustrate this, Figure 7.18 shows a spreadsheet that has been set up to record the monthly expenditure of a GNVQ Health and Social Care student.

The student has entered the months as text in cells B1 to F1 to provide column headings, and has entered spending

	A	B	C	D	E	F
1		Jan	Feb	March	April	May
2	Food	80	74	82	76	85
3	Clothes	20	35	12	18	20
4	Entertain	70	75	50	67	54
5	Books	50	12	35	50	22
6	Savings	29	30	41	24	32
7						
8						
9						
10						
11						
12						
13						
14						

Figure 7.18   *A student's expenditure record before refinement*

categories as row headings in cells A2 to A6. The amounts spent per month have then been entered into the appropriate cells. The computer recognises which cell entries are text and aligns them over to the left, whereas numbers are aligned to the right.

Each entry has been made by positioning the active cell highlight to the required position and typing. The entry appears in the active cell, and also in a special part of the screen outside the main spreadsheet area. You can edit the entry until you are satisfied and then you press the enter key to confirm it.

	A	B	C	D	E	F
1		Jan	Feb	March	April	May
2	Food	£80	£74	£82	£76	£85
3	Clothes	£20	£35	£12	£18	£20
4	Entertainment	£70	£75	£50	£67	£54
5	Books	£50	£12	£35	£50	£22
6	Savings	£29	£30	£41	£24	£32
7						
8						
9						
10						
11						
12						
13						
14						

Figure 7.19   *Refinements introduced into the student's records*

The look of a spreadsheet can be improved by changing the sizes of rows and columns, and by formatting the text and number entries to suit your requirements. For example, the word 'entertainment' will not fit in the space provided, but this can be solved by increasing the width of the A column to provide enough room. Also, the numbers entered are amounts of money – so a £ sign would help. These adjustments will leave the spreadsheet looking like Figure 7.19.

Task

Now you may wish to begin to create your own spreadsheet. First you must decide on the information you want to store and what column and row labels you will need. When you have decided what information to store in your spreadsheet you will need to find out:

- *how to set up a new spreadsheet and enter text and numbers in the cells you wish to use*
- *how to change the appearance of your spreadsheet by varying column widths and altering the format in which text and numbers are displayed.*

The planning and creation of your spreadsheet can be used as evidence towards the IT core skill unit.

As we have seen, the spreadsheet is a very neat way to display numbers. However, its real power lies in its ability to use formulae to perform calculations on the numerical contents of cells.

Formulae

Formulae use mathematical and other symbols to operate on the contents of different cells in the spreadsheet. A formula is entered into the active cell and operates on the contents of other cells in the spreadsheet. The result is calculated and displayed in the active cell.

On a computer the symbols used for the four basic arithmetic calculations are: + for add, – for subtract, *for multiply, / for divide. These are all available on the keyboard. Maths symbols like these which are used in formulae are called *mathematical operators*.

Formulae can also include a range of mathematical, statistical and scientific symbols, and your equipment will have a set of symbols that it will recognise and use. You can also use parentheses, or brackets, in formulae as you would in mathematical calculations (see Chapter 6).

Writing formulae

Suppose that you want to add the contents of cell A1 to the contents of cell B1 and display the result in cell C1. Firstly you use the *arrow* keys to make C1 the active cell. You then need to tell the computer that you are entering a formula. Your machine will recognise a particular symbol as indicating a formula, *and it is essential that you enter it correctly otherwise your formula will be treated as a text cell entry.* Now type the first cell reference, followed by an operator, then the final cell reference. The formula in cell C1 would look like this:

=A1+B1

Note that in this example we have used the equals sign (=) to signify a formula.

Like other cell entries, the formula appears *both* in the active cell *and* outside the spreadsheet area *until you press Enter to confirm your entry.* When you press Enter the formula is no longer displayed in the cell but the result of the calculation appears there instead. The formula remains visible in the other part of the screen so that you can recognise that the spreadsheet is displaying the result of a calculation.

=A1+B1

	A	B	C	D	E	F
1	8	12	=A1+B1			
2						
3						
4						

Figure 7.20 *Entering a formula*

The top part of Figure 7.20 shows how a spreadsheet might look before our formula is confirmed as the contents of cell C1. When you press Enter the computer will add the number 8 in cell A1 to the number 12 in cell B1 and the result (20 of course) is displayed in cell C1.

=A1+B1

	A	B	C	D	E	F
1	8	12	20			
2						
3						
4						

Using formulae means that results are automatically *recalculated* when changes are made to the contents of a cell that has been referred to in a formula. For instance, if we change the contents of cell A1 from 8 to 10 the result displayed in cell C1 automatically changes to 22.

In the GNVQ Health and Social Care student's expenditure spreadsheet that we have looked at (Figure 7.19) it would be useful to find out what the total spending was in each month. This can be done by entering formulae into the cells where you want the results to appear. So to display the total spending for January at the bottom of the Jan column we need to enter a formula in cell B7 that adds together the contents of cells B2, B3, B4, B5 and B6.

We could simply enter B2+B3+B4+B5+B6 which would do the job, but spreadsheets will accept certain short-cut commands which make formulae easier to write. We can use the command SUM to add together the contents of a number of cells along a row or down a column. First highlight cell B7 as the active cell, then enter the formula SUM(B2:B6), remembering to indicate that this is a formula and not ordinary text. The symbol ':' has been used here to tell the computer to include all the cells from B2 to B6 in the calculation (your machine may use different symbol). When Enter is pressed the result is calculated and displayed in cell B7 as shown in Figure 7.21.

=SUM(B2:B6)

	A	B	C	D	E	F
1		Jan	Feb	March	April	May
2	Food	£80	£74	£82	£76	£85
3	Clothes	£20	£35	£12	£18	£20
4	Entertainment	£70	£75	£50	£67	£54
5	Books	£50	£12	£35	£50	£22
6	Savings	£29	£30	£41	£24	£32
7		£249				
8						
9						
10						
11						
12						
13						
14						

Figure 7.21 *Using a formula to obtain a column total*

Now we need to enter formulae in other cells of row 7 to calculate the total spending for the other months. You *could* do this column by column, changing the cell references in each formula so that it adds the contents of the cells above. However, there is a much better way to repeat similar formulae along a row or down a column.

Copying formulae

You are able to copy cell contents to other cells in a spreadsheet, whether the cell contains text, numbers or a formula. There may well be occasions when you want to copy text or numbers, but the ability to copy formulae to other cells is especially useful. This is because the cell references in the formula adjust to the new location so that the formula now refers to a different range of cells.

For example, if the contents of cell B7 in Figure 7.21, which is the formula SUM(B2:B6), is copied to cell C7 it changes to the formula SUM(C2:C6). Now the result displayed in cell C7 is the total of the contents of cells C2 to C6. Cell references in formulae which are able to change in this way are called **relative cell references**, and the formulae we have seen so far have contained only relative cell references as we have not indicated otherwise to the computer.

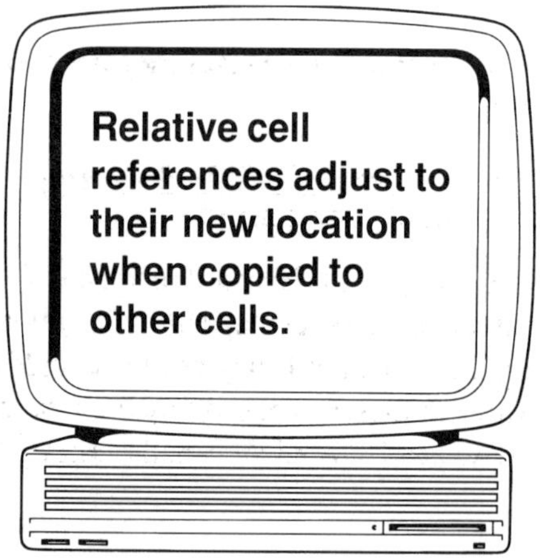

> Relative cell references adjust to their new location when copied to other cells.

If we wanted to *fix* a cell in a formula, so that it doesn't change when the formula is copied to a different cell, we can indicate this using a symbol that the computer recognises. Cell references in formulae which have been fixed in this way are called **absolute cell references** and we will look at them in more detail in a moment.

Copying the formula in cell B7 to cells C7, D7 and so on can be made even easier by using the spreadsheet's ability to copy the contents of one cell to a number of other cells. First you select a group of cells along a row or down a column, beginning with the one containing the formula you wish to copy. You then fill the formula into the selected cells either across or down as appropriate. All the relative cell references in the formula will adjust to suit their new location and the results of their calculations will be displayed.

So to copy the formulae into all the cells from cell B7 to cell F7, we first select these cells as shown in Figure 7.22. Then the computer is instructed to fill all the selected cells with the formula. When Enter is pressed the formula is copied and the totals for these months are displayed in their correct places.

=SUM(B2:B6)

	A	B	C	D	E	F
1		Jan	Feb	March	April	May
2	Food	£80	£74	£82	£76	£85
3	Clothes	£20	£35	£12	£18	£20
4	Entertainment	£70	£75	£50	£67	£54
5	Books	£50	£12	£35	£50	£22
6	Savings	£29	£30	£41	£24	£32
7		£249				
8						
9						
10						
11						
12						
13						
14						

Figure 7.22 *Copying a formula across cells*

The students' results

Now that you have seen some of the features of the spreadsheets we will look at how Sharon, Aysha and Jason have used one to record their results.

The students' questionnaire form contained five questions:

1 Do you think that smoking is bad for your health?
2 Do you think smoking can harm other people's health?

3 Do you think smoking should be allowed in enclosed public places like cinemas and restaurants?

4 Do you smoke cigarettes?

5 Would you go out with someone who smoked cigarettes?

For questions 1 and 2 the answer 'yes' shows that the respondent is aware of the dangers of smoking, and for questions 3,4 and 5 the answer 'no' would indicate this. The students plan to record these 'aware of the dangers' answers on a spreadsheet, separating the responses from males and females so that any difference of attitude between the sexes can be picked up.

Figure 7.23 shows the spreadsheet that they have created to display their results before any formulae are put in.

	A	B	C	D	E	F
1		Smoking Awareness Survey – Results				
2		Q.1	Q.2	Q.3	Q.4	Q.5
3	Male	12	10	11	9	5
4	Female	11	9	10	8	3
5	Total					
6						
7						
8						
9						
10						
11	People asked					
12	Male	16				
13	Female	14				
14	Total	30				

Figure 7.23 *The data entered*

They have used row 1 to provide a title and have entered the question numbers as column headings in cells B2 to F2. Cells A3, A4 and A5 contain the row labels Male, Female and Total. The results have been recorded in the appropriate cells so that the number of males and females giving 'aware' answers to each question is displayed. Cells A11 to A14 and B11 to B14 have been used to display the total number of the people asked.

They now need to calculate the totals in cells B5 to F5 and are going to use a formula for this. They make B5 the active cell and enter the formula B3+B4, which will calculate the total 'aware' responses for question 1 and display the result in cell B5 as they require. To total the remaining columns

they copy the formula across as far as cell F5 *using the methods described earlier.* As the formula uses relative cell references their copies adapt to their new location and calculate the correct totals in B5 to F5.

The students also want to show their results as a *percentage* of people asked so that they can more easily compare attitudes between male and female respondents. They enter row labels in cells A7, A8 and A9 so that the spreadsheet now looks like Figure 7.24.

	A	B	C	D	E	F
1		Smoking Awareness Survey – Results				
2		Q.1	Q.2	Q.3	Q.4	Q.5
3	Male	12	10	11	9	5
4	Female	11	9	10	8	3
5	Total	23	19	21	17	8
6						
7	% Males					
8	% Females					
9	% Total					
10						
11	People asked					
12	Males	16				
13	Females	14				
14	Total	30				

Figure 7.24 *Preparing to calculate percentages*

To calculate the percentage responses they need to use a formula like this:

$$\frac{\text{Number of 'aware' responses}}{\text{Number of people asked}} \times 100$$

in the cells where they want the result to appear. For example, to calculate the percentage of males giving an 'aware' response to question 1 they need to divide the number of aware responses in cell B3 by the total number of males asked, which is in cell B10, and multiply the result by 100.

They have earmarked cell B7 as the place to display the result, so they make B7 the active cell and need to enter the formula B3/B12*100.

As you know, when the formula is copied to other cells in row 7 the relative cell references will adjust to their new locations. However, the students want the reference to cell

B12 to remain fixed since the total number of males asked doesn't change. The answer is to include a special symbol in the formula so that cell B12 is given an *absolute* cell reference which will remain exactly the same when the formula is copied to other cells. We will use the symbol $ to indicate an absolute cell reference, but your equipment will have its own way of recognising this.

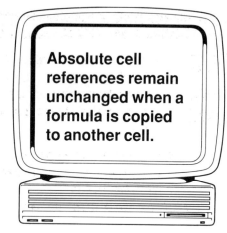

Absolute cell references remain unchanged when a formula is copied to another cell.

Sharon, Aysha and Jason therefore enter their formula in cell B7 as shown in Figure 7.25. They can now copy the formula into cells C7, D7, E7 and F7 and the absolute cell reference will remain unchanged. For instance, the formula copied into cell E7 will be adjusted to E3/$B12*100.

B3/$B12*100

	A	B	C	D	E	F
1		Smoking Awareness Survey – Results				
2		Q.1	Q.2	Q.3	Q.4	Q.5
3	Male	12	10	11	9	5
4	Female	11	9	10	8	3
5	Total	23	19	21	17	8
6						
7	% Males	75				
8	% Females					
9	% Total					
10						
11	People asked					
12	Males	16				
13	Females	14				
14	Total	30				

Figure 7.25 *The first calculation completed*

The students then enter formulae into cells B8 and B9 to calculate the percentage of 'aware' answers from female

respondents, and the percentage of 'aware' responses from all respondents. They copy these formulae, including the appropriate absolute cell references, to the necessary cells in rows 8 and 9. All the results are calculated by the computer and their final spreadsheet looks like Figure 7.26.

B5/$B14*100

	A	B	C	D	E	F
1		Smoking Awareness Survey – Results				
2		Q.1	Q.2	Q.3	Q.4	Q.5
3	Male	12	10	11	9	5
4	Female	11	9	10	8	3
5	Total	23	19	21	17	8
6						
7	% Males	75	62.5	68.7	56.2	31.2
8	% Females	78.1	63.9	71	56.8	21.3
9	% Total	76.7	63.3	70	56.7	26.7
10						
11	People asked					
12	Males	16				
13	Females	14				
14	Total	30				

Figure 7.26 *The final table of results*

Task

Now you may wish to enter formulae into your own spreadsheet. Decide what calculations you need to make and try writing them down using spreadsheet cell references in your formulae. Decide whether you need to use any absolute cell references in your formulae.

To enter formulae into your spreadsheet you will need to find out:

- *what symbol to use on your equipment to indicate that a formula is being entered*
- *what symbol your equipment recognises as indicating an absolute cell reference*
- *what range of mathematical and statistical and other operators your spreadsheet is able to use in formulae.*

To copy formulae along rows and down columns you need to find out how to:

- *select a range of cells along rows and down columns*
- *copy a formula along a row and down a column.*

Your equipment may well have sophisticated presentation features to make your spreadsheet look better when printed. Experiment with these, and when you have completed your spreadsheet obtain a printout. Remember to save your spreadsheet file in an appropriate directory on a floppy disk.

The work that you do creating, editing, saving and printing your spreadsheet can be used as evidence towards the IT core skill unit.

· CREATING A CHART OR GRAPH ·

The spreadsheet does an excellent job of recording and performing calculations on numerical data, but often we want to display the results in a form that emphasises the point we wish to make. A good way to do this is by the creation of a chart or graph from part of a spreadsheet. As you will have seen in Chapter 6, charts can be made in a variety of forms, such as the bar chart (Figure 6.6) and the pie chart (Figure 6.8).

Sharon, Aysha and Jason want to create a chart from the results of their smoking awareness research. First they need to decide which cell contents they want to display in the chart, and the percentage results in Figure 7.26 are chosen.

Next they decide what type of chart will display the results best. They agree that a bar chart will show up the

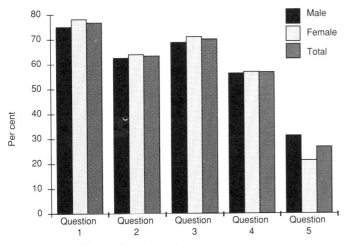

Figure 7.27 *The students' bar chart*

differences in responses that they wish to highlight in the final report. Figure 7.27 shows the results produced by the spreadsheet.

The chart file can be saved in a suitable directory on a floppy disk, ready to incorporate into their report. It will need a suitable title.

Task

You may be able to create a chart or graph with your equipment, either using data from a spreadsheet or by inputting data with the keyboard. You need to:

- *decide what data you want to make a graph or chart from, and what type of presentation your data needs*
- *find out how to create a chart or graph on your equipment*
- *experiment with the range of chart and graph styles available to you.*

When you are satisfied with your work, save your file on a floppy disk and obtain a printout of the finished chart. The work that you do in creating and printing a chart from your spreadsheet results can be used as evidence towards the IT core skill unit.

· PUTTING THINGS TOGETHER ·

When you have completed a research project like the one Sharon, Aysha and Jason have been working on, the best tool to help you compile your final report is the word-processor. We have already seen some of the word-processor's capabilities, and the creation of a longer and more detailed document introduces other features.

Importing data

Sharon, Aysha and Jason have created a word-processor file and are typing in the text of their smoking awareness research report. They want to put the charts that they have created into the report, and to attach as an appendix a sample questionnaire form and letter and a list of the cinemas and restaurants contacted.

The software applications they are using are able to share data between them, and so the students use this facility to **import** their charts into the report file. They run the word-processor and load their report file. The cursor is moved to the part of the document where the first chart is to appear and the import procedure is begun. The computer must be given the path and file name of the chart file, and the disk containing it must be put into the computer's floppy disk drive. The chart is copied into the word-processor file at the insertion point and the original chart file on the floppy disk is unaffected.

Sharon, Aysha and Jason decide to import copies of their letter and questionnaire form into the report file rather than print separate copies from the original files. This is because they intend using the computer to insert *page numbers* on the report and want the appendix to be included in the numbering. The procedure is similar to that used for the charts, except that this time they are importing another word-processor file, and of course the path and file names are different.

Next, data from the database is imported in the form of a list of cinema and restaurant names. They only require a list of the contents of the Name and Type fields and need to specify this when importing the data.

When importing data you must specify the file name and path correctly.

Formatting

All that remains now is to arrange the document for printing. The pages of a word-processed document can be formatted in several ways before printing. The word-processor prints text between four margins on each page, the left, right, top and bottom.

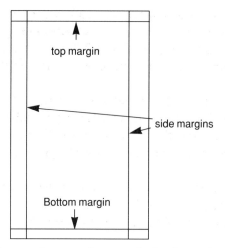

Figure 7.28 *There are four margins to set during formatting*

The text wraps on to the next line automatically when you reach the right margin, and in a similar way a new page is begun when you reach the bottom margin. The page margins can be altered so that text gets closer to or further from the page edges. This can be used to alter the look of a document and to vary the number of pages by fitting more or less on each sheet.

There may be an occasion when you want to keep part of the text on its own page, without the possibility of it being spread into a second page if you later add text to an earlier part of the document. This can be done by inserting *hard page breaks*. A hard page break is an instruction to the computer to begin a new page regardless of how far down the current page you have got. Insert a page break before the section you are concerned with and it will begin on a new page; insert one after and it will be printed on a page of its own.

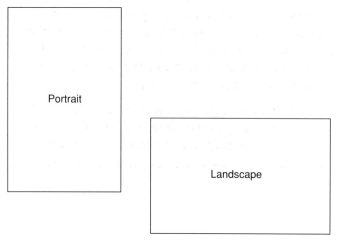

Figure 7.29 *Portrait and landscape options*

Another option in page design is which way round the paper is printed on. You can choose either portrait layout or landscape layout (Figure 7.29). Work is still confined within the margins whichever layout is used.

It is also possible to add page numbers automatically throughout the document. The page number can be omitted from the first page so that it can be used as a *title page*, and numbering will then begin on the second sheet.

These are just a few of the ways in which a word-processor can help you to deal with longer documents . Your equipment will have its own range of additional features.

Task

Use the word-processor to create the final report for an assignment you are completing as part of your studies. Try importing relevant data from other files such as spreadsheets, databases, and other word-processed documents. Adjust the format of your document before printing to reduce paper usage, and add a cover page and page numbers. Save and print your file. You need to find out how to:

- *import into the word-processor data from files created in other applications*
- *format your document by adjusting margins and including page breaks*
- *add page numbers to your document.*

You can use these techniques together with those we have looked at earlier to create a well-organised and smartly presented report. Remember to plan your use of IT when you begin an assignment so that you can carry out each part more effectively, and are able to bring your results together easily in a neat final report.

Evidence of your planning can be used towards the IT core skill unit, and quality of planning is one of the factors taken into account in the awarding of Merit and Distinction grades.

Final remarks

These are by no means the only applications that are available, and you may well have access to other useful software that you can use to effect during your studies. For example, there could be a *graphics* application on your equipment which you can use to create plans and illustrations. As you use the computer you will find out what is available if you make good use of IT staff who may be there to help you.

Fast facts

Absolute cell reference   In a **spreadsheet** formula an absolute cell reference remains unaltered when the formula is copied to other **cells.** See also **relative cell reference.**

Application   A word used for the set of instructions that the computer carries out. The word application refers to **software** that has been designed to be applied to a particular task such as word-processing or spread-sheeting. See also **software** and **program.**

Byte   A single piece of information. Bytes are used as a measure of computer memory size. See also **kilobyte** and **megabyte.**

Cell   In a **spreadsheet** a cell is the area where an item of data or a formula is stored.

Cell reference   The unique address of a cell in a spreadsheet. The cell reference is given by the row and column headings which apply to the cell.

Compatibility   The ability of **hardware** and **software** to work together.

Cursor   A blinking line or dash on the screen which indicates where your typing will appear, or your editing take place.

Cut and paste   A term used for the process of selecting and moving text.

Database   A database manager (usually referred to simply as a database) is a **software** application used to deal with information in the form of lists. Strictly speaking a database is any listed information, and so a telephone directory or your address book are databases.

Directories   Electronically created compartments on a disk that are used to group **files** you wish to keep together.

Field   A category of information contained in a **database**. Records contain data entered into fields.

File   A piece of work that has been created and saved on the computer.

Floppy disk   A portable piece of **hardware** used to store data. Floppy disks are small, lightweight and reasonably durable.

Form letter   A word-processed letter that contains **merge fields** linked to a **database.** Form letters are used to create mass mail-shots.

Formatting floppy disks   The process of electronically dividing a floppy disk into tracks and sectors. Disks must be formatted before **files** can be saved on them.

Formatting text   This refers to alterations made to the way text looks, either by changing character size and type or by varying the arrangement of paragraphs.

Graphics application   A **software** application designed to deal with graphical information. Graphics applications are used to produce artworks and plans.

Hard disk   A piece of **hardware** used to store information. The hard disk is permanently fixed inside the computer's case and cannot be removed from it.

Hardware   The physical equipment used in IT. This includes the computer, the monitor, the keyboard, cables and other devices such as printers.

Information technology   The term is used to refer to modern, scientific ways of handling information. It is applied to the fields of computing, video and telecommunications and the rapidly developing links between them.

Landscape layout   Work printed with the long edge of the paper horizontal.

Margins   The boundaries within which your work is printed. There are margins at the top and bottom of the page, as well as on either side.

Megabyte   A measure of amount of information. One megabyte (Mb) = 1024 **kilobytes** = 1,048,546 **bytes.**

Kilobyte   A measure of amount of information. One kilobyte (Kb) = 1024 **bytes.**

Merge fields   Specially marked parts of a form letter which contain the titles of **fields** in a **database.**

Operating system   **Software** which starts the computer running and controls its activities. The operating system must be running before you can run other types of software.

Portrait layout   Work printed with the long edge of the paper vertical.

Program   A word used for the set of instructions that the computer carries out. See also **software** and **application.**

RAM   Stands for Random Access Memory. The RAM holds the information and instructions that are being used by the computer during your work sessions. It is completely cleared when you switch the computer off.

Record   The information held in a **database** on a particular item. Each record consists of data entered into **fields.**

Relative cell reference   In a **spreadsheet** formula a relative cell reference adjusts to its new location when the formula is copied to other cells. See also **absolute cell reference.**

Scrolling   Bringing other parts of a document into view on the screen.

Selecting   Identifying certain parts of a file with a highlight so that the selected text can be deleted, moved or copied.

Spreadsheets   A **software application** designed to deal with numerical information.

Software   A word used for the set of instructions that the computer carries out. See also **program** and **application.**

Word-processor   A **software application** that is designed to deal with text-based information. Pie

ANSWERS

Answers to questions on page 21

1 Standards are definitions of what has to be demonstrated and assessed in order to get GNVQ awards and qualifications. Standards don't explain what has to be studied – only what gets assessed. Standards provide an alternative to exam-based qualifications. Exam-based qualifications are like a competition, only the people who come in top do well. With standards, it only matters if people can demonstrate what's needed.

2 Standards often contain technical words and descriptions. People will need to know a great deal about an area before standards for that area can be easily understood. At the beginning of a programme, people often don't have the knowledge to understand what is meant by particular element and performance criteria statements. Understanding standards is part of the learning goals for GNVQ.

3 Assessment to standards requires evidence. The standards define what is needed for an award; evidence is the information that shows that a person has done what was needed. They have reached 'the standard'. When all the appropriate standards have been reached, the person is qualified.

4 Action plans enable individuals to work out how they will collect evidence to meet 'evidence indicators'. Action plans can also be used to plan assignments, practical demonstrations and placement and project work. Action plans might be useful in helping candidates to meet standards requirements. Action plans are necessary for Merit and Distinction grades, as candidates have to show skills in planning and in monitoring courses of action. Records of planning will be needed to provide evidence of planning and monitoring skills.

5 Yes! A candidate can work out what is needed, and provided they do the work and submit the necessary evidence, they should be able to guarantee the grade they want. GNVQs are not a competition – grades don't depend on some final assessment of group results. Candidates can get advice and guidance as they go through the programme, to ensure that they have the necessary evidence for Merits or Distinctions.

6 Evidence of: independent action planning, monitoring courses of action, independent identification of information needs and independent identification and use of 'sources' to obtain information. All these criteria or standards might be assisted by action planning work.

7 A portfolio is a portable collection of evidence which aims to demonstrate that national standards have been met. The portfolio will, therefore, include an index of assignment evidence and core skills and grading evidence. This will be used by assessors and verifiers who will check the quality of a candidate's work.

The portfolio will be complicated and work on it should start early in the programme. Leaving the design of the portfolio to the end of the programme may make it difficult to achieve Merit or Distinction grades. If the collection of evidence is regularly 'self-assessed' or checked, then candidates can change their work to ensure that it meets the requirements for these grades.

If the records are not kept, or not checked, then it may become too late to do the right kind of work at the end of the programme.

8 They should revise their own portfolio of evidence for the unit, discuss unit content with other people, make notes of their work! Discussion might help memory. Use the Fast Facts sections of this book as an aid to recognising concepts and ideas.

9 Good grades on GNVQ depend on independent planning and monitoring. Candidates have to plan to provide enough evidence for assessment. A good way to make sense of all this work is to self-assess the evidence before presenting it. The development of self-assessment skills would cover much of what is needed for Merit and Distinction grades.

10 Reflection is a skill which enables people to experiment with their ideas until the ideas work in a useful way. Reflection is a skill that will enable self-assessment and evidence collection. Reflection will also enable a carer to help others to clarify their thoughts and feelings, it is part of the necessary knowledge for Unit 1.

Answers to questions on page 57

1 The correct answer from the nursery nurse was **c**. The child was being given an opportunity to share the sadness. Not to talk about sad happenings doesn't make the sadness less, it just makes it stay inside the unhappy person.

2 It is usually important to have good eye-contact with someone to show you are listening to them. Reflecting back proves that you were listening to them. Asking questions doesn't always mean that we have listened – sometimes we ask questions because we have lost track of what the other person is saying.

3 You could use the sense of touch to offer the client support. You could make sure your tone of voice conveyed your meaning clearly.

4 A client with impaired hearing might rely more heavily on body language, including eye-contact, facial expression (tone of voice should be normal).

5 An angry person will be likely to fix their eye-contact on the person offending them and not look away.

6 If a client was unhappy or distressed, a care worker could offer emotional support by speaking in a slower, calm and varied voice.

7 Someone sitting stiffly upright in a group meeting might be likely to make the other people feel they were in a very formal situation. The person sitting stiffly might be seen as attempting to dominate or be 'superior.'

8 You can learn to understand your clients by:

a watching their non-verbal behaviour

b listening to what they tell you (perhaps using reflective techniques)

c checking your guesses with your clients (perhaps by asking questions).

9 A closed question closes down the range of answers possible. A closed question usually requires a short, simple, fixed type of answer: 'How old are you?' Ans. 17! An open question suggests an open reply – the other person might have to talk for a while to give an answer. Open questions suggest that all sorts and types of reply are possible.

10 **b** is the open question because all sorts of types of answers are possible – it could lead to a long discussion. The answer to **a** is yes/no or 'shut-up!' The answer to **c** is 98 pence or 'I'm not saying!' **a** and **c** are closed questions.

11 **a** is a probe – checking to see what the other person really might have meant

b is a prompt – suggesting an answer 'not worth it' to see if the person agrees

c isn't a probe or a prompt – it's a statement – not a questioning technique like probes and prompts.

12 Behaving in exactly the same way would ignore each client's individuality, their feelings and their views. Behaving the same way would mean that some people's self-esteem needs might be ignored. Failure to value others and meet their individual self-esteem needs might cause conversations and care relationships to stop. Clients might become angry or depressed.

13 **a** Probable messages include: 'I don't want to be part of this group'. 'I don't want to join in'. 'I'll join in only if I decide I will'. 'I'm not part of this group'.

b Another member could ask the isolated person why he doesn't come round and join the group – ask a question! He might say 'don't want to', which could confirm his non-verbal behaviour; but he might say 'there's no space – the table's too heavy', in which case he is not intending to send a non-verbal message with his behaviour.

14 The main difference involves the number of people! Groups will contain various individuals each with their own separate individuality. Value and respect has to be communicated to each person; interest, warmth and sincerity has to be communicated to each group member. Conversation is harder to monitor, and turn-taking and reflection can be harder to demonstrate.

15 Reflective listening is saying back what another person has said, either exactly as they said it or else in your own words. Non-verbal messages and the use of silence have to be used appropriately to support reflective listening.

Reflective listening is used to keep a conversation going, but more importantly to help other people sort out their thoughts and feelings. Reflective listening is one technique for increasing understanding of other people's self-esteem needs.

16 **a** and **b** are good ideas. **c** is silly – how many people, who aren't working in caring, could answer such a difficult question? It takes a lot of conversation to learn about another person's individuality. **d** might keep a conversation going – but do you want a conversation about buses to keep going?

17 Respect and value help to keep a conversation going. Lack of respect and value will stop caring from working. Respect and value for others is a basic starting point for understanding others' self-esteem needs and for providing emotional support.

18 **a** and **c** – it would be very annoying and would sound like a parrot at work.

19 Cultural differences in non-verbal communication. It's very difficult to display respect and value if other people's culture is not understood. Apparently, everyone got very confused – some soldiers chose insults in the Greek system – after all, Churchill started it. Some tried to show respect by offering an insult in the British system – this may not have been appreciated! The only way out was to wave instead!

20 **b**! Action **a** would often be understood as aggression or as something being wrong. **c** would be perhaps both laid-back and defensive.

21 **c** The other two answers are judgemental and/or patronising.

22 Sincerity is being yourself, not using fixed phrases or copying what you have seen other people doing or saying when they care for others.

23 Other people might talk about things which they value, such as their achievements, their religion, the way they have chosen to live and so on. Non-verbal communication can show that we are interested and that we think it is important to learn about these things. Smiles, head-nods, eye-contact and body posture can show interest and warmth. Interest and warmth may meet others' self-esteem needs.

24 Organised question sequences are approaches which help to get clear answers from people by leading the conversation across a range of issues. Funnelling is an example of organised question sequences. These sequences are important when designing a survey or questionnaire (core skills) but they can also be used in supportive conversation.

25 Tone of voice often gives part of the meaning to a spoken phrase or sentence. Words can mean different things depending on the stress put on them when they are spoken. Sometimes people take more notice of the tone of voice something was said in, than the words that were used.

Answers to questions on page 92

1 Norms are **a**, **b** and **d**. **c** is a belief.

2 It is called a role.

3 The very influential socialisation that takes place within the family during early childhood.

4 Our family and our peer group.

5 The group's culture.

6 Peers are people who share a similar social situation to ourselves and whom we regard as our equals.

7 Occupation.

8 All of these (**a**, **b**, **c**, **d** and **e**).

9 Both **a** and **c** are income.

10 Housing, food, transport, clothing.

11 Self-esteem is the value a person places on him- or herself.

12 Commitments are things which need regular payments, such as mortgages and loan agreements.

13 To treat a person differently from the way others are treated.

14 They have been labelled.

15 A stereotype is an image of a 'typical' member of a group. People who have been labelled as members of a group may be expected to think and behave according to the stereotyped image of a group member.

16 Race, gender, age and disability.

17 Ethnicity refers to a person's cultural background, whereas race refers to biological differences between people that are perceived by others.

18 Exclusion.

19 Judgements based on stereotypes, and exclusion through lack of access.

20 People can come to see themselves in terms of the stereotype that they have been labelled with, so that their self-concept is altered.

21 b They relate to an increased cholesterol level.

22 c Lung disease.

23 a Growth and repair of cells.

24 Unprotected sexual intercourse; sharing of needles; passing body fluids (e.g. blood) between people and between mother and foetus.

25 Cirrhosis of the liver; cancers of the throat and liver; increased weight gain; damage to a developing foetus; depression; stomach disorders.

26 Include wholemeal bread or cereals; more fresh fruit and/or vegetables; bran food.

27 Warming up prepares the muscles for the exercise to follow. If you do not warm up you run the risk of injury (e.g. pulling a muscle).

28 Several agencies work together and pool their resources to ensure all the needs of the client are addressed.

29 Breathing in smoke when you are not actually smoking yourself. This can be voluntary (i.e. you choose to be in that situation) or involuntary (i.e. you have no choice).

30 You are working closely with other people and poor personal hygiene is unpleasant.

31 Boredom; curiosity; peer pressure; escape from problems.

32 Swimming develops the ability of the heart muscles to work for long periods of time under pressure.

Answers to questions on page 121

1 c Blistering.

2 d Choking.

3 d Complaint of pain.

4 c Check that it is safe for you to approach the crashed vehicles.

5 b The carotid pulse.

6 d Airway, Breathing and Circulation.

7 a A temporary loss of consciousness.

8 **c** Making sure the daughter does not injure herself.

9 **d** You are giving oxygen to the casualty.

10 **c** Halving the distance and halving the lowest half.

11 **a** One breath to every five compressions.

12 **b** More than three minutes.

13 **c** Lower the head and raise the legs.

14 **b** Wads of paper – like a telephone directory.

15 **a** Aspirin.

16 Faintness, dizziness, weakness; rapid shallow breathing; nausea perhaps vomiting; pale cold clammy skin; weak, maybe irregular pulse.

17 No carotid pulse; colour blueish-grey; pupils dilated.

18 Support the back of the casualty's neck; place hand on forehead and tilt head backwards; pull chin upwards and forwards.

19 Dial 999 and call ambulance; reassure; rest and make comfortable; half sitting half lying position; nothing to eat or drink; support knees and shoulders; monitor vital signs (breathing, pulse and consciousness levels).

20 No creams, gels or ointments; no sticky dressings like plasters; leave blisters alone.

Answers to questions on page 154

1 **b** Appointment with the GP.

2 **a** GP, practice nurse and health visitor.

3 **b** Well-person clinics.

4 A rest home provides for the more independent and mobile older person. A nursing home cares for more dependent people who require a lot more nursing care – up to 24 hours a day.

5 **a** A service provided by law.

6 **c** Controlled by the district Health Authority.

7 **c** They provide health and care services.

8 **d** They are paid for by the people who use them.

9 **a** They control their own budgets.

10 **a** True, **b** False, **c** True, **d** False, **e** False, **f** False, **g** False.

11 Any people using the health and care services.

12 Freedom from discrimination, dignity, independence, choice, confidentiality, and health and safety.

13 Setting conditions for access to things such as employment or services which exclude members of certain groups.

14 To promote client rights so that people are able to have more control over their own lives.

15 An image of a typical member of a group which is applied to a real person and used to make judgements about them.

16 By ensuring that people are given as much privacy as is safely possible, and by taking care never to talk about them in their presence as if they were not there.

17 **c** Choice.

18 Keeping secret something that you have been told in confidence.

19 By helping them to communicate in writing or through gestures.

20 Practice which promotes the rights of all people to freedom from discrimination on the basis of their personal characteristics.

ICONS FOR PHOTOCOPYING

Photocopy any of the range of icons below and paste onto your GNVQ assignments. This will enable you and your tutor to see at a glance those areas which have been covered in your evidence collection.

 Communication

 Application of Number

 Information Technology

 I did this on my own without help

 I did most of my own work but my tutor gave me guidance

 My tutor suggested areas of research and helped me to structure my project

 Providing Emotional Support

 Influences on Health and Well-being

 Health Emergencies

 Health and Care Services

 Independently draw up action plans that 'prioritise' or explain the order of activities.

 Independently identify information needs for tasks.

 Identify the need to monitor action plans and revise or change them when necessary.

 Independently find and collect information. This might involve the 'sources of information' column on the action plan.

The page numbers in brackets
refer to Fast Facts.